REPRESENTATIVE AMERICAN SPEECHES 1981–1982

edited by OWEN PETERSON
Professor, Department of Speech Communication,
  Theatre, and Communicative Disorders
Louisiana State University

THE REFERENCE SHELF

Volume 54, Number 5

THE H. W. WILSON COMPANY

New York   1982

THE REFERENCE SHELF

The books in this series contain reprints of articles, excerpts from books, and addresses on current issues and social trends in the United States and other countries. There are six separately bound numbers in each volume, all of which are generally published in the same calendar year. One number is a collection of recent speeches; each of the others is devoted to a single subject and gives background information and discussion from various points of view, concluding with a comprehensive bibliography. Books in the series may be purchased individually or on subscription.

The Library of Congress cataloged this title as a serial.

Main entry under title:

Representative American speeches, 1981–1982.

New York, H. W. Wilson Co.
v.21.cm.annual. (The Reference Shelf)
Editors: 1937/38–1958/59, A. C. Baird.–1959/–1969/70,
L. Thonssen.–1970/71–1979/80, W. W. Braden,-O. Peterson.
  1. American orations.   2. Speeches, addresses, etc.
I. Baird, Albert Craig, ed.   II. Thonssen, Lester, ed.
III. Braden, Waldo W., ed.   IV. Peterson, Owen, ed.   V. Series.
PS668.B3   815.5082   38-27962

International Standard Book Number 0-8242-0669-x
PRINTED IN THE UNITED STATES OF AMERICA

CONTENTS

THE PRESS AND THE PUBLIC

IN TRANSIT

OF HEROES

TECHNOLOGY AND THE FUTURE

With some regularity articles and essays appear bemoaning the decline and even the demise of oratory. *Time* magazine published such an article by Lance Morrow in August, 1980. Morrow's thesis was that "Today, oratory seems in serious, possibly terminal, decline." He argued that probably the last great speech most Americans heard was Martin Luther King Jr.'s address at the 1963 civil rights march in Washington. Dr. King's speech unquestionably was eloquent, but when Morrow cites former Tennessee governor Frank Clement and the late Senator Everett Dirksen as other memorable speakers, it becomes clear that what Morrow finds missing in speeches today is the bombastic, table-pounding speech which has been on the decline ever since Franklin D. Roosevelt mastered the art of radio fireside chats. Clement and Dirksen were two of the most forgettable orators in recent history.

It can be said that there has been a *change,* rather than a *decline,* in the style of oratory, and Morrow rightly attributes it to television. When a speaker delivers an address on television, even though his listeners may number several million, his audience consists of small groups of two or three people sitting in the quiet of their homes watching the television screen. The kind of bombast appropriate to a convention keynote address or a mass protest rally is totally inappropriate when speaking to a few persons in the privacy of their homes.

Much more discomforting than Morrow's piece are the observations of Melvin Maddocks in the *Christian Science Monitor* (May 10, 1982). He observes:

Ever since the television tube took over from the back platform of a train as the proper podium for a candidate, every little mayorality campaign has been burdened by strategic analyses of 'communication skill' and those sub-skills of 'image' and 'style.' There was just no stopping the search for candidates with 'communication skills' once it became the conventional wisdom that

Richard M. Nixon lost the 1960 election to John F. Kennedy because he went into a TV debate well-informed, but with shoddy make-up and a questionable shave.

But what do we mean by this umbrella term, 'communication'? Certainly not a grace and prevision in our spoken and written language. 'Verbal skills,' as we all know, have withered as 'communication skills' have boomed. Do we mean that more and more brilliant, urgent, and exciting ideas are being circulated? Alas, no again. Does 'good communication' then mean that poeple, at the least, are coming across as human beings to other people? This reassuring thought would also be hard to prove.

We may be heard to complain that we live in a time of unprecedented confusion and extraordinary estrangements. And yet we continue to talk about 'communicating' as if it were something we and our leaders are particularly expert at.

Can it be that by 'communication skills' we mean only a soothing murmur, a winning smile, a certain vigor in body language—a comforting impression, transmittable by microphone and camera? . . . Do we all have buttons—anxieties, insecurities, fears—that 'communicators' can punch, whether they are advertisers or politicians, and make us feel they are The Answer? . . .

Is 'communication' turning into something very like manipulation, on the one hand—all artful suggestions and subliminal? And, on the other hand, a taped monologue delivered by a network of robots with a gift for nonsequitur? . . . What we get, in either case, is technique. What we long for is substance—not just the voice but a meaning. We hunger for content—for wisdom or love or humor. Anything please, but mere performance. For it will be the worst of ironies in this Age of Communication if we learn how to say everything, and find we have nothing to say.

With increased knowledge and sophistication concerning the control of audiences and the greater use of these manipulative techniques by politicians, religious leaders, executives, and groups and individuals promoting a variety of special interests, Mr. Maddock's observations can be viewed as a cause for concern.

To quote three former editors of this collection, Lester Thonssen, A. Craig Baird, and Waldo W. Braden, in their book *Speech Criticism*, it is important to recognize "that public address functions within the framework of a social and political milieu. . . . Rhetoric and politics, age-old partners, cannot be divorced." Because the election of Ronald W. Reagan as President of the United States was widely regarded as a rejection of many programs and policies developed over four decades, much of the speaking in 1981–1982 reflected a "wait and see" attitude. Initially, leaders in many areas adopted a course of caution. The new President's skill in winning support for his programs in the early months of his administration, coupled with a recognition of his abilities as a communicator, held off criticism during his first few months in office. During the traditional "honeymoon" period of grace granted new presidents by all but their fiercest critics, the main question was whether Reagan would remain true to his election campaign promises. Only when it became clear that he fully intended to abide by his campaign rhetoric did he and his proposals come under attack—from liberals, women, labor, blacks, and media, and others.

An important development in 1981–1982 was the growth of political activism. For the first time since a decade earlier when protests against the war in Vietnam convulsed the nation, many Americans were becoming involved in organizations and activities directed against government policies. The principal concern was the threat of a nuclear holocaust. Scientists, physicians, clergymen, educators, and students were active in a "nuclear freeze" movement to stop the proliferation of nuclear weapons. Labor, badly hurt by inflation and the recession, sponsored a successful "Solidarity" march on Washington and began openly to combat the President's economic program.

What were the best forums for speakers wishing to influence public opinion in 1981–1982? Certainly not speeches on the floors of the houses of Congress, which are largely unlistened to, unreported, and concerned with details of legislation being considered. The President can command a nationwide audience on television and, occasionally, other prominent spokesmen will be accorded national air-time because of the person's office, reputation, or special knowledge. However, these channels are limited. The speaker's best chances of making his views known and influencing public opinion today are the television talk show, the college lecture circuit, commencement exercises, and conventions of important national organizations and associations.

I could not compile this volume without the assistance of many people whose contributions I would like to acknowledge.

First and foremost, I wish to express my thanks and appreciation to Beth Wheeler. Her help and careful attention to detail has been invaluable.

I am grateful to the following persons who contributed to this volume by providing me with speech texts, background information, biographical data, and other research assistance: John H. Bennitt, Richard Collins, C. David Cornell, Huynh Huynh, Peter Kingsley, James Lubetkin, Rory Maher, Barrett McGurn, Saul Miller, Ruth Mraz, Richard B. Muller, Caroline P. Shoemaker, Nancy Cowger Slonim, Richard Troutman, and Joan E. Twiggy.

I also thank my colleagues and associates at Louisiana State University who have assisted me in a wide variety of ways. Thank you Steve Cooper, Mary Frances Hopkins, Jean Jackson, Lisa Matherne, Francine Merritt, Harold Mixon, and John Pennybacker.

OWEN PETERSON

Baton Rouge, Louisiana
May 16, 1982

NATIONAL PRIORITIES

A NEW FEDERALISM:
STATE OF THE UNION ADDRESS[1]

Ronald W. Reagan[2]

On January 26, 1982, President Ronald W. Reagan presented his first State of the Union message to the joint houses of Congress assembled in the chamber of the House of Representatives, before a television audience of millions. All State of the Union addresses are important as indicators of the direction the President hopes to take in the forthcoming year, but, because of the far-reaching and highly controversial changes in the role of the federal government proposed by Reagan, this address was particularly significant.

For years, Reagan advocated a "new federalism" which would transfer many federal activities and programs back to the states and localities and now he returned to that theme. The *New Republic* described the address a follows:

> In a beautifully delivered State of the Union address on January 26, he made the most revolutionary proposal for government changes in the past fifty years: in a 'single bold stroke' Washington would turn over to the states forty federal programs for operation. ... He proposed a widespread transfer of government operations to increase the authority of the states and reduce that of Washington. (TRB, "A Game of Risk," *New Republic,* F. 10, '82, p 4)

The *New York Times* said of the speech, "For months, the suspense had been building. Would Ronald Reagan remain true to himself? The surprise last week was how true he turned out to be." (Ja. 31, '82, p 4)

During his first year in office, President Reagan had impressed political observers—both supporters and critics—with his skill as a communicator. Columnist Jeff Greenfield wrote, "Mr. Reagan gives the best-crafted speeches of any president since John Kennedy, and he's probably even better than the Kennedy-Sorenson team." (Baton Rouge *State-Times,* Ja. 26, '82, p 6B) *New York*

---

[1] Delivered before the joint houses of Congress assembled in the United States House of Representatives on January 26, 1982.

[2] For biographical note, see Appendix.

Times writer Tom Wicker observed, "Ronald Reagan is the master of television. No politician in the brief history of the medium has known better how to use it, as a campaigner first and now as president, or done so with more confidence." (Ag. 4, '81, p 2J) According to Hedrick Smith, "To the electorate, he has come across as Mr. Nice Guy, with the Eisenhower grin and the infectious optimism of the boy next door." (*New York Times Magazine*, Ag. 9, '81, p 12) Sir William Rees-Mogg, former editor of *The Times* of London and himself an accomplished orator observed:

> As a communicator he is more skillful than any American president since John F. Kennedy, and in some ways perhaps more skillful than any since Franklin D. Roosevelt. . . . On a number of issues, as he has already shown in his dealings with Congress, President Reagan can mobilize public opinion on his side. (*The Times*, London, Jl. 13, '81, p 10)

The immediate response to the State of the Union message was mixed. The Associated Press reported, "Reagan was interrupted by applause 20 times, but most of it came from the Republican side of the aisle. And at one point, Reagan was jeered by a handful of Democrats when he conceded that 'the budget deficit will exceed our earlier expectations'." (Baton Rouge, *State-Times*, Ja. 27, '82, p 1) Steven R. Weisman stated, "The general skeptical reaction" to the speech centered on Reagan's new federalism plan (*New York Times*, Ja. 31, '82, p 4:1), and Marvin Tolchmin agreed, saying the proposal "was hailed as 'brilliant' and 'creative' by many Republicans and some conservative Democrats. . . . But many Democrats and some moderate Republicans denounced the proposal." (*New York Times*, Ja. 27, '82, p 9)

Many television viewers wondered whether the President had memorized the entire 46-minute speech because of direct eye contact and lack of manuscript or notes. In actual fact, Reagan was well-acquainted with the speech but had not memorized it in its entirety. He used a TelePrompter, out of the viewers' range.

Immediately following Reagan's message, the three networks presented viewers with a 28-minute Democratic answer to the speech taped earlier in the month. How this rebuttal affected the public cannot be determined. The *Christian Science Monitor* probably best sums up the general reaction:

> President Reagan no doubt scored highly with many Americans with his first State of the Union message. His buoyancy, unselfconscious patriotism, and feisty determination to stick by his guns are qualities of leadership having great popular appeal. Even those who disagree

with his policies cannot but admire his abilities as a persuader. (Ja. 28, '82, p 24)

Ronald Reagan's speech: Mr. Speaker, Mr. President, distinguished Members of the Congress, honored guests, and fellow citizens:

Today marks my first State of the Union address to you, a constitutional duty as old as our Republic itself.

President Washington began this tradition in 1790 after reminding the nation that the destiny of self-government and the "preservation of the sacred fire of liberty" is "finally staked on the experiment entrusted to the hands of the American people." For our friends in the press, who place a high premium on accuracy, let me say: I did not actually hear George Washington say that. But it is a matter of historic record.

But from this podium, Winston Churchill asked the free world to stand together against the onslaught of aggression. Franklin Delano Roosevelt spoke of a day of infamy and summoned a nation to arms. Douglas MacArthur made an unforgettable farewell to a country he loved and served so well. Dwight Eisenhower reminded us that peace was purchased only at the price of strength. And John F. Kennedy spoke of the burden and glory that is freedom.

When I visited this chamber last year as a newcomer to Washington, critical of past policies which I believed had failed, I proposed a new spirit of partnership between this Congress and this administration and between Washington and our state and local governments. In forging this new partnership for America, we could achieve the oldest hopes of our Republic—prosperity for our nation, peace for the world, and the blessings of individual liberty for our children and, something for all of humanity.

It's my duty to report to you tonight on the progress that we have made in our relations with other nations, on the foundation we've carefully laid for our economic recovery, and finally, on a bold and spirited initiative that I believe can change the face of American government and make it again the servant of the people.

Seldom have the stakes been higher for America. What we do and say here will make all the difference to auto-workers in Detroit, lumberjacks in the Northwest, steel-workers in Steubenville who are in the unemployment lines; to black teenagers in Newark and Chicago; to hard-pressed farmers and small businessmen; and to millions of everyday Americans who harbor the simple wish of a safe and finan-cially secure future for their children. To understand the state of the Union, we must look not only at where we are and where we're going but where we've been. The situation at this time last year was truly ominous.

The last decade has seen a series of recessions. There was a recession in 1970, in 1974, and again in the spring of 1980. Each time, unemployment increased and inflation soon turned up again. We coined the word "stagflation" to de-scribe this.

Government's response to these recessions was to pump up the money supply and increase spending. In the last 6 months of 1980, as an example, the money supply increased at the fastest rate in postwar history—13 percent. Inflation re-mained in double digits, and government spending increased at an annual rate of 17 percent. Interest rates reached a stag-gering 21½ percent. There were 8 million unemployed.

Late in 1981 we sank into the present recession, largely because continued high interest rates hurt the auto industry and construction. And there was a drop in productivity, and the already high unemployment increased.

This time, however, things are different. We have an eco-nomic program in place, completely different from the artifi-cial quick-fixes of the past. It calls for a reduction of the rate of increase in government spending, and already that rate has been cut nearly in half. But reduced spending alone isn't enough. We've just implemented the first and smallest phase of a 3-year tax-rate reduction designed to stimulate the econ-omy and create jobs. Already interest rates are down to 15¾ percent, but they must still go lower. Inflation is down from 12.4 percent to 8.9, and for the month of December it was running at an annualized rate of 5.2 percent. If we had not acted as we did, things would be far worse for all Americans than they are today. Inflation, taxes, and interest rates would all be higher.

A year ago, Americans' faith in their governmental process was steadily declining. Six out of 10 Americans were saying they were pessimistic about their future. A new kind of defeatism was heard. Some said our domestic problems were uncontrollable, that we had to learn to live with this seemingly endless cycle of high inflation and high unemployment.

There were also pessimistic predictions about the relationship between our administration and this Congress. It was said we could never work together. Well, those predictions were wrong. The record is clear, and I believe that history will remember this as an era of American renewal, remember this administration as an administration of change, and remember this Congress as a Congress of destiny.

Together, we not only cut the increase in government spending nearly in half, we brought about the largest tax reductions and the most sweeping changes in our tax structure since the beginning of this century. And because we indexed future taxes to the rate of inflation, we took away government's built-in profit on inflation and its hidden incentive to grow larger at the expense of American workers.

Together, after 50 years of taking power away from the hands of the people in their states and local communities, we have started returning power and resources to them.

Together, we have cut the growth of the new federal regulations nearly in half. In 1981 there were 23,000 fewer pages in the *Federal Register* which lists new regulations, than there were in 1980. By deregulating oil we've come closer to achieving energy independence and helped bring down the cost of gasoline and heating fuel.

Together, we have created an effective federal strike force to combat waste and fraud in government. In just 6 months it has saved the taxpayers more than $2 billion, and it's only getting started.

Togther we've begun to mobilize the private sector, not to duplicate wasteful and discredited programs, but to bring thousands of Americans into a volunteer effort to help solve many of America's social problems.

Together we've begun to restore that margin of military

safety that ensures peace. Our country's uniform is being worn once again with pride.

Together we have made a New Beginning, but we have only begun.

No one pretends that the way ahead will be easy. In my Inaugural Address last year, I warned that the "ills we suffer have come upon us over several decades. They will not go away in days, weeks, or months, but they will go away . . . because we as Americans have the capacity now, as we've had it in the past, to do whatever needs to be done to preserve this last and greatest bastion of freedom."

The economy will face difficult moments in the months ahead. But the program for economic recovery that is in place will pull the economy out of its slump and put us on the road to prosperity and stable growth by the latter half of this year. And that is why I can report to you tonight that in the near future the state of the Union and the economy will be better—much better—if we summon the strength to continue on the course that we've charted.

And so, the question: If the fundamentals are in place, what now? Well, two things. First, we must understand what's happening at the moment to the economy. Our current problems are not the product of the recovery program that's only just now getting underway, as some would have you believe; they are the inheritance of decades of tax and tax and spend and spend.

Second, because our economic problems are deeply rooted and will not respond to quick political fixes, we must stick to our carefully integrated plan for recovery. That plan is based on four commonsense fundamentals: continued reduction of the growth in federal spending; preserving the individual and business tax reductions that will stimulate saving and investment; removing unnecessary federal regulations to spark productivity; and maintaining a healthy dollar and a stable monetary policy, the latter a responsibility of the Federal Reserve System.

The only alternative being offered to this economic program is a return to the policies that gave us a trillion-dollar debt, runaway inflation, runaway interest rates and unemployment. The doubters would have us turn back the clock with tax increases that would offset the personal tax-rate reductions already passed by this Congress. Raise present taxes to cut future deficits, they tell us. Well, I don't believe we should buy that argument.

There are too many imponderables for any one to predict deficits or surpluses several years ahead with any degree of accuracy. The budget in place, when I took office, had been projected as balanced. It turned out to have one of the biggest deficits in history. Another example of the imponderables that can make deficit projections highly questionable—a change of only one percentage point in unemployment can alter a deficit up or down by some $25 billion.

As it now stands, our forecast, which we're required by law to make, will show major deficits starting at less than a hundred billion dollars and declining, but still too high. More important, we're making progress with the three keys to reducing deficits: economic growth, lower interest rates, and spending control. The policies we have in place will reduce the deficit steadily, surely, and in time, completely.

Higher taxes would not mean lower deficits. If they did, how would we explain that tax revenues more than doubled just since 1976; yet in that same 6-year period we ran the largest series of deficits in our history. In 1980 tax revenues increased by $54 billion and in 1980 we had one of our all-time biggest deficits. Raising taxes won't balance the budget; it will encourage more government spending and less private investment. Raising taxes will slow economic growth, reduce production, and destroy future jobs, making it more difficult for those without jobs to find them and more likely that those who now have jobs could lose them. So, I will not ask you to try to balance the budget on the backs of the American taxpayers.

I will seek no tax increases this year, and I have no intention of retreating from our basic program of tax relief. I promise to bring the American people—to bring their tax rates down and to keep them down, to provide them incentives to rebuild our economy, to save, to invest in America's future. I will stand by my word. Tonight I'm urging the American people: Seize these new opportunities to produce, to save, to invest, and together we'll make this economy a mighty engine of freedom, hope, and prosperity again.

Now, the budget deficit this year will exceed our earlier expectations. The recession did that. It lowered revenues and increased costs. To some extent, we're also victims of our own success. We've brought inflation down faster than we thought we could, and in doing this, we've deprived government of those hidden revenues that occur when inflation pushes people into higher income tax brackets. And the continued high interest rates last year cost the government about $5 billion more than anticipated.

We must cut out more nonessential government spending and root out more waste, and we will continue our efforts to reduce the number of employees in the Federal work force by 75,000.

The budget plan I submit to you on February 8th will realize major savings by dismantling the Departments of Energy and Education and by eliminating ineffective subsidies for business. We'll continue to redirect our resources to our two highest budget priorities—a strong national defense to keep America free and at peace and a reliable safety net of social programs for those who have contributed and those who are in need.

Contrary to some of the wild charges you may have heard, this administration has not and will not turn its back on America's elderly or America's poor. Under the new budget, funding for social insurance programs will be more than double the amount spent only 6 years ago. But it would be foolish to pretend that these or any programs cannot be made more efficient and economical.

The entitlement programs that make up our safety net for the truly needy have worthy goals and many deserving recipients. We will protect them. But there's only one way to see to it that these programs really help those whom they were designed to help. And that is to bring their spiraling costs under control.

Today we face the absurd situation of a federal budget with three-quarters of its expenditures routinely referred to as "uncontrollable." And a large part of this goes to entitlement programs.

Committee after committee of this Congress has heard witness after witness describe many of these programs as poorly administered and rife with waste and fraud. Virtually every American who shops in a local supermarket is aware of the daily abuses that take place in the food stamp program, which has grown by 16,000 percent in the last 15 years. Another example is Medicare and Medicaid—programs with worthy goals but whose costs have increased from 11.2 billion to almost 60 billion, more than 5 times as much, in just 10 years.

Waste and fraud are serious problems. Back in 1980, federal investigators testified before one of your committees that "corruption has permeated virtually every area of the Medicare and Medicaid health care industry." One official said many of the people who are cheating the system were "very confident that nothing was going to happen to them." Well, something is going to happen. Not only the taxpayers are defrauded; the people with real dependency on these programs are deprived of what they need, because available resources are going not to the needy, but to the greedy.

The time has come to control the uncontrollable. In August we made a start. I signed a bill to reduce the growth of these programs by $44 billion over the next 3 years while at the same time preserving essential services for the truly needy. Shortly you will receive from me a message on further reforms we intend to install—some new, but others long recommended by your own congressional committees. I ask you to help make these savings for the American taxpayer.

The savings we propose in entitlement programs will total some $63 billion over 4 years and will, without affecting social security, go a long way toward bringing federal spending under control.

But don't be fooled by those who proclaim that spending cuts will deprive the elderly, the needy, and the helpless. The federal government will still subsidize 95 million meals every day. That's one out of seven of all the meals served in America. Head Start, senior nutrition programs, and child welfare programs will not be cut from the levels we proposed last year. More than one-half billion dollars has been proposed for minority business assistance. And research at the National Institute of Health will be increased by over $100 million. While meeting all these needs, we intend to plug unwarranted tax loopholes and strengthen the law which requires all large corporations to pay a minimum tax.

I am confident the economic program we've put into operation will protect the needy while it triggers a recovery that will benefit all Americans. It will stimulate the economy, result in increased savings and provide capital for expansion, mortgages for homebuilding, and jobs for the unemployed.

Now that the essentials of that program are in place, our next major undertaking must be a program—just as bold, just as innovative—to make government again accountable to the people, to make our system of federalism work again.

Our citizens feel they've lost control of even the most basic decisions made about the essential services of government, such as schools, welfare, roads, and even garbage collection. And they're right. A maze of interlocking jurisdictions and levels of government confronts average citizens in trying to solve even the simplest of problems. They don't know where to turn for answers, who to hold accountable, who to praise, who to blame, who to vote for or against. The main reason for this is the overpowering growth of federal grants-in-aid programs during the past few decades.

In 1960 the federal government had 132 categorical grant programs, costing $7 billion. When I took office, there were approximately 500, costing nearly a hundred billion dollars— 13 programs for energy, 36 for pollution control, 66 for social services, 90 for education. And here in the Congress, it takes at least 166 committees just to try to keep track of them.

You know and I know that neither the President nor the Congress can properly oversee this jungle of grants-in-aid; indeed, the growth of these grants has led to the distortion in the vital functions of government. As one Democratic governor put it recently: The national government should be worrying about "arms control; not potholes."

The growth in these federal programs has—in the words of one intergovernmental commission—made the federal government "more pervasive, more intrusive, more unmanageable, more ineffective and costly, and above all, more (un)accountable." Let's solve this problem with a single, bold stroke: the return of some $47 billion in federal programs to State and local government, together with the means to finance them and a transition period of nearly 10 years to avoid unnecessary disruption.

I will shortly send this Congress a message describing this program. I want to emphasize, however, that its full details will have been worked out only after close consultation with congressional, state, and local officials.

Starting in fiscal 1984, the federal government will assume full responsibility for the cost of the rapidly growing Medicaid program to go along with its existing responsibility for Medicare. As part of a financially equal swap, the states will simultaneously take full responsibility for Aid to Families with Dependent Children and food stamps. This will make welfare less costly and more responsive to genuine need, because it'll be designed and administered closer to the grassroots and the people it serves.

In 1984 the federal government will apply the full proceeds from certain excise taxes to a grassroots trust fund that will belong in fair shares to the 50 states. The total amount flowing into this fund will be $28 billion a year. Over the next 4 years the states can use this money in either of two ways. If they want to continue receiving federal grants in such areas as transportation, education, and social services, they can use their trust fund money to pay for the grants. Or to the extent they choose to forego the federal grant programs, they can use their trust fund money on their own for those or other purposes. There will be a mandatory pass-through of part of these funds to local governments.

By 1988 the states will be in complete control of over 40 federal grant programs. The trust fund will start to phase out, eventually to disappear, and the excise taxes will be turned over to the states. They can then preserve, lower, or raise taxes on their own and fund and manage these programs as they see fit.

In a single stroke we will be accomplishing a realignment that will end cumbersome administration and spiraling costs at the federal level while we ensure these programs will be more responsive to both the people they're meant to help and the people who pay for them.

Hand-in-hand with this program to strengthen the discretion and flexibility of state and local governments, we're proposing legislation for an experimental effort to improve and develop our repressed urban areas in the 1980s and '90s. This legislation will permit states and localities to apply to the federal government for designation as urban enterprise zones. A broad range of special economic incentives in the zones will help attract new business, new jobs, new opportunity to America's inner cities and rural towns. Some will say our mission is to save free enterprise. Well, I say we must free enterprise so that together we can save America.

Some will also say our states and local communities are not up to the challenge of a new and creative partnership. Well, that might have been true 20 years ago before reforms like reapportionment and the Voting Rights Act, the 10-year extension of which I strongly support. It's no longer true today. This administration has faith in state and local governments and the constitutional balance envisioned by the Founding Fathers. We also believe in the integrity, decency, and sound, good sense of grassroots Americans.

Our faith in the American people is reflected in another major endeavor. Our Private Sector Initiatives Task Force is seeking out successful community models of school, church, business, union, foundation, and civic programs that help community needs. Such groups are almost invariably far more efficient than government in running social programs.

We're not asking them to replace discarded and often discredited government programs dollar for dollar, service for service. We just want to help them perform the good works they choose and help others to profit by their example. Three hundred and eighty-five thousand corporations and private organizations are already working on social programs ranging from drug rehabilitation to job training, and thousands more Americans have written us asking how they can help. The volunteer spirit is still alive and well in America.

Our nation's long journey towards civil rights for all our citizens—once a source of discord, now a source of pride—must continue with no backsliding or slowing down. We must and shall see that those basic laws that guarantee equal rights are preserved and, when necessary, strengthened.

Our concern for equal rights for women is firm and unshakable. We launched a new Task Force on Legal Equity for Women and a Fifty-States Project that will examine state laws for discriminatory language. And for the first time in our history, a woman sits on the highest court in the land.

So, too, the problem of crime—one as real and deadly serious as any in America today. It demands that we seek transformation of our legal system, which overly protects the rights of criminals while it leaves society and the innocent victims of crime without justice.

We look forward to the enactment of a responsible Clean Air Act to increase jobs while continuing to improve the quality of our air. We're encouraged by the bipartisan initiative of the House and are hopeful of further progress as the Senate continues its deliberations.

So far, I've concentrated largely, now, on domestic matters. To view the state of the Union in perspective, we must not ignore the rest of the world. There isn't time tonight for a lengthy treatment of social—or foreign policy, I should say, a subject I intend to address in detail in the near future. A few words, however, are in order on the progress we've made over the past year, reestablishing respect for our nation around the globe and some of the challenges and goals that we will approach in the year ahead.

At Ottawa and Cancún, I met with leaders of the major industrial powers and developing nations. Now, some of those I met with were a little surprised that I didn't apologize for

America's wealth. Instead, I spoke of the strength of the free marketplace system and how that system could help them realize their aspirations for economic development and political freedom. I believe lasting friendships were made, and the foundation was laid for future cooperation.

In the vital region of the Caribbean Basin, we're developing a program of aid, trade, and investment incentives to promote self-sustaining growth and a better, more secure life for our neighbors to the south. Toward those who would export terrorism and subversion in the Caribbean and elsewhere, especially Cuba and Libya, we will act with firmness.

Our foreign policy is a policy of strength, fairness, and balance. By restoring America's military credibility, by pursuing peace at the negotiating table wherever both sides are willing to sit down in good faith, and by regaining the respect of America's allies and adversaries alike, we have strengthened our country's position as a force for peace and progress in the world.

When action is called for, we're taking it. Our sanctions against the military dictatorship that has attempted to crush human rights in Poland—and against the Soviet regime behind that military dictatorship—clearly demonstrated to the world that America will not conduct "business as usual" with the forces of oppression. If the events in Poland continue to deteriorate, further measures will follow.

Now, let me also note that private American groups have taken the lead in making January 30th a day of solidarity with the people of Poland. So, too, the European Parliament has called for March 21st to be an international day of support for Afghanistan. Well, I urge all peace-loving peoples to join together on those days, to raise their voices, to speak and pray for freedom.

Meanwhile, we're working for reduction of arms and military activities, as I announced in my address to the nation last November 18th. We have proposed to the Soviet Union a far-reaching agenda for mutual reduction of military forces and have already initiated negotiations with them in Geneva on intermediate-range nuclear forces. In those talks it is essential that we negotiate from a position of strength. There must be a real incentive for the Soviets to take these talks seriously. This requires that we rebuild our defenses.

In the last decade, while we sought the moderation of Soviet power through a process of restraint and accommodation, the Soviets engaged in an unrelenting buildup of their military forces. The protection of our national security has required that we undertake a substantial program to enhance our military forces.

We have not neglected to strengthen our traditional alliances in Europe and Asia, or to develop key relationships with our partners in the Middle East and other countries. Building a more peaceful world requires a sound strategy and the national resolve to back it up. When radical forces threaten our friends, when economic misfortune creates conditions of instability, when strategically vital parts of the world fall under the shadow of Soviet power, our response can make the difference between peaceful change or disorder and violence. That's why we've laid such stress not only on our own defense but on our vital foreign assistance program. Your recent passage of the Foreign Assistance Act sent a signal to the world that America will not shrink from making the investments necessary for both peace and security. Our foreign policy must be rooted in realism, not naivete or self-delusion.

A recognition of what the Soviet empire is about is the starting point. Winston Churchill, in negotiating with the Soviets, observed that they respect only strength and resolve in their dealings with other nations. That's why we've moved to reconstruct our national defenses. We intend to keep the peace. We will also keep our freedom.

We have made pledges of a new frankness in our public statements and worldwide broadcasts. In the face of a climate of falsehood and misinformation, we've promised the world a season of truth—the truth of our great civilized ideas: Individual liberty, representative government, the rule of law under God. We've never needed walls or minefields or barbed wire to keep our people in. Nor do we declare martial law to keep our people from voting for the kind of government they want.

Yes, we have our problems; yes, we're in a time of recession. And it's true, there's no quick fix, as I said, to instantly end the tragic pain of unemployment. But we will end it. The process has already begun and we'll see its effect as the year goes on.

We speak with pride and admiration of that little band of Americans who overcame insuperable odds to set this nation on course 200 years ago. But our glory didn't end with them. Americans ever since have emulated their deeds.

We don't have to turn to our history books for heroes. They're all around us. One who sits among you here tonight epitomized that heroism at the end of the longest imprisonment ever inflicted on men of our Armed Forces. Who will ever forget that night when we waited for television to bring us the scene of that first plane landing at Clark Field in the Philippines, bringing our POW's home? The plane door opened and Jeremiah Denton came slowly down the ramp. He caught sight of our flag, saluted it, said, "God bless America," and then thanked us for bringing him home.

Just 2 weeks ago, in the midst of a terrible tragedy on the Potomac, we saw again the spirit of American heroism at its finest—the heroism of dedicated rescue workers saving crash victims from icy waters. And we saw the heroism of one of our young government employees, Lenny Skutnik, who, when he saw a woman lose her grip on the helicopter line, dived into the water and dragged her to safety.

And then there are countless, quiet, everyday heroes of American life—parents who sacrifice long and hard so their children will know a better life than they've known: church and civic volunteers who help to feed, clothe, nurse, and teach the needy; millions who've made our nation and our nation's destiny so very special—unsung heroes who may not have realized their own dreams themselves but then who reinvest those dreams in their children. Don't let anyone tell you that America's best days are behind her, that the American spirit has been vanquished. We've seen it triumph too often in our lives to stop believing in it now.

A hundred and twenty years ago, the greatest of all our Presidents delivered his second State of the Union message in this chamber. "We cannot escape history," Abraham Lincoln warned. "We of this Congress and this administration will be remembered in spite of ourselves." The "trial through which we pass will light us down, in honor or dishonor, to the latest generation."

Well, that President and that Congress did not fail the American people. Together they weathered the storm and preserved the Union. Let it be said of us that we, too, did not fail; that we, too, worked together to bring America through difficult times. Let us so conduct ourselves that two centuries from now, another Congress and another President, meeting in this chamber as we are meeting, will speak of us with pride, saying that we met the test and preserved for them in their day the sacred flame of liberty—this last, best hope of man on Earth.

God bless you, and thank you.

THE ARMS RACE vs. THE HUMAN RACE[1]
GEORGE S. McGOVERN[2]

In 1981-1982, the country witnessed a revival of the kind of political activism that had been missing since the late '60s—more than a decade earlier—when protests against the war in Vietnam, racial discrimination, and student rights convulsed the nation. The issue that bothered many citizens and prompted them to express concern was nuclear proliferation and the possible extinction of the human race. With the United States and the Soviet Union having stockpiles of nuclear weapons "equivalent to four tons of TNT for every man, woman, and child presently on this planet" (Richard Strout, *Christian Science Monitor*, Ap. 2, '82, p 23), a growing number of Americans began seriously to ponder the unthinkable—the possibility of a nuclear holocaust.

In the forefront of this concern were prominent experts on American foreign policy and national defense including Robert S. McNamara, Secretary of Defense, 1961–1968; McGeorge Bundy,

[1] Delivered at the commencement exercises, Oberlin College, Oberlin, Ohio, at Tappan Square, at 11 A.M. on May 25, 1981.
[2] For biographical note, see Appendix.

national security advisor, 1961–1966; Gerald Smith, who headed the Strategic Arms Limitation Talks, 1969–1972; and George F. Kennan and Thomas J. Watson Jr., both former ambassadors to Moscow. They were joined by scientists, physicians, lawyers, and religious leaders who had been organizing a variety of groups to publicize the danger and rally support for a nuclear freeze. A National Clearinghouse for the Nuclear Freeze Campaign was established by volunteer groups to coordinate the efforts of organizations throughout the country to halt the buildup of nuclear arms. To focus attention on the threat, Roger C. Molander, a former expert at the Defense Department and National Security Council, organized Ground Zero, a week-long series of seminars, teach-ins, "dances against death," "run for your life" marathons, and other activities at 450 campuses and more than 750 communities throughout the country in mid-April, 1982.

Also indicative of growing concern about possible nuclear holocaust was the revelation in *Publisher's Weekly* that 130 "nuclear fear" books had been published in the past two years. The catalyst for the growing movement was the publication in *The New Yorker* in the spring of 1982 of a 90,000 word essay by Jonathon Schell; it was later published as a book, which attracted international attention.

As the campaign progressed, more and more politicians began to shed their inhibitions and speak out on the issue. By March 1982, 17 United States senators and 122 representatives had signed a congressional resolution calling for a nuclear freeze. The *Christian Science Monitor* wrote of the movement in an editorial:

> Whether or not one agrees with the concept of a nuclear arms freeze, this growing public movement is salutary and encouraging. If nothing else, it focuses national and world attention on perhaps the most perilous and difficult problem of our times. (Mr. 17, '82, p 4)

A defeated presidential candidate and rejected member of the United States Senate by his electorate in 1980, George McGovern clearly and eloquently addressed the issue of the threat of nuclear annihilation in a speech at the commencement exercises of Oberlin College on the morning of May 25, 1981. This was the 148th commencement at Oberlin, a school that prides itself on being the first to open the doors of higher education to women and blacks.

The commencement exercises took place on Tappan Square, in an open area, where chairs and a podium had been set up on the grass, under the shade of surrounding trees. Approximately 4,000 persons heard the address, including 650 graduating seniors, their families, friends, faculty, administrators, and townspeople. An academic procession and brief speeches by the presidents of the college and senior class preceded McGovern's address. A light rain began falling on the audience and Senator McGovern as the procession began, but it ended well before he began to speak at 11 A.M.

George McGovern's speech: Early in this century the distinguished Cambridge Professor of Economics, Alfred Marshall, warned that "students of social science must fear popular approval; evil is with them when all men speak well of them. . . . *It is,*" he said, *"almost impossible for a student to be a true patriot and have the reputation of being one at the same time."* (*Memorials of Alfred Marshall,* by A. C. Pignon, ed., London, MacMillan, 1925, p 89)

In 1952 the late Adlai Stevenson issued a similar warning about those of us who follow the profession of politics: "Beware," he said, "of the politician who tries to please you on every issue. He is probably the biggest charlatan of them all." With those words in mind, I invite you to look honestly at the most important challenge to Americans and, indeed, to much of humanity. I refer to the unprecedented danger to our survival posed by the nuclear arms race—a contest that has been gathering force between the United States and the Soviet Union since the end of the second world war.

If the nuclear race between Russians and Americans is not halted and reversed soon, those two societies will destroy each other along with much of the rest of human civilization. I have long been deeply concerned by the treacherous character of Soviet-American relations in the nuclear age. No other danger has prompted more reading, thinking, writing and speaking on my part—first as a student and teacher of history and then during 25 years in political life.

But since leaving the U.S. Senate in January [1981], I have looked even more intently and perhaps more clearly at the mounting prospect of nuclear annihilation. It is now my considered conviction that the mutual destruction of the United States and the Soviet Union in nuclear war is more likely than the possibility of escape through mutual recognition of the imperatives of peace. If I now had to place a wager in some gigantic gamble as to the future of the human race, I would have to say that the odds are stronger for annihilation than for survival. For the first time, I fear that the biblical prophecy of Armaggedon—that final terrifying destruction of humanity—may take place in our time.

I hasten to affirm that humankind, God willing, has the capacity to be saved if we and the Russians become determined to do so. But I can only repeat that from all present indications the probability of destruction is greater than the probability of survival.

On what factors do I base this frightful analysis of our future prospects?

First there is the stark fact that for the first time in human history, at least two nations each has the capacity to destroy the other and much of the rest of humankind in an hour's time.

In August of 1945, two American atomic bombs incinerated the people in Hiroshima and Nagasaki. The Japanese government quickly sued for peace and the world recoiled in wonderment at the terrible new power that had been unleashed. At that time only a handful of these nuclear monsters existed—all of them in American hands. Now, 36 years later, according to Dr. Wolfgang Panofsky, Director of the Stanford Linear Accelerator Center, there are 50,000 nuclear warheads stockpiled worldwide.

Dr. Panofsky has said recently that the arms race is now "set for disaster."

"Once nuclear war is initiated by any power," he warns, "under any doctrine, in any theater for any strategic or tactical purpose, the outcome will involve truly massive casualties and devastation, leading to incalculable effects on the future of mankind. No national leader," he cautions, "should assume that he can fine-tune the use of nuclear weapons in an actual conflict."

Believing that arms negotiations represent the most urgent of priorities, Dr. Panofsky calls upon all nuclear powers to "consider unilateral steps in decreasing nuclear armament."

The scientists who publish *The Bulletin of the Atomic Scientists* predict in a recent issue that humanity is fast accelerating toward a nuclear exchange. Since 1945, this distinguished scientific journal has carried a clock on its cover warning that mankind is moving toward atomic death. In 1980 the hands of the clock were set at seven minutes before the midnight doomsday. In 1981 the clock was set at four minutes before midnight.

Most of the deliverable weapons in the world's vast arsenal are in American and Russian hands. In terms of the most destructive deliverable strategic nuclear weapons, the United States and the Soviet Union now have a rough parity. Beyond our thousands of tactical nuclear weapons, the United States has approximately 10,000 heavier strategic nuclear warheads—each of them more devastating than the bomb that long ago incinerated Hiroshima. The Soviets have about 6,-000, but some of their systems are larger than ours. Together, the Soviet Union and the U.S. now have nuclear arsenals with one million times the explosive power of the Hiroshima bomb that crushed Japan in 1945. Long ago, Russia and the United States each reached and has now vastly exceeded the point at which it would have been able to absorb a first nuclear strike and still retaliate with a society-destroying conflagration. George Kennan, perhaps the best informed American on Soviet-American relations, estimates that each side has at least five times as many nuclear weapons as it needs to deter the other from attacking—even if one assumes either side actually wanted to attack. We have had a mutual suicide pact with the Russians for three decades. Both sides know that a nuclear war means the end of both countries.

Most of the nuclear structures being manufactured as the two superpowers scramble for nuclear supremacy represent a costly and totally irrational "overkill" that serves no purpose other than the ill-defined hunger to have more than the other side—or in the words of the nuclear war game-playing strategists, to increase the number of "options" once the nuclear conflagration begins.

Each nation having long ago passed the point of being

able to destroy the other no matter who hits first, the vast accumulations since then have added nothing either to deterrence or security. Indeed, it is this maddening race beyond deterrence and beyond reason that is the deadliest enemy of both superpowers.

One of our leading American authorities on the Soviet Union and, indeed, one of our wisest men, former Ambassador George Kennan, has warned recently: "Modern history offers no example of the cultivation by rival powers of armed force on a huge scale that did not in the end lead to an outbreak of hostilities." Then Professor Kennan articulated what he believes desperately needs to be said to the decisionmakers of the two superpowers:

> For the love of God, of your children, and of the civilization to which you belong, cease this madness. You have a duty not just to the generation of the present; you have a duty to civilization's past, which you threaten to render meaningless, and to its future, which you threaten to render nonexistent. You are mortal men. You are capable of error. You have no right to hold in your hands—there is no one wise enough and strong enough to hold in his hands—destructive powers sufficient to put an end to civilized life on a great portion of our planet. No one should wish to hold such powers. Thrust them from you. The risks you might thereby assume are not greater—could not be greater—than those which you are now incurring for us all.

Beyond the sobering knowledge that two countries can now pulverize the planet in a few minutes time, there is a second factor in my present fear about the survival of the race. It is the current growth of a public doctrine which holds that it may be feasible to fight and survive the next war with the use of nuclear weapons. The urgency of reaching an accommodation between ourselves and the Russians is being set aside by false pride and by a paranoid fear that only a vast new escalation of nuclear power can prevent us from becoming a second-rate people overwhelmed by Soviet wickedness and military might. The same mad doctrine has its counterpart among some Russian strategists.

We are being told that on top of the 10,000 strategic nuclear warheads in our arsenal and the 20,000 tactical nuclear devices under our control in Europe and elsewhere, we now need a vast new underground missile system in Utah and Nevada—the MX. This biggest and most costly of all military systems, probably costing a hundred billion dollars to build, would simply lead to an offsetting buildup in the Soviet Union. Thus the nuclear level would move to a much higher, more dangerous level with no relative increase in U.S. power over the Soviet Union.

Meanwhile, some nuclear strategists are now talking openly about our need to view nuclear war as a viable strategy that might kill *"only"* 20 or 30 million Americans. One of these strategists noted in a recent article in the *Foreign Policy Quarterly* that such an experience would be unpleasant but not fatal to the nation.

No one can give any such assurance about the limitations of nuclear war, but even if they could, can we really contemplate as a viable instrument of U.S. policy a war scenario that at best would kill 20 million of our fellow citizens and leave the survivors stranded to sicken and die in a poisoned, radioactive environment?

The blunt truth is that the only alternative to co-extinction in nuclear war is co-existence through détente and arms limitation.

The highest duty of every American citizen is to cast his or her influence on the side of saving our civilization from nuclear annihilation.

Eighteen years ago, the Soviet Union and the United States signed the Limited Nuclear Test Ban Treaty to end the testing of nuclear weapons in the atmosphere. That treaty has stopped the deadly practice of polluting the atmosphere with radioactive fallout from American and Russian test bombs. In making the closing speech in support of that treaty—one of the few speeches that I have heard during eighteen years in the Senate which actually changed any votes—the late Senator Everett Dirksen, the Republican leader of the Senate, said:

Mr. President, late the other night I went back to refresh myself on a little history. One of the classic reports made in our generation was the one made by John Hersey to *The New Yorker*, on what happened at Hiroshima. . . .

As he relates the story, it was 8:15 in the morning of a bright, sunny day. The weather was a little humid and warm. At 8:15 things happened. Out of the 20th Air Wing, Col. Paul W. Tibbetts Jr., flying that B-29, and with two escort observation planes, flew over the center of Hiroshima, a town of probably 375,000 persons. Then, for the first time, the whole bosom of God's earth was ruptured by a manmade contrivance that we call a nuclear weapon.

Oh, the tragedy . . . the dismay . . . the blood . . . the anguish. When the statisticians came to put the cold figures on paper, they were as follows: As a result of 1 bomb—66,000 killed; 69,000 injured (many to die later); 62,000 structures destroyed. That was the result of that one bomb, made by man in hope of stopping that war. Little did he realize what this thermonuclear weapon would do, and the anguish that would be brought into the hearts of men, women and children. At Hiroshima it caused a mass incineration such as never before had been witnessed in the history of the whole wide world. The result was almost too catastrophic to contemplate.

In the accelerated march of history, how quickly we forget. But there is the account, for all to read; and it all happened at 8:15 on a bright and shining morning, when God's day began, and when, I suppose, hundreds of thousands of people were thinking that, despite the war, they have been privileged to live another day.

Mr. President, that happened 18 years ago last month. Since then, what have we done? What steps have we taken? How far have we moved?

The President calls this treaty a first step. What sort of steps have we taken except steps to make the bombs that fell on Hiroshima and Nagasaki look like veritable toys when compared to the heavy-duty, heavy-yield weapons of today.

I want to take a first step, Mr. President. I am not a young man; I am almost as old as the oldest member of the Senate, certainly am older than a great many senators. One of my age thinks about his destiny a little. (When they bury me at Pekin, Illinois), I should not like to have written on my tombstone, 'He knew what happened at Hiroshima, but he did not take a first step.' "

Recalling the words of Senator Dirksen in the summer of 1963, let us not have it written on our tombstones: "We knew what happened at Hiroshima, but we did not take a first step."

WHAT AMERICANS WANT IN FOREIGN POLICY[1]

David D. Newsom[2]

The Georgetown University School of Foreign Service is the nation's oldest institution for training diplomats. The Institute for the Study of Diplomacy at Georgetown University was organized in 1978 by some of the country's most experienced diplomats in order to bring together "those who have borne the Ambassadorial flag and those who have built the finest in the traditions of diplomatic education." The Institute's purpose is "to learn from a knowledge of diplomacy of the past and to define the requirements for the diplomacy of the future." The Institute draws on an exceptional pool of experts in diplomacy and foreign relations to carry out its program, which includes publishing case studies in diplomatic experience and problems, gathering panels of experts to discuss issues pertinent to the diplomatic process, awarding prizes in recognition of diplomatic achievement, and the researching of aspects of diplomacy by staff members and visiting fellows.

On the afternoon of January 6, 1982, David D. Newsom, former Undersecretary of State and Ambassador and currently Director of Administration and Programs for the Institute, delivered a lecture to an audience of approximately fifty senior members of the United States Foreign Service and the armed services. The occasion was a meeting of the Foreign Service Institute's Executive Seminar, which is the senior training course for foreign service officers and selected members of other executive departments and the armed forces. The seminar met in one of the Institute's classrooms.

In his lecture, Ambassador Newsom sought to give an answer to the question: What do Americans want in their country's foreign policies? Writing in the *Christian Science Monitor* (F. 24, '82, p 23), Newsom stated that in the year since leaving government service, he had been speaking to groups and individuals around the country, seeking an answer to that question. This experience had led him to conclude that,

[1] Delivered at a meeting of the Foreign Service Institute's Executive Seminar on the afternoon of January 6, 1982, in a Study of Diplomacy classroom at Georgetown University, Washington, D.C.
[2] For biographical note, see Appendix.

Obviously, there are many Americans and many views. There are strong advocates of emphases on arms control, human rights, economic aid, population programs, environmental concerns, and many more. Clearly, also, the foreign policies of the Carter years were not popular with many people, even though, in the eyes of those who worked with that administration, there were many solid accomplishments.

Newsom stated in the article that his first impression from the year's experience was that the perception of policies is, perhaps, more important than the policies. He then went on to observe that "the perception of policies depends in large measure on how they seem to fit with one or more of four basic American concerns." These were: (1) We must be number one; (2) We are special; (3) Every problem has a solution; and (4) The Soviets should be our primary concern.

He concluded in the *Monitor* article that,

... whatever policies the United States pursues, whether radical or imaginative or cautious, must, to be acceptable, be expressed in ways which do not too strongly challenge our pride, our optimism, our impatience, and our basic suspicions of the Soviet Union.

David Newsom's speech: What does it take to create and effectively present U.S. foreign policy? First, of course, it requires an understanding of the world outside and second, an understanding of our own country: our fundamental attitudes toward the world, and the kind of actions and stances toward the rest of the world that the U.S. public is prepared to tolerate and support.

It is the task of specialists in the field of foreign affairs to understand and, hopefully, explain the world beyond our borders. But foreign affairs specialists must also understand the attitudes that determine and support policy in our own country. Not only must they effectively explain the United States to those abroad, but many, whether in civilian or military careers, must help the political leadership in this country communicate policies to the Congress and to the public.

To examine this dynamic between the formation and the explanation of U.S. foreign policy, it is useful to review briefly the Carter Administration and to ask why that Administration is perceived by so many in this country as having failed. In many ways the Carter Administration had a sophisticated view of the outside world. Its officials, particularly Secretary Vance, genuinely looked for solutions to problems. They sought, for instance, to relate the United States more effectively to the Third World. Much was accomplished, but each success carried a political liability because of opposing domestic attitudes.

The Camp David accords were a remarkable accomplishment, and yet I have been asked repeatedly "What significant accomplishment did Carter achieve in the Middle East?" The American public, it appears, is more prepared to criticize the Camp David agreement because it did not achieve all that was hoped for than they are to applaud the remarkable diplomacy which changed the strategic, military and political alignment of the Middle East.

Other examples are the SALT II and Panama Canal treaties. SALT II created severe opposition here at home, the result being almost total rejection of that treaty, not only in the Congress but by the public in general. It was the Carter Administration that finally concluded a Panama Canal Treaty, removing from our relations with Latin America one of the major irritants over many, many years. Yet that treaty was immediately attacked and squeaked through the Senate only by the addition of some very difficult and questionable amendments. The normalization of relations with China, the foundations of which were laid in the Nixon Administration, brought not praise but the Taiwan Relations Act and the consequent political problems that exist today in reconciling our responsibility toward Taiwan with our responsibilities to and agreements with China.

The transformation of isolated Rhodesia into independent Zimbabwe was again a major triumph of diplomacy. Those of us who had dealt with that problem in earlier administrations understood the depth of difference between the various parties. It was ultimately British diplomacy that resolved that problem, but the very effective groundwork laid by Secretary

Vance, Ambassador Young, Anthony Lake, Richard Moose, and others made the resolution possible. The long drama of the hostages in Iran and their ultimate release under terms which were honorable for this country was a triumph of diplomacy. Yet while the hostages were welcomed home warmly, the diplomacy that released them was severely criticized by their fellow citizens.

Support for other policy initiatives of the Carter Administration—human rights and nonproliferation, for example—was lukewarm in the public although stronger in the Congress.

What then are the domestic attitudes affecting our diplomatic maneuverability, our reactions to events abroad? Generalizations in a matter of this kind are very risky. Attitudes vary with time, circumstances, regions and other variables, yet there are certain core attitudes our people hold toward ourselves as a nation and toward the world outside. These attitudes need to be recognized in the creation of foreign policy. They need to be identified singly as strands affecting the creation and reception of U.S. foreign policy; they need also to be considered as a whole, as a world view. Along these lines, Professor William McNeill, Professor of History at the University of Chicago, has written:

Truth, in short, does not reside in the exact recording of every detail. It never has. It resides in myth—generalizing myths that direct attention to what is common amid diversity by neglecting trivial differences of detail. Such myths make subsequent experience intelligible and can be acted on. When results conform to expectations, truth has been tested and the mythical formulation gains or retains plausability. When experience contradicts expectation, it is time to mend the myth if one can, to look for limiting conditions or overriding patterns that somehow distort its acceptability.

What I'm talking about today are myths in that sense. This is not an indictment of this country. Many attitudes which are criticized by some abroad are also strengths. Our interest in the world outside, our determination, our desire to resolve issues are seen as impatience. Yet, for many who criticize our character, the worst fear is that the United States will lose interest. Nor are we alone in our generalized myths about the world around us. Others certainly have theirs based on history, on prejudices, on current conflicts; Europe is a caldron of myths.

But the possession of attitudes toward ourselves and toward the rest of the world is particularly complicated in this country for three reasons: (1) the undeniable overriding significance of what this country does in terms of the future of the world, in terms of war and peace; (2) the degree to which ethnic and ideological advocates bring their debates to our shores, whether from Eastern Europe or from Latin America or from the Middle East. We are the judge and jury, handing down verdicts on other societies and on our relations with those societies, through the decisions we make on aid, on arms sales, on diplomatic gestures. Moreover, to an extent which I think is unparalleled in any other country, the advocates, the various points of view, seek to influence the attitudes that exist in this country. They play upon our views of the world, often with very considerable accuracy, and so these views are important, not just in the creation of our own policies, but in the course of events in other countries as well; (3) our lack of control over how others see us. We cannot calculate and present to the rest of the world an official view of how we would like to be seen. Our society is open. Our films, our media, our books convey in a totally unrestricted fashion how this nation is seen, not just by its government, but by its artists, its people, its reporters. However much the government might wish to structure how attitudes are perceived, they are really perceived through the sum and substance of the private media extensions abroad.

Two prevailing frustrations are often at the heart of the reactions of our people to events abroad. The first is a deep frustration over the inability of this country to control, to foresee, or to change circumstances that we don't like abroad. There is a deep belief that through the CIA we should be able to alter political circumstances which seem to be going against our interests. There is a deep belief that we have a power, an influence through our programs or indeed through the very fact that we are Americans, so that when change goes against us, it is not very often seen as the natural result of elements in a distant country, but is somehow seen as the fault of U.S. officials who lost "X." My experience appearing before congressional committees after a revolution abroad has been that the questions are not—at least initially—"Why did this happen?" but "Why didn't we know it was going to happen?" "Wasn't there something we could have done to prevent it and can't we now do something to put the pieces back together again?" There is often in this country, a country which is on the one hand, very sensitive to political currents within its own borders, a remarkable insensitivity to the fact that other countries have internal politics as well.

Because of this frustration, we have a special problem with the United Nations. That leads me to the second of the basic frustrations that our people have in looking at the rest of the world: the fact that others so often seem to equate us with the Soviet Union. We are not in their eyes something special; we are one of the super powers. Out of this frustration grows the belief that our virtues are not seen because of our failure to tell our story effectively. As a result, this Administration has emphasized a resurgence of the view that the Voice of America and International Communication Agency programs should be devoted to telling people the truth about the Soviet Union and to telling people the truth about us.

What we forget is that the view of the United States abroad will be far more than just what our own voice disseminates, and further, that the voice will only be effective if it is credible. We either forget or are ignorant of the fact that if we are seen as anti-Arab it is going to be very, very difficult to have the United States seen as totally benign in the Middle East. A similar dynamic exists in Black Africa and elsewhere.

The cacophony of statements coming out of the United States makes it difficult for people abroad to separate out the official statement from the Congressional statement or from the editorial statement. In many places they are all seen as Americans speaking and the picture becomes confused.

These two frustrations, the fact that we can't control events and that people see us as just one more super power, arise from certain basic interrelated attitudes, attitudes that exist in both political parties and in every administration. Let me name six: First, we must be number one, (2) we are a special country, (3) we are impatient, (4) we believe in free enterprise, (5) we fear the Soviet Union and judge other countries on the basis of their attitudes toward the Soviets, (6) we see relations in terms of friendship.

Let me elaborate briefly on each one of these. We must be Hertz, not Avis. Our intense spirit of competitiveness at home carries over into our approach to foreign affairs. We still believe in unchallenged power. If we don't have it, we should have it. If we are not number one, something should be done to make us number one.

We believe that we have a special character through the freedom that we have created and espoused through our democratic institutions. Through our demonstrated altruism, we derive the belief that we are among the most generous of countries, and we hold an underlying, if perhaps not often spoken, belief that the world should ultimately, if it is to be peaceful and free, conform to the paths that we have charted.

And, in fact, we are special, as the flow of refugees to this country shows, as demonstrated by the emulation of things American around the world, and by the expectations that people have of us. Yet there are paradoxes in our view. We emphasize how good we are, we emphasize our humanitarian approach to the world, and yet in no area have we had greater difficulty in responding to the competition of the Soviet bloc than in placing doctors, nurses, and educators in countries which are still in balance between the Soviet Union and ourselves.

We are impatient—don't just stand there, do something. When a Foreign Service Officer in the Department takes a new issue to a Secretary of State or to one of the Secretary's senior aides, the question is not likely to be "What are the facts; do we *need* to do something?" The question is going to be, "What *are* we going to do about it?" Diplomacy is slow and suspicious to Americans if we do not have a clear idea of where we are going. I think we are still deeply affected by the fact that the major efforts that this country made in World War I and World War II resulted relatively quickly in forms of unconditional surrender. Vietnam showed many things, but it showed, among other things, our unwillingness as a nation to endure a sustained effort.

We believe that every problem has a solution and preferably a quick solution. As a country we are fascinated with the military option over diplomacy. The U.S. public cheered the *Mayaguez;* as stated earlier, they were far less enthusiastic about the negotiations which led to the hostage release.

There is no view more unpopular than that there are some problems that we cannot resolve but only manage. On one hand, we are a country that responds dramatically and generously to disasters. We are also a country that has great difficulty in agreeing to the kind of sustained, long-term efforts necessary for sensible economic development in the Third World. There is an underlying belief in free enterprise, a belief that comes naturally out of a country built on the risks and motivations of the free enterprise system. There is a fear of the term "socialism." We have an inadequate view/understanding of the differing conditions underlying the development of other nations, and we have an ahistorical understanding of our own national development. Thus there is a lack of understanding of the nature of development problems in many countries, so that we see free enterprise as a pattern that should automatically be adaptable to other countries as well. We make a myth of our economic success story and forget the special advantages that we had as a nation: the rich continent that lay ahead of us, our relatively small population, and the very basic help which we received initially at the beginning of our nationhood.

Perhaps the most fundamental concern is apprehension, ranging from fear among some to curiosity among others, over the intentions and competitiveness of the Soviet Union as a country and of communism as a philosophy. The fear is of the Soviet Union specifically, but also of the communist philosophy, which if given a chance to flourish, it is believed, will result in taking away that which we have as individuals and as a nation. This apprehension is fed in part by refugees from Eastern Europe who believe that this country is the only hope of reversing the Soviet domination of Eastern Europe. Fear of the Soviets is evident in our attitudes on international human rights. In contrast to the great debate over attitudes on human rights in other countries, there is virtually none on our need to make a diplomatic and political issue out of human rights in the Soviet Union. Our attitude toward political change reflects our suspicion of the Soviets and communism. We welcome the emergence of a free trade union movement in Poland. We welcome people fighting tanks in the streets of Berlin, but we have difficulty in relating to revolution against non-communist governments. We have difficulty relating positively to the image of the barefoot, open-shirt revolutionary, and so all revolutions tend to get bound up in our basic attitudes and concerns over the intentions of the Soviet Union.

There is no fundamental belief that politicians can less afford to challenge than this one. In the famous 1976 debate with Carter, Ford's statement that Poland did not lie in the Soviet sphere of influence probably cost him the election. Similarly Carter's statement after the Afghanistan incursion that he was discovering the nature of the Soviet Union probably did him an equal amount of harm.

In the Third World as a whole, we tend to see issues in terms of the global conflict with the Soviet Union much more than in terms one might expect from a country with a tradition of humanitarian concern.

Finally, we see the world in terms of friendship, not in terms of interest. If you want to receive a very severe challenge, if not a reprimand when speaking to an audience in this country, say that we should view the world from a standpoint of where our interests lie and not from a standpoint of who our friends are. Friendship we define more on the basis of another country's view of the Soviet Union than on the basis of a country's embrace of democratic institutions and processes. Thus we count Argentina and Chile as friends but

we have a very ambivalent attitude toward India, the world's
largest democracy.

We personalize our view of governments, leaders and
problems so that we see friendship in terms of individuals,
one phenomenon that brings about our problem of identification with regimes and rulers. Actions and rhetoric based on
friendship cannot help but create an image of support and
identification. Friendship tends to be easier with the English-
speaking, well-dressed oligarch than it does with the revolutionary. And so again President Carter praises Iran under the
Shah as an island of stability just a few months before the
Shah was overthrown. Vice President Bush speaks positively
about a democracy in the Phillipines seriously eroded by
Marcos' autocratic rule. Both statements were made in the
context of demonstrating our friendship.

Each of these attitudes has implications for regional policy. Europe, more united now than ever before, does not accept that we are necessarily number one. They have a different view of the Soviet Union and of socialism. They look upon
foreign policy as based more on interests than on friends.

Central America does not acknowledge our preeminence
or our ability to control events publicly. Because of our attitude toward friendship, we have difficulty in maneuvering
through a very changing revolutionary situation in much of
Latin America.

In the Middle East we are constantly confronted with the
fact that we can only manage problems, not resolve them,
and management is considered failure. When Ambassador
Habib went out and stilled the guns for the first time in Leba-
non—a remarkable diplomatic feat—his mission was labelled
by much of the press and public as a failure. And in the Middle East we have difficulty reconciling our desire to support
the friendly country of Israel with the problems of preserving
access to energy in Arab countries less willing to acknowledge our friendship.

These basic sentiments present any policymaker with a
dilemma, because the world is not prepared fully to accept
our premises. We never have had a capacity totally to foresee

and control events; to suggest that we did or should seems to many abroad presumptuous. To expect acceptance on our terms ignores the fact that others see us in the light of our attitude toward their problems: the Arabs judge us on our view toward Israel, the Africans on our view toward South Africa, the Europeans on how we see nuclear war. To look for quick and sometimes violent solutions is to ignore the benefits of patient diplomacy and the risks of precipitate action.

There is little argument that the Soviets represent the major threat to us, militarily. The argument is whether we meet that threat by a total concentration on the Soviets and on others' attitudes toward them or on the conditions in other countries which they exploit.

There are variations in attitudes by region, by race, by background. Whatever these variations, however, whatever policies the United States pursues, whether radical, or imaginative, or cautious, must, to be acceptable, be expressed in ways which do not too strongly challenge our pride, our optimism, our impatience, and our basic suspicions of the Soviet Union.

MAINTAINING THE BALANCE OF POWER IN GOVERNMENT

THE PEOPLE SHOULD GOVERN, NOT THE COURTS[1]

William French Smith[2]

On January 25, 1982, in an address to the House of Delegates of the American Bar Association, Attorney General William French Smith asked his fellow lawyers to join him in urging the courts to stop "political policy-making," which, he said, undermines "popular support for our legal profession" and "threatens the legal profession" as well as the courts. It was not an unfamiliar theme for the Attorney General; three times in the preceding three months he had made major speeches on the subject.

Smith's remarks on "judicial activism" echoed those of former Senator Sam Ervin Jr. ("Judicial Verbicide: An Affront to the Constitution," *Representative American Speeches*, 1980–1981, p 61+) and found favor with many conservative legislators. Senator Jesse Helms said, ". . . the soundness of the Attorney General's position is obvious. The rights and responsibilities of state legislatures and the Congress should not be violated by activist federal judges" in a statement accompanying one of Smith's speeches which appeared in the *Congressional Record* (No. 4, 1981, S12910). Senator Strom Thurmond placed a later speech on the same thesis in the *Record* of April 22, 1982 (S3904) with the following observation,

> I would like to take this opportunity to say that I have come to know Attorney General Smith as a man of great integrity, capacity, and dedication. I have found him to be an outstanding public servant dedicated to the preservation of ordered liberty based on sound principles of law.

Not everyone agreed with these assessments. *New York Times* syndicated columnist Anthony Lewis wrote:

> Even more amazing than Smith's obsession with a non-existent problem, voracious courts gobbling up democ-

---

[1] Delivered to the House of Delegates of the American Bar Association at 11 A.M. on January 25, 1982, in the Grand Ballroom of the Hyatt Regency Hotel in Chicago.
[2] For biographical note, see Appendix.

racy, is his failure to see a real threat to the American constitutional system—many would say the most profound threat in years. That is the legislation pending in Congress to strip the Supreme Court and lower federal courts of jurisdiction to decide certain constitutional issues. More than 30 bills, introduced by Senator Jesse Helms and others of the extreme right, now await action in the two houses. Their purpose is to undo decisions on such subjects as school prayer, busing, and abortion. Their method is simply to say that the courts have no power to decide any cases in those areas. (*Oakland Tribune*, Ja. 29, '82)

The same group that Smith addressed in this speech had, in August, 1981, voted overwhelmingly against any legislative curtailment of the jurisdiction of the courts and in support of "the integrity and independence of the federal courts." The president of the American Bar Association, David R. Brink, had embarked upon a speaking campaign to try to prevent any curbs on the powers of the courts. One of Mr. Brink's speeches on this issue appears immediately after Mr. Smith's in this volume (see p 54).

In a sense, the Attorney General's remarks in this address can be regarded as a personal defense of his statements in an earlier speech to the Federal Legal Council which had been criticized in the *American Bar Association Journal* and elsewhere for seeking to politicize the courts when he suggested the courts should heed "the groundswell of conservatism evidenced by the 1980 election."

Smith delivered his speech at 11 A.M. in the Grand Ballroom of the Hyatt Regency Hotel in Chicago to an audience of approximately 450. The occasion was the midyear meeting of the American Bar Association's House of Delegates, the policy-making body of that organization. Those present included the 385 delegates, media representatives, and members of the ABA staff. Preceding the Attorney General's remarks, ABA president David R. Brink addressed the group and the delegates voted on several issues. Most of the audience was probably aware that Smith is a wealthy Los Angeles lawyer who before being appointed Attorney General had not only been a personal friend and financial consultant to President Ronald Reagan, but also a member of Reagan's "kitchen cabinet" of informal advisors.

William French Smith's speech: It is a special pleasure to appear before this prestigious House of Delegates, which represents perhaps the world's largest voluntary professional association. Naturally, my pleasure is heightened by my longtime membership in the association you govern.

For the past year, as Attorney General of the United States, I have gained new insight into the role of lawyers in our society and the public's understanding of that role. The Attorney General, like all lawyers, represents clients and is the advocate for their interests in the courts. In addition, however, the Attorney General owes another allegiance, as do all lawyers, an allegiance to our Constitution and legal system, to the effective operation of the legal system and to its preservation and improvement.

Over the past year, I have often been struck, and sometimes bemused, by the confusion evinced in the press over those two roles. I can personally attest to the accuracy of what is called Knoll's Law of Media Accuracy: "Everything you read in the newspapers is absolutely true except for the rare story of which you happen to have firsthand knowledge."

Let me illustrate. During my first months in Washington, one obscure publication called me a "somnambulist," but *Time* magazine said I was "wide awake." Several columns reported that the Justice Department was "out of control" and "runaway." To the contrary, others said that the department had been "steamrolled by White House politicos" or that the "White House . . . is calling the policy shots on sensitive legal issues." One journal added, in bold headlines, "Justice Department 'Betraying' Conservatives." *National Review* countered that I was "the point man of the Reagan social counter-revolution." And *Time* confirmed that I had "given marching orders to (the) department to execute a right face."

As a result, I was not surprised when *Newsweek* commented that "describing the new attorney general has become a Capital Rorshach test."

I was surprised, however, when this association's press organ, the *ABA Journal*, became caught up in the journalistic confusion. Concerning the main subject of my remarks today, the need for a new measure of judicial self-restraint, our *Journal* commented that I was reflecting the Administration's "desire to politicize the federal judiciary and constitutional law." Nothing could be further from the truth. Indeed, my remarks on this subject, including a piece in the present issue of the *ABA Journal*, suggest the grave dangers to the federal courts, and hence the country, when judges stray into the thicket of political policy-making, which the Constitution wisely entrusted to the popularly elected branches of government.

Today, I want to consider the similar danger to the legal profession of a shift in policy-making responsibilities from elected representatives to the courts. I also want to urge the organized bar to join in supporting what is a matter not of politics but of constitutional principle. In doing so, however, I intend to correct some of the mischaracterizations of my previous remarks on judicial restraint.

First, I have called for judicial *self*-restraint in obedience to the constitutional limits placed upon the courts. I have said that the Justice Department will encourage that self-restraint. And I believe that it is important that lawyers in general understand and support this call to principle. I do not mean that lawyers should be less than zealous advocates for their clients in court. I do mean that your special knowledge of law should elicit your support for the constitutional principle of separation of powers.

Second, judicial restraint does not require judges to abdicate their role under the Constitution as interpreters of that instrument's limits upon legislative and executive authority. It means only that judges should respect the limits upon their own role and recognize the breadth as well as the limitations of the role envisioned by the Constitution for the elected branches of government. Clearly, courts review legislative enactments. Just as clearly, they should overturn them as unconstitutional only when a legislative objective either falls beyond the scope of legislative authority or possesses no rational connection to the legislative means adopted. There is no bright line marking those distinctions. Nevertheless, the more uncertain the logical connection between constitutional text and judicial interpretation, the more disinclined judges should be to substitute their own judgments for those of elected representatives.

Lawyers, above all others in society, should and must understand the importance of these principles. The inclination of lawyers as a group to turn every social issue into a legal question requiring judicial resolution can only exacerbate the public's suspicion of the legal profession. Those issues resolved by the courts, and especially those issues resolved on constitutional grounds by the courts, are removed temporarily or permanently from democratic or popular resolution. And the resolution is instead worked through lawyerly language and procedures that usually bewilder the public's understanding.

Our country was founded upon the revolutionary notion that the people should govern. To the extent important social issues are judicially removed from popular debate and democratic resolution, the people inevitably feels its will thwarted by the legal system itself. Each such frustration exacts a toll upon popular support for our legal system, especially when an ultimate resolution requires years of tortuous twists in the courts.

A critique of judicial activism is neither "conservative" nor "liberal" in terms of the substantive results ordered by the courts. It is merely a recognition of the importance to our constitutional system of the popularly elected branches of government. In 1941, after serving as President Franklin Roosevelt's Solicitor General, Robert Jackson wrote the following:

After the forces of conservatism and liberalism, of radicalism and reaction, of emotion and of self-interest are all caught up in the legislative process and averaged and come to rest in some compromise measure such as the Missouri Compromise, the N.R.A., the A.A.A., a minimum-wage law, or some other legislative policy, a decision striking it down closes an area of compromise in which conflicts have actually, if only temporarily, been composed. Each such decision takes away from our democratic federalism another of its defenses against domestic disorder and violence. The vice of judicial supremacy, exerted for ninety years in the field of policy, has been its progressive closing of the avenues to peaceful and democratic conciliation of our social and economic conflicts.

Though far removed from that time, we should remember that Jackson's critique of judicial activism followed a conservative Supreme Court's thwarting the economic and social policy decisions of the New Deal era.

At different points in our history, the federal courts have overstepped their constitutional authority and removed questions of policy from resolution by the political branches. Invariably, bad policy has resulted, as have serious attacks upon the independence and legitimacy of the courts. In an early example, the *Dred Scott* decision, the Supreme Court overturned an attempt by Congress to limit the spread of slavery. This limitation, which the Court imposed upon the ability of Congress to limit or eliminate slavery, was overturned only by the War Between the States. During the subsequent Reconstruction period, the Court continued to be viewed as so political an institution that Congress felt no qualms about manipulating the number of justices for purely political purposes.

In the early years of this century, the Supreme Court again entered upon an era of judicial over-reaching at the expense of legislative authority. In the 1905 case of *Lochner* v. *New York*, the Court overturned the New York legislature's attempt to ameliorate sweat-shop conditions in the baking industry. So began an era of judicial supremacy that lasted about one-third of a century. The policies implicit in the substantive due process decisions of that era were subsequently repudiated. In addition, by 1937 they had provoked the court-packing assault upon the "nine old men" of the Supreme Court.

I do fervently believe that it was wrong for the Supreme Court to use the constitutionally fictitious concept of substantive due process to strike down democratically arrived at decisions of legislative bodies. Four decades later, I believe that a similar critique applies to many court decisions today overturning legitimate legislative determinations. And I believe that, irrespective of the "liberal" or "conservative" result that flows from any court's decision.

The effort to encourage judicial restraint is most emphatically not an effort to engage the courts in politics or to undermine their independence. This audience should recognize that the courts themselves engage in politics if they exceed their constitutional role and intrude on the policy-making responsibilities of the political branches. The promotion of judicial restraint is thus an effort to secure the independence of the judiciary, not undermine it. Justice Felix Frankfurter recognized this when he wrote that,

the independence of the judiciary is jeopardized when courts become embroiled in the passions of the day and assume primary responsibility in choosing between competing political, economic, and social pressures.

Or, as Robert Jackson put it:

It is precisely because I value the role the court performs in the peaceful ordering of our society that I deprecate the ill-starred adventures of the judiciary that have recurringly jeopardized its essential usefulness. . . . By impairing its own prestige through risking it in the field of policy, it may impair its ability to defend our liberties.

Judicial restraint by the courts would serve to protect the independence of the judiciary and to ensure popular support for its role. Unrestrained intrusion by the courts upon the domain of the states and the elected branches would thrust the courts into the political arena.

It is for these reasons that, in a speech to the Federal Legal Council last October 29th, I announced a new and major effort by the Department of Justice to urge judicial restraint upon the courts.

Three areas of judicial policy-making are of particular concern. First, the erosion of restraint in considerations of justiciability. Second, the expansion of several doctrines by which state and federal statutes have been declared unconstitutional, in particular the analyses that have multiplied so-called "fundamental rights" and "suspect classes." And third, the extravagant use of mandatory injunctions and remedial decrees. Constructs employed by the courts in these areas have resulted in substitution of judicial judgment for legislative judgment.

In all of these areas the courts have engrafted upon the Constitution interpretations at best tenuously related to its text. Thereby, they have substituted judicial policy determinations for legislative policy determinations. They have removed policy-making from the will of the majority expressed through popularly and regularly elected legislative bodies. In a democracy, that insulation of policy decisions from popular opinion is exceedingly troubling. Further, judicial policy-making is inevitably inadequate or imperfect policy-making. The fact-finding resources of courts are limited and inordinately dependent upon the facts presented to the courts by the interested parties before them. Legislatures, on the other hand, have expansive fact-finding capabilities that can reach far beyond the narrow special interests being urged by parties in a lawsuit. When policy judgments are to be made by government, the values of the people expressed by their elected representatives, rather than the personal predilections of unelected jurists, should control.

Therefore, in all of these areas we shall urge judicial restraint whenever the very nature of the issues presented both practically and constitutionally require the resources of a legislature to resolve. It is to resolve those kinds of issues that the Constitution created a Legislative Branch. We intend to do everything possible to ensure that the federal courts, through excess zeal to do what they consider right, do not undermine the powers confided in the other branches by the Constitution.

I believe that it is important that this association join in the effort to encourage judicial self-restraint, not only because such an effort is necessary to secure the well-being and independence of the judiciary, a primary concern of all lawyers, but because judicial policy-making threatens the legal profession as well.

Throughout America's history, lawyers have been viewed

by the public with suspicion, if not outright hostility. Lawyers were unwelcome in many of the thirteen original colonies. Massachusetts Bay actually prohibited pleading for hire, as did, for example, Virginia, Connecticut, and the Carolinas. Similarly unkind views of attorneys continued even after the American Revolution. In 1782, the author of the famous *Letters from an American Farmer* wrote:

Lawyers are plants that will grow in any soil that is cultivated by the hands of others; and when once they have taken root they will extinguish every other vegetable that grows around them.

The historic hostility to lawyers in America has not abated in recent years. In 1978, a *Time* magazine cover story chronicled "Those [expletive deleted] Lawyers!" Just last year, *U.S. News & World Report* considered "Why Lawyers Are in the Doghouse" and cited as the public's indictment: dishonesty, incompetence, and greed. When one survey asked what institutions retained the "high confidence" of Americans, law firms finished last in a list of 13, behind the Congress, the press, and labor unions.

The age-old complaints about lawyers have, however, assumed a graver importance in recent years. The reason is simple. As the *Time* magazine cover story noted, lawyers are today "hard to live with—and without." Among the reasons cited by *Time:*

... the past quarter-century has brought a particularly explosive burst of growth in the legal industry. Since the mid-1950s the courts have discovered a spate of new constitutional rights, protections and entitlements for whole groups of peoples.

The historic suspicion toward the legal profession is particularly a matter of concern because lawyers have become so seemingly necessary. It should therefore be of grave concern to the organized bar that many now contend the legal system is usurping responsibilities that constitutionally belong to the popularly elected branches of government—the branches most responsive to all of the people, not just lawyers.

I believe that our adversary system is one of the finest developments in legal history. It guarantees the just application of democratic law to the particular circumstances of individuals with conflicting legal claims. As a result, I recognize the central importance of Canon 7 of our Code of Professional Responsibility: "A Lawyer Should Represent a Client Zealously Within the Bounds of the Law." As EC 7-4 states, a lawyer's "conduct is within the bounds of law, and therefore, permissible, if the position taken is supported by law or is supportable by a good faith argument for an extension, modification, or reversal of law." Nevertheless, the code also prescribes another equally important duty for lawyers. Canon 8 requires that "A Lawyer Should Assist in Improving the Legal System." And EC 8-1 states that lawyers should therefore "participate in proposing and supporting legislation and programs to improve the system, without regard to the general interests or desires of clients or former clients."

A lawyer knows the excesses as well as the successes of our legal system. A lawyer is schooled in its mysteries. I believe firmly that lawyers can do much to raise their standing in the eyes of the public by working, for example, to simplify and streamline the resolution of legal disputes.

More fundamentally, however, lawyers should recognize that judges, like other human beings, can overstep their constitutional roles. The result is judicial policy-making, the usurpation of the popular authority that the Constitution confided in the elected branches. If lawyers are best suited to recognize the excess, they should also join in the effort to curb that excess.

Individual lawyers appearing in court must, of course, zealously represent their clients. But individual lawyers both as citizens and as members of the ABA, and this association itself, should also urge self-restraint upon the courts. Our very concept of self-government is at stake. Lest some think that lawyerly duties end within the courtroom, let me remind them that 31 of the 55 delegates to the Constitutional Convention were themselves lawyers. As those lawyers of old framed our unique constitutional system of separated powers, the lawyers of today should work to preserve it. The independence of the judiciary and public respect for our legal system demand that of us all.

In recent years, over half the members of Congress and

one-fifth of the state legislators have been lawyers. When it comes to making law, lawyers have, and should retain, an important role. They should do so, however, as voters and as legislators, not as judges. The Constitution and the public envision no more. Neither should the A.B.A.

CAN WE AVOID CONSTITUTIONAL CRISIS?[1]

DAVID R. BRINK[2]

During 1981–1982, more than 30 pieces of legislation designed to limit the jurisdiction of the courts were placed before the 97th Congress. Most of the bills were introduced by conservatives bent on curbing the power of the judiciary in cases involving various social issues such as abortion, school busing, and prayers in the public schools. Each bill proposed, in one way or another, sought to reduce or to take away entirely the authority of the federal courts to act and to return control of public policy in those areas exclusively to state governments.

Many lawyers, jurists, and legal scholars believe that such bills imply that Congress could by statute profoundly alter the structure of American government and, if actually passed, would thoroughly put askew the traditional balance of power between the three branches.

In August, 1981, the 380-member House of Delegates of the American Bar Association voted overwhelmingly to "oppose the legislative curtailment of the jurisdiction" of the federal courts with only one person speaking against the resolution. A report adopted by the delegates stated that "irrespective of the subject involved and regardless of our individual beliefs with respect to any of them, the overriding consideration is that we support the integrity and independence of the federal courts . . . and the integrity and inviolability of the amending process."

One of the most concerned delegates was David R. Brink, president of the American Bar Association. Brink believes that these bills posed the "greatest constitutional crisis since the Civil War" and he embarked upon a speaking campaign to mobilize state and

---

[1] Delivered at a monthly meeting of the Hennepin County Bar Association in the Gopher Room of the Minneapolis Athletic Club at noon on December 7, 1981, in Minneapolis, Minnesota.

[2] For biographical note, see Appendix.

local bar associations, as well as public opinion, in opposition to the legislation. By the end of 1981, Brink had spoken on the issue nine times to groups such as the University of Bridgeport Law School, the National Jewish Community Relations Advisory Council, the National Conference of Bar Presidents, the Conference of Chief Justices, the Leadership Conference on Civil Rights, and the Bar Leadership Institute, the American College of Probate Council, and the National Press Club.

The speech reproduced here was delivered to the Hennepin County Bar Association in Brink's home town of Minneapolis at its monthly meeting in the Gopher Room at the Minneapolis Athletic Club, at noon on December 7, 1981. It happened to take place on the fortieth anniversary of the Japanese attack on Pearl Harbor and the outbreak of World War II. The speech was presented to approximately 100 lawyers from Hennepin County, most of whom were probably familiar with Brink, since he had served as president of both the Hennepin County Bar Association and the Minnesota State Bar Association. Having broad experience in public speaking, Brink has spoken on many subjects of interest to practicing lawyers, including better representation of the profession, better service to lawyers, specialization, and future planning for the profession and organized bar.

David Brink's speech: You were kind enough to give me a choice of topics today. I considered telling you what I have been doing as ABA (American Bar Association) president, giving you a laundry list of issues before the bar, or entertaining you with stories.

But then I thought a little longer. I remembered a day exactly 40 years ago to the hour—Pearl Harbor day—when I stood in the offices of the *Minnesota Law Review* and heard news I couldn't believe, that our country was being forced into a fight for its life. I thought about what it means to have survived that fight and what it means to be a lawyer in our free country. I thought about the great traditions of the Hennepin County Bar Association and the Minnesota State Bar Association as national leaders among lawyers. And I reflected that our associations represent, at its best, the great American legal tradition described in 1775 by Edmund Burke, called by Dr. Samuel Johnson "the greatest man you had ever seen." Burke said: "In no country perhaps in the

world is law so general a study (as in America). . . . This study
renders men acute, inquisitive, dexterous, prompt in attack,
ready in defense, full of resources. . . . They augur misgovern-
ment at a distance, and snuff the approach of tyranny in every
tainted breeze." I thought about Fred Stinchfield, the last
member of this association who was an ABA president, and
the fight he had to lead against the plan to pack the United
States Supreme Court. And then I concluded that I wanted to
talk to you about a single serious great issue—one that we
should "snuff (as) the approach of tyranny." I speak of the 31
proposals now before the Congress that would strip our federal courts of jurisdiction or the power to grant remedies in
constitutional cases. Those proposals are not dissimilar to the
court-packing plan of 45 years ago.

These proposals pose a possible constitutional crisis that
could prove the most serious since our great Civil War. For
the proposals now in Congress could threaten our Constitution, our separation of powers, and our very system of government.

Many of our citizens today look back to simpler, and perhaps happier, days when, in their view, we enjoyed more traditional values of home, family, and religion. As a response to
that view, a number of lawmakers are proposing legislation to
enforce more traditional moral and social views in the areas
of abortion, prayer in schools, and busing as a means of school
desegregation. Those are indeed troubling questions on which
we are entitled to our own strong individual opinions. But the
means being used—taking those questions away from our federal courts—are what threatens the crisis.

This nation serves the world as a model of representative
democracy through a written Constitution and Bill of Rights.
The genius of that model is the doctrine of separation of
powers that divides government into three branches, each
having an assigned role and each operating to a degree as a
check and balance on the others. We have conferred on the
executive a role of policy making and administration, on the
legislative the power to respond with laws to serve changing
public needs, and on the judicial the interpretation of law and

the preservation of the fundamental rights secured to our citizens by our organic document.

Assuming that the public truly desires a change in our mandated moral standards, how far should we go in our search for a solution? Some argue that we should go however far the solution requires, at whatever cost. But the founders of this nation said, no—there are limits. And they set down those limits in the Constitution and Bill of Rights. Sometimes our strong emotions on social and moral questions tempt us to tear down the limits. But for two hundred years we have remained a land of liberty and freedom. Unless we intend to give up that liberty or that freedom, those limits must stand. If we truly believe that, we must test every legislative proposal against the Constitution and the fundamentals of our system of government. If we can justify violating the Constitution merely by claiming we need to, our Constitution will soon be a scrap of paper. Two hundred years ago, William Pitt said, "Necessity is the plea for every infringement of human freedom. It is the argument of tyrants; it is the creed of slaves." If we are to remain free, necessity must yield to the Constitution and our system of government.

The current proposals respond to the view of some today that our traditional moral and social values have gone astray through constitutional interpretations of our federal courts. They pose challenges to our Constitution and to the independence and supremacy in constitutional questions of the federal trial and appellate courts and of the United States Supreme Court itself. In other words, they challenge our very form of government by threatening elimination of the third branch of federal government, the judicial.

I am not prepared to say today that all measures to curb the authority of the federal courts in these areas are flatly unconstitutional. That is a question for the courts themselves to decide. And if that question could be answered easily and definitely and if it did not lead to a confrontation among our three branches of government, there would be little difference between it and other constitutional questions that are disposed of daily by our federal courts. It is precisely because the present *legal* question is not free from doubt that a constitutional crisis is threatened and that lawyers must be especially vigilant to fight for the voluntary *policy* that has given our judicial branch its independence, power, and ultimate supremacy in dealing with constitutional cases.

It is true that constitutional scholars have expressed a variety of views on the proper interpretation of the Constitution respecting these bills in Congress. The materials from which the debate is made come from the Constitution itself and from our national history. Article III confers on our Supreme Court the supreme judicial authority, subject to such exceptions as the Congress may make, and gives Congress the power to create so-called inferior federal courts. Article VI makes the Constitution and federal laws and treaties the supreme law of the land. Article V creates procedures for the amendment of the Constitution. The first ten amendments to our Constitution—our Bill of Rights—date from 1791 and, like some other provisions of the original Constitution and further amendments, guarantee all our citizens certain fundamental rights that may not be abridged by government. The Supreme Court of the United States does not have the capacity to hear all federal cases and, therefore, Congress, under its Article III power, has created the District Courts and Courts of Appeal. But the hearing of constitutional cases has gone on in these federal courts for so many years as to become well-nigh a vested right to a hearing before them.

To me, the most reasonable deduction from these materials is that Congress has no power to make any exceptions to the jurisdiction of the Supreme Court that would limit the fundamental rights guaranteed our citizens by the Constitution and Bill of Rights. Congress doubtless can remove the jurisdiction of inferior federal courts to consider purely statutory matters or can create new courts or shift their responsibilities. But, considering the physical inability of the Supreme Court to hear all cases, it seems unreasonable that Congress can, by abolishing lower courts or limiting their subject matter or available remedies, deprive citizens of their Article III right to be heard on constitutional questions in the federal courts. Therefore, in my personal view, all bills that would limit the power of the federal courts at any level to consider or grant remedies in cases affecting the fundamental rights of citizens under the Constitution should be held unconstitutional.

Some have expressed an extreme contrary view, that the exceptions clause of Article III grants Congress unlimited power to take away the jurisdiction of the Supreme Court, and that the power of Congress to create inferior Article III courts implies the power to abolish those courts or any part of their jurisdiction. If that view prevailed, a door would be opened that would permit a future Congress to wipe out federal jurisdiction in *all* constitutional cases. At best, we would have 50 federal constitutions—one for each state. But there are even worse possibilities. If state legislatures followed the example of Congress and deprived state courts of constitutional jurisdiction, we would have no judicial review at all in constitutional cases. And what if Congress, exercising powers like the commerce power, in the name of federal supremacy, then undertook by statute to regulate all our citizens in every state to the exclusion of state law? We would have a purely central parliamentary system of government without an enforceable written Constitution.

But whether all the current proposals are constitutional or not, they represent dangerous policy and threaten constitutional crisis. The admitted purpose and intent of these bills is to change the constitutional law as interpreted by the branch of federal government to which the power of interpretation was entrusted by the Constitution. That intent demonstrated a conviction that our forefathers' trust in the federal judiciary was misplaced. It also betrays a terrible cynicism about our state judicial systems, for it is based on the belief that variations that are pleasing to current local majorities will be read into our national organic document by local courts. If that belief is unfounded, the bills are pointless. If it is well founded, it tells us that the proponents are willing to convert America into a kind of league of independent states instead of one nation. It is a kind of nonshooting civil war. It is an internal Pearl Harbor.

I cannot believe that any American today really wants a

league of states rather than a nation. What is happening is that today's expediencies are blinding us to the fundamentals. We have come to take for granted our strength standing together as a nation, governed by one wise Constitution that has served well, under our federal courts, to protect the fundamental rights of all of us against the transient whims of local majorities and the shifting policies of our successive elected executive and legislative representatives.

But suppose, for a moment, that our Constitution or its interpretation by the courts are wrong or are perceived wrong in changing times. We are not frozen into an inflexible document. Changing circumstances produce new cases and new court interpretations. If those interpretations are also deemed wrong, the framers wisely gave us the amendment process to change our organic document itself. It is true that the amendment process is cumbersome or, as Justice Frankfurter said, "leaden-footed." And so it should be. Before we alter our Constitution, we should be required to take more than usual care that we do not destroy the very fabric of our system. If we permit Congress, or even the people, to avoid this process at will by simple majorities, we have, at best, but a parliamentary system. We have lost our Constitution as the supreme law of this land. And if we lose that, we lose our system of government.

Abraham Lincoln strongly disagreed with the Dred Scott decision of the United States Supreme Court. Yet he said, "We think its decisions on constitutional questions, when fully settled, should control, not only the particular cases decided, but the general policy of the country, subject to be disturbed only by amendments of the Constitution as provided in that instrument itself. More than this would be revolution."

Congress over many years has rejected the temptation to heed calls from either the right or the left to substitute its role for that of the federal courts. In the past we have weighed the perceived needs of our time against the fundamental values of our unique system of government and have wisely concluded that, as a matter of policy, those values vastly outweigh our momentary needs. We have avoided the constitutional crisis—the ultimate confrontation of the legislative or executive branches with the judicial. We must do so once again—whatever the pressures may be. Benjamin Franklin said, "They that can give up essential liberty to obtain a little temporary safety deserve neither liberty nor safety."

For I have a deep concern, a concern that I believe it is the duty of every lawyer to put above all else, that far outweighs our concern as citizens over change in moral values. That is the concern that we may take for granted what we achieved at such cost. I am concerned that as Americans, as a people who have lived with liberty for two hundred years, it is becoming difficult for us to believe that that liberty will ever vanish. I am concerned that we no longer believe that we can ever be anything but free. That concern should be the business of every citizen, but it is the special responsibility of lawyers as guardians of the rule of law.

We must never lose our love for this nation and the liberty it bestows upon us. We must feel deeply what it means to be free and contemplate the alternative. We must glory in the genius of our Constitution and Bill of Rights. We must never forget that it is the federal courts that guarantee us our precious constitutional rights. So long as we guard our system and preserve the proper function of each branch of government, we cannot help but remain American and free. We can do no less if we are to be true to those who defended our nation against external attack forty years ago.

TO REDUCE CRIME AND REHABILITATE THE CRIMINAL

CRIME AND THE DECLINE OF VALUES[1]

MARK W. CANNON[2]

On June 4, 1981, Mark W. Cannon delivered an address on the subject, "Crime and the Decline of Values," which attracted widespread attention. In his speech, Dr. Cannon stated:

> The possibility of reducing the scourge of crime exists. In addition to skilled, often courageous law enforcement and speedy, just courts, achieving this goal will require devotion, creative energy, and a more widespread commitment to values.

The speech apparently touched a nerve because even though it was presented to a small, unpublicized conference in the Southwest, ten different legal and educational journals, with a combined circulation of more than 200,000, reprinted the address. Dr. Cannon speculates that,

> The apparent high interest in the speech may have derived from a growing apprehension that crime is threatening all that is of value in our society; and a massively growing unease and distress over a deterioration of the individual values which engender a lawful and responsible society, and at the cavalier way many institutions have been treating the need for and encouragement of such values.

Mark Cannon is the first incumbent to hold the position of Administrative Assistant to the Chief Justice of the United States, a position created in 1972, in which he works on an array of projects designed to improve the functioning of the Judiciary. The speech was made at the Southwestern Judicial Conference, an annual meeting of state justices, judges, and legal officials from Arizona, Nevada, New Mexico, and Utah, which was held in Santa Fe, New Mexico. Cannon spoke at the conference banquet at 7:30 P.M. to an audience of 150 people (100 judges and their guests).

---

[1] Delivered to the Southwestern Judicial Conference at the Hilton Inn, Santa Fe, New Mexico, at 7:30 P.M. on June 4, 1981.
[2] For biographical note, see Appendix.

As the speech was organized according to the problem-solution pattern, Cannon defined the problem as "our failure to transmit positive values, norms, and attachments from one generation to another." In analyzing the problem, the speaker discussed the effects of this failure first and then focused on its causes, the decreased teaching of traditional values and mores in our society and the rise of mass media as teachers of values. For a solution to the problem, Cannon proposed strengthening "institutions that encourage positive norms and a sense of personal responsibility." Dr. Cannon's scholarly background is revealed in the breadth of his knowledge of studies relating to this problem and his skillful use of testimony of authorities to bolster his argument.

Mark Cannon's speech: Justice Stanley Reed has reported that when the Supreme Court was deliberating over *Public Utilities Commission v. Pollock,* Justice Felix Frankfurter felt so strongly opposed to transit companies forcing audio advertising on their riders that he told the Justices he would disqualify himself. Justice Reed responded, "Felix, how can you feel so strongly about protecting captive audiences? You have been using the rest of us as a captive audience ever since you came here."

I appreciate the opportunity to address a captive audience of so many distinguished judges who are leaders in their states and communities.

Matthew Cossolotto, aide to Congressman Leon Panetta, wrote in the *Washington Post* about walking up to the front door of his home on Capitol Hill at 10:35 P.M.:

It was then that I heard the gate squeak open behind us. . . . I felt the hard cool steel of a handgun against my head. . . . The handgun told me to open the door. . . . I realized that my world of values, of reason—in fact, my life itself—counted for little. I opened the door and, under the gun's command, turned off the burglar alarm. . . . was forced to lie face down. . . .

We were at the mercy of the two feral men. We did not know what they wanted from us, nor whether the next few moments might be our last.

Then suddenly they disappeared into the night, taking . . . $31 and credit cards. Such was the extent of our tribute to the terrible god of crime, who for some unknown reason spared us. . . .

Early last Thursday morning one of the best loved gentlemen on Capitol Hill, delicatessen owner Charles Soloman, was beaten to death after he returned to his deli. He had become a foster father to many of his customers and they were left shocked and choked with tears at the tragic death of this kindly man.

Recently a 17 year-old youth of a loving black family failed to return home for dinner, or to sleep. The family members were beside themselves. Their fears were realized the next day when he was found strangled, victim number 27 in Atlanta.

Last year, virtually one-third of all homes were victimized and a reported 23,000 Americans were killed by criminals. This was up from 16,000 in 1970 and was four times as many Americans as were killed in combat per year in the Vietnam War.

If an illness suddenly struck one-third of our households, killing 23,000 Americans and costing us $125 billion per year, or if foreign-supported terrorists did the same, would we not rise up in alarm and mobilize our best intellects and harness our collective energies and resources to try to stop such devastation? We would devote ourselves unceasingly to the eradication of such an enemy.

A *Newsweek* survey revealed that 53 percent of Americans are afraid to walk in some areas within a mile of their homes at night. Although there is no panacea which will eliminate crime, anything which may reduce this malignancy requires our attention.

Instead of attempting to prevent crime, we rely on law enforcement. But as Cossolotto says, "Police are society's bouncers, there to rid us of anti-social behavior after it occurs." Thoreau long ago stressed prevention, saying "For every thousand hacking at the branches of evil, there is one striking at the roots." Yet to examine the roots of crime is perplexing.

Numerous theories attempting to explain the causes of crime and delinquent behavior have been advanced. Some assert that anti-social behavior is often "neurological" or "psychological" and, hence, uncontrollable. Others maintain that sociological and cultural factors, including poverty and class-based frustrations, contribute heavily to crime. Crime is even viewed by some to be a "rational response" to the inequities of our capitalistic economic system. The sheer profitability of crime is cited as a cause, as is the use of alcohol and drugs. One study showed that only 29 percent of offenders had taken neither drugs nor alcohol before the offense.

Though alcoholism, poverty, and perceived social injustice all contribute to crime, there is a deeper force that is causing a breakdown of our society. These merely tip the raft of social order, while a deep current is moving the entire raft at a startling speed. That deep current is our failure to transmit positive values, norms, and attachments from one generation to another.

As Justice Powell has observed: "We are being cut adrift from the type of humanizing authority which in the past shaped the character of our people." He was not referring to governmental authority, but to "the more personal forms we have known in the home, church, school, and community which once gave direction to our lives."

The U.S. Constitution, perhaps the most enduring product of western democracy, assumed two components of a well-ordered polity: a political system which prescribed *how* people should live and a metaphysical theory that explained *why* they should comport themselves thusly. Each component is inextricably bound to the other. James Madison, the architect of the Constitution, urged that in its adoption, people should "perceive a finger of that Almighty hand which has been so frequently . . . extended to our relief." But much of our intellectual community has in recent decades dismissed the metaphysical part as superstition or imagination.

We consequently live in a society where spirituality is denigrated. Arianna Stassinopoulous, former president of the Cambridge Union, wrote recently:

The relegation of religion and spirituality to the irrational has been one of the most tragic perversions of the great achievements of Western Rationality and the main reason for the disintegration of Western Culture.

Similarly recognizing the tremendous effect of spirituality and religious commitment upon society is Alexander Solzhenitsyn. He stated at Harvard:

How did the West decline? . . . I am referring to the calamity of a despiritualized and irreligious humanistic consciousness. . . . It will exact from us a spiritual upsurge.

Not only has spirituality declined, but families have been weakened. Thirty percent of all children under six years of age live with just one parent or no parents at all. Michael Novak noted in *Harpers:*

The family nourishes 'basic trust.' From this spring creativity, psychic energy, social dynamism. If infants are injured here, not all the institutions of society can put them back together. Familial strength that took generations to acquire can be lost in a single generation, can disappear for centuries. If the quality of family life deteriorates, there is no 'quality of life.'

Ironically, the very system that depends upon families for its subsistence too often undermines them through its institutions and legislation. "Almost everything about mobile, impersonal, distancing life in the United States—tax policies, real-estate policies, the demands of corporations, and even the demands of modern political forms—makes it difficult for families to feel ancient moral obligations," writes Novak.

Concomitant with the weakening of the family structure is the diminishing emphasis on ethics and values in our public schools. The Thomas Jefferson Research Center, a nonprofit institution studying America's social problems, reports that in 1775 religion and morals accounted for more than 90 percent of the content of school readers. By 1926 the figure was only six percent. Today it is almost nonexistent. A study of third grade readers reported that references to obedience, thoughtfulness, and honesty began to disappear after 1930.

A majority of parents have considered the private school alternative, according to *Newsweek.* The desire of parents to have a "clear moral framework" for their children's education is one of the factors contributing to declining public school enrollments and increases in private schools.

Is it mere conjecture that values relate to crime or is there evidence? Few people have studied this question. Searching for such studies is like panning for gold. However, since they are both little known and yet important to the curtailing of crime, they warrant more emphasis than would be usual in a speech.

Sean O'Sullivan of Columbia University, in a study of families in the Bedford-Stuyvesant area of New York, found that law abiding youth most often came from homes where the father was present and the mother was active in church. "Discipline in a family cuts the chances of drug addiction in half," reported O'Sullivan. He also found a close link between drug addiction and fighting, skipping school, drinking, and driving without a license. O'Sullivan concluded that the "complete nuclear family," combined with discipline and religious faith was the best insulation from anti-social behavior and, therefore, efforts at prevention of drug abuse and delinquency should concentrate on strengthening such families.

A thorough investigation by Peter O. Peretti indicates that when parents separate, youngsters tend to "lose interest" in their values. Peretti adds, "It might be assumed that religion does play a part in inculcating youth and adults alike with the socially desirable values of a society." Albert Rhodes and Albert Reiss, in their significant article "The 'Religious Factor' and Delinquent Behavior," after elaborate statistical analysis found that boys with no religious preference committed twice as many crimes per thousand as those "having a religious preference."

The vitality of traditional values is shown by their relationship to achievement. Many people are astounded to learn that most young achievers hold much more traditional values than others their age. A 1980 poll of *Who's Who Among American High School Students*, with 24,000 responding, revealed:

Eight out of ten belong to an active religion and 71% attend services regularly.

Nearly half don't drink and 88% have never smoked cigarettes.

A vast majority (94%) of these teens have never used drugs, including marijuana.

Eighty percent do not think marijuana should be legalized and 90% wouldn't use it if it were.

76% of these teens have not had sexual intercourse.

Some 87% of the survey group favor a traditional marriage.

A good number (52%) watch less than 10 hours of television a week.

Allen Bergin, former professor of clinical psychology at Columbia, observed:

If one considers the 50 billion dollars a year we spend on social disorders like venereal disease, alcoholism, drug abuse, and so on, these are major symptoms of social problems. Their roots, I assume, lie in values, personal conduct, morality, and social philosophy.

Alberta Siegel of Stanford wrote,

Every civilization is only twenty years away from barbarism. For twenty years is all we have to accomplish the task of civilizing the infants . . . who know nothing of our language, our culture, our religion, our values, or our customs of interpersonal relations.

The increasing number of student assaults on unfortunate teachers, under-reported at 113,000 last year, is a commentary on how America has been "civilizing" its children.

Historically, families, churches, and schools perpetuated societal norms and values. The deterioration of these institutions, however, has left a void which is being filled by such institutions as television and motion pictures. Do the mass media influence behavior?

Television brings into our homes such outstanding programming as the voyage of the space shuttle, Pavarotti and the Met, and in-depth features on most important issues. But these are not the shows primarily watched by youth. A child entering school has seen television more hours than would be spent in the classroom during four years of college. By the age of fourteen, the average child has witnessed on television the destruction of more than 12,000 people.

Many studies, reports, and articles on the audio-visual media's impact on our society underscore the concerns of many responsible analysts and leaders of the media.

An emerging body of scholarly literature indicates that violence is idealized on television; violent methods are the ones used most frequently for goal attainment. Many shows promulgate and encourage instant gratification. Deferment of gratification, often essential to the attainment of a larger reward later, is, on the other hand, subtly denigrated by many shows. One study showed that only half as many frequent television watchers were concerned about planning for the future as non-frequent watchers. Psychologist Victor Cline, editor of a collection of essays and empirical studies on values and the media, went so far as to state:

Concerning probably no other issue in the social sciences has the evidence been so overwhelming or convincing as that regarding the influence of media violence on values and behavior. Television and motion pictures are powerful teachers of values, behavior, and social conduct.

The Surgeon General of the United States reported, "The overwhelming consensus and the unanimous Scientific Advisory Committee's report indicate that televised violence, indeed, does have an adverse effect on certain members of our society."

Alberta Siegel asks, regarding many television shows:

How many instances are there of constructive interventions to end disagreement? What other methods of resolving conflict are shown? How many instances of tact and decency could an avid televiewer chronicle during the same hours? How often is reconciliation dramatized? What strategies for ameliorating hate are displayed? How many times does the child viewer see adults behaving in loving and helpful ways? What examples of mutual respect does he view? What can he learn about law and order? How many episodes of police kindness does he see? How frequently does the glow of compassion illuminate the screen?

Self-indulgence is often promoted and sensitivity and sympathy belittled.

Shifting values may explain the increasing tendency of delinquents to blame others—society, other people, and their social and economic conditions—for their actions. Last fall I visited the Union Gospel Mission in Seattle, which provides free beds and meals to thousands of unfortunate, rootless people. The Reverend Stephen Burger said a significant difference from the past was that "older down-and-outers readily admit having 'messed up their lives.' But the younger men have no moral concept that they have done anything wrong."

In short, the decreased teaching of traditional values and mores in our society and the rise of mass media as teachers of values have produced results which challenge our ingenuity.

Crime and delinquency cost us at least 125 billion dollars per year, forcibly alter our lives, destroy people, frighten and demoralize us, and may even threaten our civilization. The vast resources we commit each year to law enforcement, the courts, correctional institutions, rehabilitation, and crime prevention efforts have unfortunately not curtailed the surge of crime. We must therefore regroup, and explore additional methods to reduce and prevent crime.

Institutions that encourage positive norms and a sense of personal responsibility should be strengthened. If Americans successfully fortify the foundations of pro-social behavior, rather than simply combat the symptoms of anti-social behavior, some embryonic crime will be eliminated. We must focus on the roots of the problem—some of which are the beliefs, values, and attitudes being adopted by the young.

An illustration of how an established institution can help the young was shown by the Harvard Public Health School. As part of its preventive medicine program, it targeted smoking in junior high schools. Dr. Albert McAlister worked with non-smoking student leaders who had classroom discussions on questions such as why people smoke, showed films, and set up role playing on such problems as resisting taunts. He found that in some schools the number of new smokers could be cut in half. He also reported positive results dealing with alcohol and drugs.

Since the family, the church, the school, and the community have traditionally encouraged pro-social behavior by teaching values of integrity, accountability, planning for the future, service, and respect for others' rights, efforts should be made to strengthen people's affiliations with these entities. Strong ties to one or more of these encourage adherence to rules. Theories which maintain that people "stay out of trouble" because of their association with traditional institutions, termed "bonding theories," are becoming increasingly accepted by sociologists and criminologists.

Schools should strengthen and expand programs encouraging broad student participation, particularly by those who generally hang back, thereby providing more students with a sense of personal success. Successful involvement in meaningful activities, with clear and consistent reinforcement for positive behavior, strengthens the bonds which help prevent delinquent behavior. Such activities may be athletics, music, student government, special-interest clubs, or drama and dance. Major goals of these activities should be to heighten each student's sense of personal success, attachment to teachers and to school, and belief in moral order. Committed and competent teachers can also encourage student involvement and satisfaction with learning. John Steinbeck put it well:

In her classroom our speculations ranged the world. She breathed curiosity into us, so that each morning we brought in new questions, cupped and shielded in our hands like captured fireflies. When she left us we were sad, but the light did not go out. She had written her indelible signature on our minds. I have had many who have taught me soon forgotten things, but only a few who created in me a new direction; a new energy. I suppose, to a large extent I am the unsigned manuscript of such a teacher. What deathless power lies in the hands of such a person.

The Center for Action Research reports, "The only important conventional affiliations for most young persons are the school and the family. When these deteriorate, there is usually nothing left. In practice, many youth do not even have the luxury of two independent affiliations." The number of conventional ties open to young people should be increased. An obvious option is through employment. Though many "make-work" programs have demonstrated little success in deterring delinquent behavior, the Center reports that significant "employment that creates an affiliation that the young worker does not want to jeopardize through misconduct . . . should deter delinquent behavior."

Special benefits come from youth helping youth through such volunteer activities as tutoring, day care centers, and counseling their peers. The National Committee on Resources for youth has documented 1500 successful examples of such programs.

Community-focused youth participation projects can increase attachments to the neighborhood and community and thereby help prevent delinquency. Community planning committees should include youths, organize activities, and seek to provide an environment for pro-social behavior. A major goal should be to include young people who are not typically involved in leadership roles in their schools.

Another possibility for increasing ties is through organized religion and service groups. By providing programs for youth and adults in athletics, arts, crafts, music, and community service, religious affiliations could be broadened and involve an increased proportion of young people. This, of course, should be done by church groups, since public schools are prohibited from promoting religions.

In short, we must find ways to increase the number of meaningful "bonds" our youth have with institutions encouraging pro-social behavior. If we do not, many youth will find reinforcement from less worthwhile sources.

One of the most effective ways to offset negative norms and behavior is to promote values in our schools—even though this is difficult in a pluralistic society. Increased use of curricular materials and emphases that provide both the incentive and the resources for confronting problems of moral commitment and choice is a necessary first step. The Hon. Charles E. Bennett testified before a House sub-committee:

The home and the church can no longer be solely relied upon. Today they are least available where most needed. These institutions today are no longer equipped to handle the job without help from our schools. Those children who are most in need of instruction are getting it least.

Congressman Bennett hopes that young people can "learn to formulate their own values in an open academic atmosphere where free discussion may improve and strengthen our culture."

A recent Gallup poll found that 79 percent of the public favored "instruction in the schools that would deal with morals and moral behavior." Only fifteen percent were opposed. As the Center for Action Research points out, such instruction could be carried out completely "within Constitutional limitations."

In 1967, Sandrah L. Pohorlak published a study conducted at the University of Southern California. She found that in over half the states, schools were required to teach ethics. Yet although many laws *required* instructors to teach ethics, states provided *nothing* in the way of texts, guides, or other materials to help teachers deal with ethics and character in the classroom.

Amoral America, a book published in 1975, summarized a study by political scientists George C. S. Benson and Thomas S. Engeman. "Contemporary western society," wrote Dr. Engeman, "suffers from inadequate training in individual ethics. Personal honesty and integrity, appreciation of the interests of others, non-violence, and abiding by the law are examples of values insufficiently taught at the present time." Dr. Engeman continued, "Our thesis is that there is a severe and almost paralyzing ethical problem in this country. . . . We believe that we can demonstrate that unlawful behavior is in part the result of the absence of instruction in individual ethics."

The Thomas Jefferson Research Center has identified case histories where dedicated, competent teachers have achieved remarkable improvements in discipline and deportment by emphasizing ethics and character in the classroom. For example, the Character Education Curriculum, developed by the American Institute for Character Education is a systematic program in ethical instruction for kindergarten through sixth grade. It has been tested in more than 400 schools in 19 states with dramatic success in a number of instances.

The Character Education Curriculum has been in continuous use at Wendell Phillips Public School #63 in a poverty area of Indianapolis since September 1970. Principal Beatrice M. Bowles described the school before character education:

The building resembled a school in a riot area. Many, many windows had been broken, and the glass had been replaced with masonite. . . . Most of the pupils were rude, discourteous, and insolent to the members of the faculty. . . . The children had no school pride, very poor self-image, and were most disgruntled because they had to attend "that old school."

Mrs. Bowles reported surprising results during the six years after all of the teachers began using the character development program. "There has been less than $100 of glass breakage and this has been accidental. Student attitude has greatly improved. . . . There is a feeling of one for all and all for one." Mrs. Bowles reported that "discipline and vandalism are no problem. . . . Our children are well behaved, courteous, and with few exceptions, achieving at maximum potential. . . . The program has been a tremendous success for us and our children."

Literature reinforcing traditional values need not be dull. Far from it. Much adult literature has become nihilistic, empty of moral content, and reflective of the view that life is meaningless and purposeless. Nevertheless, it is interesting that an author who has been popular with young people is Ray Bradbury, who unabashedly believes America is a great success. His science fiction is cheerful and reflects a clear sense of moral order.

Research shows it is practical to teach ethics in junior high school, high school, and at college levels. Don Hutson, speaking before the Phi Alpha Delta Law Fraternity, said:

You don't become ethical when you pass the Bar. You don't suddenly find integrity by turning a faucet. And you can't find honesty at the corner drug store. It has to be learned, and understood, at the law schools, in the undergraduate schools, and yes even down into the high schools of America. That is where you learn the basic principles that ought to guide you as a lawyer.

Encouraging results also appear to be coming from nearly 500 "law-related education programs" established in recent years. Under these programs, information about the law, both the benefits it provides and the responsibilities it requires, is being disseminated among participating students from kindergarten to twelfth grade. This increases their ability to make informed and responsible decisions. Equally important as teaching substantive law is providing students with an understanding of the moral foundations of our legal system. Having been taught by judges, law students, and lawyers, students better comprehend and appreciate law enforcement, the judicial system, and legal concerns relevant to their personal lives and the reasons the legal system should receive support. It has been generally observed that student participation and interest in these programs is high. The first Values Education Commission in America, recently established in Maryland, found that there is "nothing in court decisions that would preclude the teaching of ethical content. It has been made equally clear that the schools have both the right and the duty to instill into the minds of pupils those moral principles which are so necessary to a well-ordered society."

Thus Frank Goble, president of the Thomas Jefferson Research Center, concluded that, based upon tens of thousands of hours of research, "an increase in quality and quantity of ethical instruction in our schools and other institutions is the only practical method to bring present exploding crime, violence, and delinquency under control."

Similarly, Owen V. Frisby, vice president of the Chase Manhattan Bank, testified: "Without materials in the curriculum and much more emphasis on character building in the classroom and in our homes, we will not produce as many future leaders as we need to solve the enormous number of problems that will face the next generation." He continued, "The benefits of such an effort in the schools, in our homes and in the media would certainly be vast. It would mean less crime, less drug addiction, less alcoholism, less violence in the classroom, less cheating on exams, less inflation because of a reduction in retail theft, more productivity, and a much happier society."

It is interesting to note that during Chief Justice Burger's February speech in Houston, the audience burst into spontaneous applause when he stated: "Possibly some of our problem of behavior stems from the fact that we have virtually eliminated from public schools and higher education any effort to teach values of integrity, truth, personal accountability, and respect for others' rights."

A backup to the more immediate socializing institutions of our society—the home, school, and church—is the community. Communities influence the development of their citizens by offering general norms and expectations for either deviant or conforming behavior. Crime rates are associated with characteristics of community areas.

Nineteen thousand Neighborhood Watch Programs have been created, providing unique protection for residential areas. Their social strategy of engaging neighborhood members in shared activities around the common goal of crime prevention develops a community pride and establishes community norms against crime. A report by the Center for Law and Justice at the University of Washington hypothesized that these norms can "contribute to a climate in which criminal actions are viewed by community youths as both risky and unacceptable rather than as a routine part of growing up." Furthermore, some junior watch programs in schools have been highly effective against drug dealers. The National Neighborhood Watch Association has taken on the important challenge of expanding and strengthening these programs, which encourage close cooperation between law enforcement officials and citizens and allow communities to overcome sentiments of frustration and helplessness with regard to rising crime. A county police officer was quoted in the *Washingtonian* magazine as saying, "Ninety-nine percent of all arrests depend on citizens giving us information." Whatever the actual percent, the value of alert neighbors who inform police cannot be overstated.

In summary, violent crime and juvenile delinquency have been ascending. Attempts to explain and fight crime have been, at best, only partially successful. The diminished influence of traditional institutions and our failure to promote ethical standards suggest another explanation for crime. Audiovisual media have partially replaced the family, church, school, and community in conveying values to the oncoming generation and these often appear to encourage hedonism and the use of force. We are in jeopardy of becoming a valueless society and of encouraging decision-making by aggression instead of by reason and democratically established law. If this is the case, then possible avenues to pursue in the prevention and elimination of crime are: teach values in our schools; promote law related education so young people understand both the rights and the responsibilities of our Constitution and legal system; increase youth activities by constructive organizations; guide children to quality media productions; increase the number of potential bonds or attachments citizens have with pro-social institutions; strengthen families and communities; and educate and constructively counsel delinquents. We must, in short, revitalize and strengthen the moral and ethical foundation of our society.

The possibility of reducing the scourge of crime exists. In addition to skilled, often courageous law enforcement and speedy, just courts, achieving this goal will require devotion, creative energy, and a more widespread commitment to values. There is evidence that more youth can be reached. A $5 million study of schools included two conclusions—smaller schools do better than large ones and it makes a difference when the school's principal is strongly committed to and encourages basic learning—showing that students are far from impervious to effectively projected values of teachers.

Indeed, the stakes are high. Since decision-making power belongs to the entire citizenry, our system requires widespread responsibility and wisdom. Yet responsibility and wisdom are not ours by nature. They must be learned. If our society neglects this teaching, we do so at our peril. During the formative period of our nation, judges, particularly while circuit riding, helped explain and increase support for the new Constitutional system. So, like your predecessors, you also can educate citizens today to civic virtue, moral responsibility, and voluntary support of law. You should call their attention to the reasons to abide by the law and to make responsible, ethical contributions to improve our society. Hopefully, this will not only deter law breaking, but will also enrich the quality of life and happiness of our citizens. May we all rise to the challenge ahead!

A MODEST PROPOSAL FOR PRISON REFORM[1]

WARREN E. BURGER[2]

With a record 48 percent of the public fearful of venturing out alone after dark in their own neighborhoods, according to a Gallup Poll, the American people in 1981–1982 were ready for innovative proposals for prison reform. Critics maintained that current prison facilities were outdated, understaffed, and not rehabilitating criminals. They also feared that a possible early release of inmates to ease overcrowding posed a threat to public safety by putting dangerous persons back on the streets. A Gallup survey in January, 1982, indicated that two-thirds of the people would be willing to pay more taxes to improve the nation's prisons.

Warren E. Burger, Chief Justice of the United States Supreme Court, addressed the issue of prison reform in a speech at the George Washington University National Law Center on May 24, 1981, in Washington, D.C. The occasion was the commencement exercises of the Law Center. The speech was delivered at 1:30 P.M. in the university's Charles E. Smith Center auditorium—an athletic facility—to approximately 2,000 graduating students and their friends and families. The presentation of awards honoring outstanding students and faculty and the conferring of an honorary Doctor of Law degree on Justice Burger preceded his address, which was covered by major newspapers, many television stations, and National Public Radio.

---

[1] Delivered at the commencement exercises of the George Washington University National Law Center in the Charles E. Smith Center auditorium at 1:30 P.M. on May 24, 1981.

[2] For biographical note, see Appendix.

Instead of using the occasion to "pass the torch" to the graduating seniors—as once was the custom at commencements—Justice Burger chose instead the increasingly frequent practice of utilizing the exercises as a forum to express his views on a significant problem: his belief in the need for prison reform. Although he disclaimed being an expert in the field of penology or corrections, he told his listeners that "close observations of criminal justice and correctional practices for 25 years have left me with certain impressions." Burger then revealed what he believed to be the purpose of imprisoning someone for committing a crime, saying:

> I have long believed—and said—that when society places a person behind walls and bars, it has a moral obligation to take reasonable steps to try to render him or her better equipped to return to a useful life as a member of society.

He devoted the rest of the speech to a discussion of two "modest" and "affordable" steps which he believed society should take to meet that moral obligation, proposing: (1) better training of prison and correctional personnel; and, (2) programs to make certain that every prison inmate was provided with educational training in the basic skills of reading, writing, and arithmetic and vocational training in the skilled and semi-skilled crafts.

Speeches by Supreme Court chief justices, always significant and of interest, may chart new directions. Burger has been a particularly outspoken justice. His earlier speeches have been reprinted in the *Representative American Speeches* volumes for 1980-1981, 1978-1979, 1976-1977, and 1970-1971.

Warren Burger's speech: The ancient American custom of commencement speeches is an innocuous one that has done very little harm to graduates and may have the benefit of teaching them the virtue of patience. And parents, now released from paying the inflated rate of keeping a student in college, are bound to be in such a happy mood today that no speech could depress them!

I have no talent in framing cosmic remarks about the future which terminate with a "handing of the torch" to the survivors of three years of the rigors of a law school. My training as a lawyer is to try to identify problems and seek solutions. That will now be your role.

If there is a "torch" in the problem I discuss today, it is one that will singe your hands and burn your pocketbooks in the years ahead—probably for the rest of your lives. Not serious burns, but some.

Now let me tell you why it is important.

In my annual report to the American Bar Association recently, I discussed the appalling and increasing rate of crime and our apparent inability to cope with it. Since then, two particularly gross criminal acts have shocked the entire world and underscored the point.

I reminded the American Bar that governments were instituted by people primarily for their collective protection. Our own system of government, established 200 years ago—as it has evolved—affords more safeguards, more protections, and more benefits for a person accused of crime than any other system of justice in the world. The resolution of guilt is marked by characteristics which make our system unique in the world:

(a) It extends over a longer period of time than in any other judicial system;

(b) It allows for more appeals and more retrials than any other system in the world;

(c) After all appeals are fully exercised, it allows—in fact it encourages—continued attacks on the conviction even though that conviction has become presumptively final;

(d) But in the final step—the correctional stage—we seem to lose interest and our performance must be judged a failure.

No one questions that a criminal conviction should always be open to correct a miscarriage of justice. But no other system in the world invites our kind of never-ending warfare with society, continuing long after criminal guilt has been established, beyond reasonable doubt, with all the safeguards of due process. Our system has moved thoughtful, sensitive observers who are dedicated to individual liberty to ask: "Is guilt irrelevant?"

On a number of occasions over the past 25 years since I have been a member of the judiciary I have undertaken to discuss the subject of corrections, correctional practices, and correctional institutions.

That is my subject today. My concern on this subject has led me to visit many such institutions in the United States and even more in the countries of Europe.

Looking back we see that over the past half century we have indulged in a certain amount of self-deception with euphemisms, sometimes to sugar coat the acid pills of reality, and sometimes to express our humane aspirations for those who break our laws: "prisons" become "penitentiaries"— places of penitence—juvenile prisons become "reform schools," and more recently we have begun "half-way houses," without being quite sure half way from what to what.

None of this is bad. I do not refer to these terms to disparage them or to question the humane impulses that led us to substitute them for the harsh term "prison." Yet it is now beginning to emerge that these terms may reveal our own confusion and our own lack of direction to achieve the universally accepted objective to lend a helping hand to those who are confined for breaking the law. That we are confused, that we lack direction, is not surprising for we deal here with an intractable problem that has plagued the human race for thousands of years.

I cannot qualify as a professional or as an expert in the field of penology or corrections, but close observations of criminal justice and correctional practices for 25 years have left me with certain impressions. Some of those impressions have changed as reality overtook early hopes and aspirations which I had shared with penologists and judges.

I have long believed—and said—that when society places a person behind walls and bars it has a moral obligation to take reasonable steps to try to render him or her better equipped to return to a useful life as a member of society.

Note, I say "try," and I use the term moral obligation, not legal, not constitutional. The constitution properly mandates due process; it mandates many protective guarantees, but it mandates nothing concerning the subject of punishments except that they be not "cruel and unusual." The laws aside, to make these people good citizens is also for our own proper self-interest—not just theirs.

Even as recently as 20 or 25 years ago, I shared the hopes of great penologists like James V. Bennett, Torsten Eriksson of Sweden, and Dr. George Sturup of Denmark, and many others that enlightened correctional programs would change and rehabilitate prisoners. With many others, I have had to recognize—to my sorrow—that, broadly speaking, prospects for rehabilitating convicted persons are a great deal less promising than the presumed experts had thought.

To do all the things that might have some chance of changing persons convicted of serious crimes will cost a great deal of money and 1981 is hardly the year in which to propose large public expenditures for new programs to change the physical plants and internal programs of penal institutions. So what I am about to propose are programs of relatively modest fiscal dimensions which I believe will help, but with no guaranteed results.

Estimates on the cost of criminal activity are necessarily speculative. How should we measure murder, rape, or assault? But those who have studied it give estimates as high as over 100 billion dollars—billion—not million. This is reflected in a range of ways: the direct loss suffered by the victims; increased insurance rates; increased security by home-owners and businesses; increased police departments; increased court facilities; and increased public assistance to victims and their families.

To approximate ideal solutions would cost a great deal of money and require a very long-term program. But we should not wait until we can do the whole job—the ideal—however that may be defined. We should begin where we can, at a level we can afford. Small steps are better than none.

Two steps could reasonably be taken within the range of

affordable expenditures. I relate them chiefly because they are affordable in an economic sense—and affordable in terms of the psychology and the political and economic realities of 1981. These proposals are closely related, both bearing on training and education—training of the inmates and training of the keepers.

In 25 years on the bench, I have observed and dealt with more criminal cases, and cases dealing with conditions inside prisons, than I can estimate. I have visited many penal institutions and I assure you a prison is not a pleasant place, it is not even a comfortable place. It probably can never be made either comfortable or pleasant; but neither pleasure nor comfort is the primary object of the enterprise. At its best, it is barely tolerable and even at that level a penal system is enormously costly—and it is paid for partly by the crime victims on the outside.

In all too many state penal institutions the personnel—the attendants and guards—are poorly trained and some are not trained at all for the difficult and sensitive role they should perform. There is an astonishing rate of turnover of guards and correctional personnel. One state, widely regarded as having an enlightened correctional system, has a 40 percent annual turnover. One state has a 54 percent, one 60 percent, another 65 percent, and another 75 percent turnover.

How can any human enterprise be effective with that rate of turnover of key personnel? The turnover reflects, in part, the appallingly low salaries paid. And I venture to say that there is a correlation between the low salary, the rapid turnover, and the amount of training.

Long ago I observed the marked contrast between the security personnel in the prisons of northern European countries and the prisons in our country. In Northern Europe, guards are carefully screened and highly trained; that is as it should be for they are dealing with abnormal people in a very demanding setting. Without special training, prison personnel can become part of the problem rather than part of the solution.

An important and lasting consequence of lack of trained

personnel is the impact on the inmate—the individual inmate—who continues his hostility toward society, toward fellow inmates, and toward prison personnel. The "keepers" come to be the immediate symbols of the society that keep them confined. Unfortunately, judicial holdings have not always discouraged this warfare. More often than not, inmates go back into society worse for their confinement. Our dreams and hopes concerning rehabilitation have not been realized.

I begin with step one.

At present, there is no single, central facility for the training of prison and correctional personnel, particularly those at the lower and middle levels who work with prisoners on a one-to-one basis. I discussed this subject in 1971 at the Williamsburg Conference on Corrections and this led to the creation of the National Institute of Corrections which has conducted regional seminars to train middle and upper echelon prison personnel since 1972.

The operation of a correctional or penal institution is no place for amateurs. It calls for substantial professional training and the highest order of sensitivity, beginning at the guard level. We need look only to the volume of complaints, the disorders, and riots in these institutions over the past decade to find abundant evidence of this. If the only problem were the control of disorders it might be manageable, even if only by use of raw force, but force is not the solution. In a limited sense these institutions can be compared with the production lines of Detroit: recidivism is the penologists word for "product recall." When prisons turn out "products" with a high rate of recall we have disaster. And our current rate of recall recidivist offenders is a disaster. And you will inherit that disaster.

Under the leadership of Norman Carlson, of the Federal Bureau of Prisons, and Allen Breed, Director of the National Institute of Corrections, much has been done to improve conditions. But more is needed.

The best of prison administrators cannot change some of the negative conditions unless those in the high-turnover, lower echelons are carefully screened, well-trained, and reasonably paid. Psychological testing of applicants is imperative to screen out people with latent tendencies of hostility. The existing statutory prohibitions on psychological screening must be reexamined. Today, those lower positions in most of the states are generally not paid adequately enough to get minimally qualified people.

One of the great, and perhaps most lasting, contributions of the Federal Bureau of Investigation was the founding of the National Police Academy by J. Edgar Hoover. For over 45 years, the F.B.I. has given advanced training to thousands of state and local police personnel. That training has vastly improved the quality of law enforcement in America, both in terms of efficiency and the kind of law enforcement a decent society should achieve. A sheriff, constable or policeman on the street cannot avoid errors under the Fourth Amendment, for example, if he or she has not been trained to appreciate the sensitive and elusive nuances of that rule of law. The cost of creating and maintaining the F.B.I. Academy is but a tiny fraction of the benefits it has conferred.

The time is ripe to extend the fine work begun in 1972 by the National Institute of Corrections and we should proceed at once to create a National Academy of Corrections to train personnel much as the F.B.I. has trained state and local police. This is especially needed for the states which have no real training resources available. The academy should also provide technical assistance to state and local institutions on a continuing basis.

The cost of establishing such an institution, particularly if it could be made as an adjunct at the F.B.I. Academy at Quantico, is not great. The physical facilities of classrooms and dormitories could be used interchangeably by both the F.B.I. police training program and the correctional academy. I am reliably informed that the faculty of such an institution could be made up of not more than a dozen permanent staff with the balance of the training conducted by an ad hoc faculty of specialists drawn from the state and federal systems. Alternatively, the United States could acquire the facilities of a small, centrally located college which is closing its operations. Such a facility could readily be adapted to this purpose.

Now, step two.

The second step for which I would urge consideration is one that would need to be phased over a longer period. We should introduce or expand two kinds of educational programs:

The first would be to make certain that every inmate who cannot read, write, spell, and do simple arithmetic would be given that training—not as an optional matter but as a mandatory requirement. The number of young, functional illiterates in our institutions is appalling. Without these basic skills, what chance does any person have of securing a gainful occupation when that person is released and begins the search for employment—with the built-in handicap of a criminal conviction? To those who view the mandatory aspect as harsh— and some will—I suggest that the total work and study hours of inmates be no greater than we demand of the 15,000 young Americans who are cadets at our service academies—or law students!

Focusing on the longer term prisoner, the second phase of this educational program would require a large expansion of vocational training in the skilled and semi-skilled crafts. So that a prisoner would not leave the institution without some qualifications for employment in the construction, manufacturing, or service industries, these vocational training programs should also be mandatory. An inmate who declines to cooperate must be motivated to do so by incentives, including shortening the sentence. Just as good behavior credit is now allowed to reduce sentences, we should allow credit on sentences for those who cooperate. We should help them to learn their way out of prison. Rewards and penalties accompany the lives of the cadets I spoke of—and of law students. Why should this not apply to prisoners?

A few days ago I visited with W. Clement Stone, a fine American business leader, who has devoted much of his time and money to improve the lot of prison inmates. He has written and lectured on the crucial role of motivation in the lives of people. Prisoners are people and we must try to motivate them, try to train them, try to instill the self-esteem that is essential to any kind of normal life. We may succeed with only a small percentage, but we must try.

One of the institutions which impressed me in my visits to correctional facilities over the last 25 years was a juvenile prison in Europe. It had on its walls in the main entry lobby four statements which added up to a carrot and a stick. Here is the first thing the new inmate sees when he arrives to begin his term:

First: "You are here because you need help";
Second: "We are here to help you";
Third: "We cannot help you unless you cooperate";
Fourth: "If you don't cooperate, we will make you."

Someone may say that this is a harsh proposition to put to the people who are unfortunate enough to be in prison. But I suggest to you that among the factors which would explain the presence of that person at that place at that time is that he or she has not been subject to the discipline calling for adherence to certain standards of work and learning. Motivation is absent, but even small successes can spark motivation and that kind of carrot and stick program provides motivation.

We know that people who have neither learned to learn nor learned to work have little basis for the self-esteem or the esteem for others that is so essential to the human existence.

There is nothing novel in what I am proposing. There are skilled people who have thought about these problems for a long time who stand ready, willing, and able to implement them if only the government will act in the areas in which only a national government can act efficiently.

These are two very small steps in the whole scheme of this melancholy picture of crime in America. They are not necessarily logical starting points, but they are a beginning. The way to get started on any solution is to face the problem and take one or two steps—however small.

Even in this day of necessary budget austerity, I hope that the President and the Congress, in whose hands such matters must rest, will be willing to consider these two modest, but important steps. No one can guarantee results, but if we accept the moral proposition that we are our brothers' keepers and that there is a divine spark in every human being—hard as that is to believe at times—we must try.

For those who are reluctant to finance moral propositions, the hard economics of the cost of crime may offer greater inducement. For yet others, these programs offer the combined appeal of Christian charity and New England frugality.

The "torch" is now yours. I hope it singes you enough while you earn large fees from affluent clients to assure your support for these steps, because the consequences of the present system will fall on you and on your children.

EDUCATION

CAN WE HAVE EXCELLENCE IN EDUCATION?[1]
DONALD J. SENESE[2]

Education has been an important concern throughout this country's history. From the early settlers, through subsequent waves of immigrants, to their descendants today, Americans have believed that education provides an opportunity for advancement, personal development, and cultural enrichment. Increasingly, in recent years, the public has become concerned with what many perceive to be a decline in the quality of education provided by our schools. Critics claim that the schools fail to teach students basic skills, are too permissive, and do not demand that students demonstrate proficiency before being promoted. They are concerned with the steady rise in the grades educators give students while their scores on standardized education tests have declined.

Donald J. Senese, Assistant Secretary for Educational Research and Improvement in the United States Department of Education, addressed these concerns in his keynote speech to the Third Annual Conference on Educational Issues and Research at the University of South Carolina on November 6, 1981. The purpose of the conference was to bring the results of recent educational research to the attention of classroom teachers and school district personnel and to provide in-service training through workshops, addresses, symposia, and discussion of papers.

The speech was given at 7:30 P.M. in the auditorium of Currell College, a room used for classes by the College of Criminal Justice and for selected public addresses. The audience consisted of approximately 80 teachers, members of the state department of education, school district representatives, and University of South Carolina College of Education faculty members, and students. Prior to the speech, awards were presented for the best paper presented at the conference and for the most promising educational research.

In his address, which was warmly received, Dr. Senese ob-

[1] Delivered at the Third Annual Conference on Educational Issues and Research at the University of South Carolina at 7:30 P.M., on November 6, 1981, in the auditorium of Currell College.
[2] For biographical note, see Appendix.

served, "I think one of the problems has been a heavy political emphasis at the federal level on access and equity in education to the extent that overall quality has been neglected. No one benefits from a lowering of standards—not even minority and disadvantaged groups"—a remark which many liberals might regard as a repudiation of government efforts to help minority groups, the underprivileged, and the handicapped. Regardless of whether one agrees or disagrees with his allegation, it should be recognized that Dr. Senese was voicing a concern felt by a number of Americans at that time.

The speech is interesting as an example of how a speaker may seek to adapt his speech to his audience and occasion. A graduate of the University of South Carolina, Senese reminded his listeners of that fact, praised other South Carolinians, and then paid tribute to three educators in the audience who had encouraged him.

Donald Senese's speech: Dean Mulhern and distinguished educators, I am proud to say that I received my master's and doctorate degree from the University of South Carolina and did research for my master's thesis and dissertation on South Carolina history.

As one walks across this campus and views the buildings—Lieber, Pinckney, Legare, Sloan, Calhoun and Barnwell—the campus is alive with those individuals who made South Carolina a great state.

I bring you greetings from Education Secretary Terrel H. Bell. South Carolina can be proud of its congressional delegation featuring Senator J. Strom Thurmond, President pro tempore of the U.S. Senate and chairman of the Senate Judiciary Committee, and Representative Floyd Spence, the Congressman from this district, who serves so ably on the House Armed Services Committee and House Ethics Committee. There is Jim Edwards, Secretary of Energy, my special assistant, Dr. George Youstra, who is from South Carolina, as well as Lee Atwater at the White House. There are distinguished South Carolinians at all levels of government in our nation's capital.

Before I officially begin, I want to pay tribute tonight to three South Carolinians who did so much to encourage me in my education, and I am pleased they are here tonight: Mrs.

Mae Clark of Cayce; Dr. Inez Eddings, who served as superintendent of the Richland County Schools; and Mrs. Myra Wyman, who taught Latin and an appreciation of Western civilization here in Columbia. They have served as an inspiration to many students.

The topic of my talk this evening, "Can We Have Excellence in Education?," may seem a surprising challenge to you, especially if you think we already have excellence in education in America.

If you are new in the field of education, you might have thought, "Can we? I thought we did!"

There is nothing like the exuberance of youth when there is a challenge to be met. We all benefit from the very presence of the indomitable spirit of youth, and new teachers, fresh out of college, make an important contribution to the faculties they join by the enthusiasm which they infuse into the school's atmosphere. I commend those of you who have answered the call to the teaching profession.

On the other hand, if you have been around awhile, and in addition to your academic degrees, you have added experience from the school of hard knocks, you are wise indeed, and you know that while we do have an outstanding educational system in our country, we have lost ground in the last decade in the area of quality of education.

We are putting children through the mills of learning, and they are exiting the twelfth grade with diplomas in hand, but are they ready for higher education or for apprenticeship in a vocation or to meet the challenges in a society growing more complex and requiring more knowledge of technology?

What has education done for them? Or, to put it another way—even more bluntly perhaps—are they really educated? That distinguished scholar of the American educational system, Dr. Russell Kirk, has put it this way: "A great many are schooled; very few are educated."

Some react to education like the old seaman once reacted to a lighthouse he used to stare at day after day as the fog rolled in from the sea: "The light shines; we ring the bell and blow the horn; but the fog comes in all the same!"

The purpose of education surely has always been to dispel the fog of ignorance and, where the fog persists, to give us a sense of direction as we make our way through it. Teachers have provided that guiding light on the long road to knowledge and wisdom.

One measure of enlightenment, or learning achievement, if you will, the SAT [Scholastic Aptitude Test] test score, has shown a steady decline nationwide for the past fifteen years.

Quantitatively, we have excelled. We have made education equally available to everyone. In 1980, enrollment in institutions of higher education reached an all-time high of 12.1 million. During this school year, expenditures for public and private education at all levels are expected to reach $198 billion, compared to outlays of $181 billion in 1980–1981. The high school graduating class of 1982 will be close to 3 million.

The estimates of the number of earned degrees to be conferred during the year 1981–1982 are: bachelor's degrees, 945,000; first-professional degrees, 72,000; master's degrees, 300,000; and doctorates, 33,000.

In spite of seemingly stupendous efforts being put into education, parents—and even students themselves—are less than satisfied with the results.

Public perception of education is that schools are failing in their responsibility to educate the youth of America.

A story that represents the widespread dissatisfaction with our schools comes to my mind. A young man complained to his mother, "I don't want to go to school. The courseware is dull. The teachers are always complaining. The students are wild and undisciplined. The cafeteria food is lousy. Give me two good reasons why I should go to school." And his mother replied, "One, you are 39 years old, and two, you are the principal."

The consumer is always explicit in his demands, and in the field of education, competency is a commodity that is in great demand. Across the length and breadth of this land, parents are demanding that schools produce students who are competent in basic skills. They know, without the benefit of a testing program, whether or not their children are competent in reading, writing, and math skills. Parents know that grades of A's and B's on a report card don't mean a thing unless they represent true achievement.

Parents aren't buying social promotion and grade inflation any longer for their children. Promotions that do not represent true progress deceive both parents and students. A student who has been pushed along with his peers may find himself in over his head and unable to catch up when basic skills, which would have provided a foundation on which to build more profound subject matter, have not been mastered.

Inflating the value of a grade reduces competition in the classroom by making it easier to get a passing grade. A student quickly learns that he can get by without really exerting himself.

For a while, students, parents, and the school administration may be fooled by inflated report cards but, eventually, as in the story of the Emperor's new clothes, people face the truth.

The moment of truth has arrived. The day of judgment is here. Parents are putting educators to the test. They are taking stock of the system and asking: What are your standards?

Parents are paying high taxes for education—the average cost for each student in public schools is $2,200 per year—and parents expect to get something for that money. Instead, they feel that they are being shortchanged. They are demanding a solution for today's crisis in the schools.

Can we blame them? We are spending more money than ever before on education, yet achievement scores have been declining with an alarming persistence. A high school diploma sometimes only affirms that a student has occupied space in school for a required number of years.

In an effort to prove their public school systems can work, most states have adopted minimum competency examinations. These require a bottom line competency or mastery of certain levels of achievement before a student can graduate.

The purpose of such tests is not to demonstrate fluency in a subject. Minimum competency means "just getting by." One problem with the concept of minimum competency testing is that when we expect little, we get little.

I think our students deserve better than that. We ought to

give equal consideration to maximum competency—a program wherein a student might aspire to something higher than himself and thereby learn to prove his worth. Certainly, we should challenge students to strive for excellence rather than allowing this generation of budding minds to settle into a dormant state of mediocrity.

Perhaps I should have chosen as my topic this evening "The Need for Greater Expectations."

I believe children will raise to the level of expectancy. If we set high standards for students, they will meet them.

We need a reformation, a return to high standards in education. Secretary Bell has said our education system has become flabby. It has. We need to put some muscle in it.

In too many instances, students are not being given a firm foundation on which to build future careers. Instead, they are being offered a marshmallow curriculum.

In California we can see what a devastating effect superficial courses have had on student achievement. Recognized as the land of adventure and promise, California has been a trendsetter in education and technology as well as in many other areas. Yet, in the past ten years California's test scores have dropped from 52nd to 34th percentile in reading and from 42nd to 28th percentile in language for seniors.

Some critics are trying to blame proposition 13 which was passed in 1978 resulting in budget cuts that would not have had an impact on the schools until fiscal year 1979. Could there be another cause for test scores to decline steadily for the past decade in California?

A recent article in the *Washington Post*—headlined "California High Schools Wearing 'National Dunce Cap' "—reported an increase in the number of students taking "Lifestyle" instead of more traditional academic courses. I don't know if "Lifestyle" courses include surfing and beachcombing, but that title certainly does not suggest academic rigor.

According to the article, seniors who were interviewed said students gravitate toward one of the new courses, "Human Physiology," as an easy way to meet the science requirement without wrestling with chemistry.

In his book, "Decadence and Renewal in the Higher

Learning," Dr. Russell Kirk, well-known author and lecturer, analyzes the decline in education standards that has characterized our schools for the last thirty years and notes the purposelessness and intellectual disorder among students that have accompanied that decline.

When our schools fail to educate the students, we are wasting our greatest resource—our mental capabilities. South Carolina's state motto should be our goal in education: "Prepared in Mind and Resources."

I think one of the problems has been a heavy political emphasis at the federal level on access and equity in education to the extent that overall quality has been neglected.

No one benefits from a lowering of standards—not even minority and disadvantaged groups.

I believe students themselves want to be challenged. They should be given the opportunity to enjoy the Sweet Taste of Accomplishment. They'll get hooked on it and come back for more.

That wise sage Aristotle observed that, "educated men are as much superior to uneducated men as the living are to the dead." To make that distinction true today, we need to quicken education with the spirit of purpose and high endeavor.

It is trite but true to say that things are not the way they used to be in the elementary and secondary classroom. Teachers do not rule the room as they once did. Combative situations between teachers and students, once unheard of—or at least rare—now occur with alarming frequency.

In some severe inner-city cases, principals should probably post signs over classroom doors—"Combat zone. Enter at your own risk."

We have so slackened the reins of discipline that no one is in control.

What has happened is that, while attempting to help minority groups, the underprivileged, and the handicapped and to rehabilitate those with psychological problems and even criminal backgrounds, our society has become so permissive that the very concept and essence of authority has been jeopardized.

The result has been that academic standards have slipped and so has the teacher's prestige.

I realize I am painting a dreary picture of the education landscape. Of course, there are schools that have outstanding administrators, teachers, and students.

Two weeks ago Herb Sang, superintendent of public schools in Jacksonville, Florida, addressed an education forum at the Horace Mann Learning Center in Washington, D.C. and described the successful turn-around that has taken place in the Jacksonville school system in the last five years. Disgraced with disaccreditation in 1964, the school system has risen to national prominence as one of the most outstanding schools systems in the country.

However, when statistics show a 15-year decline in nationwide test scores, a decline in public confidence in our schools, and an increase in violence in the classroom, we cannot take comfort in the patches of evidence of excellence that remain; we must address our failings and set about to improve our education system. Even though SAT scores seemed to stabilize last year, that is just not good enough after a decade of declining scores.

It is always easier to identify problems than it is to find solutions.

Nevertheless, I would like to enumerate for you what I believe to be the major problems facing us in education today.

Loss of prestige is a significant factor influencing the teacher job market. Once considered noble, the teaching profession has slipped from its lofty pedestal of honor to the footstool of society.

Low salaries and lack of advancement possibilities are deterring some of the better students from choosing teaching as a career. Instead, they are going into more lucrative fields, such as, law, medicine, business administration, engineering, or computer science. A side-effect of this movement has been that more parents are better educated than their children's teachers than what used to be and this has led to teachers being held in lower esteem by the communtiy.

A decline in rewards of teaching has led to teachers leaving education and finding new careers.

Without the incentives of salary, prestige, and opportunities for upward mobility, the brighter college students are not choosing education for a career, and many of the better teachers are leaving the classroom to go into administrative positions or into other careers.

In short, we are losing quality students and teachers to other fields of endeavor. This is a serious problem confronting teacher colleges everywhere, including here at U.S.C.

Without quality teachers, it is difficult, if not impossible, to have quality learning. You may have heard the story of the businessman, the lawyer, and the teacher who met at a social club. When the waiter came to take their orders, the businessman said, "I'll have an I.W."

The waiter thought a moment and then said, "All right, that's an Irish whiskey." He then asked the lawyer what he would like to have and the lawyer responded, "I'll have an I.W.W."

The waiter paused a moment and then said, "Oh, yes, Italian white wine." He then turned to the teacher, who, by the way, was a math teacher.

"I'll have a fifteen," said the teacher.

The waiter looked puzzled and finally said, "Well, you have me there. What is a fifteen?"

The math teacher quickly replied, "Oh, that's Seagram's Seven with Seven-Up."

Of course, the joke overstates the situation; but the inference gives us pause for thought. The pursuit of excellence in education must begin with quality teaching. Teacher colleges should prepare students with a solid foundation in subject matter so that teachers going into the classrooms will be as knowledgeable in their field as are doctors, lawyers, businessmen, and other professional people.

Education theory does serve a purpose, but it is also practical and quite respectable to be able to add seven and seven and get fourteen.

Now I know you would like to ask this question: If a

teacher does know his subject well, what is going to keep him from leaving the classroom for a higher paying position in industry?

One answer is that teaching historically has been more than just a career—it has been a calling, and I believe there will always be a certain number of very dedicated people who will be attracted to teaching for that reason.

This view is depicted at the end of the play, "A Man for All Seasons." You may remember the scene where Thomas Moore urges a young man to return to his university studies.

"Be a teacher, be a great teacher," Moore tells him.

"And if I am, who will know?"

Thomas Moore responds, "Yourself, your pupils, and God. Not a bad audience, sir, not a bad audience."

Such dedication deserves recompense; teachers have to eat and someone has to pay the rent. In addition to improving salaries, I think school boards are going to have to borrow a page from the businessman's handbook and offer further incentives to teachers.

Some school systems are doing just that. *Education Week* recently reported, for example, that Houston schools are paying bonuses to keep teachers. Better pay and recognition for top performance will help attract and keep good teachers.

Louisiana has recently launched a state teacher-improvement program, and many of the states, including South Carolina, have added a new requirement for teachers' certification: passing a state teachers' exam.

A good teacher with a solid grasp of his subject commands the respect of his students much more so than the teacher who is ill-prepared. The truly learned teacher also brings prestige to his profession. And, the good teacher will always be in demand.

Can we have excellence in education? Yes, but only if we have all of the ingredients that make up a good school. Herb Sang's formula, which is succeeding in Jacksonville, Florida, is: Discipline plus patriotism plus courtesy plus academics equals a successful school. Recognized nationally for his outstanding achievements, Herb Sang has been named by the

National School Boards Association as one of the top 100 school administrators in North America.

According to a study conducted by the National Institute of Education, the five ingredients most necessary for an effective school are:

1. A principal who provides strong administrative leadership, especially in regard to instructional matters.

2. An orderly climate; learning can take place only when there is an atmosphere of peace and order.

3. Basic skills; the curriculum must offer academic courses packed with substance. In order to develop intellectually, the mind needs to be nourished on the meat of academics rather than the mild and marshmallow of easy-out, introductory courses that only skim the surface of knowledge.

4. Confident teachers; teachers must believe that all children can learn, and they must set high standards for them. Where expectancy is high, learning is high.

5. Measurement; schools need to monitor and assess the learning that is taking place. When performance is measured, performance improves.

Yes, I believe we can have excellence in education. We have lost nothing that cannot be regained by a renewal of our commitment to excellence in education.

The Reagan administration has given a high priority to stimulating excellence in education. Last August Secretary Bell established a National Commission on Excellence to examine American education and to highlight its strong points. The commission has been charged with the following responsibilities:

It will review and synthesize data on the quality of learning in the Nation's schools, both public and private;

It will examine, compare, and contrast the curricula, standards, and expectations of the educational systems of several advanced countries with those of the United States;

The Commission will hold hearings, receive testimony and expert advice on efforts that could and should be taken to foster high levels of academic excellence in the nation's schools, colleges and universities; and, perhaps most important of all,

The Commission will review and describe those school programs that are recognized as preparing students who consistently attain higher than average scores on college entrance examinations.

Those are just some of the responsibilities of the Commission of Excellence, and, as I said, probably their most important task will be to find out and tell the rest of us how those schools who consistently turn out top students are doing it. We need to know the reasons for their success.

One means of reaching a greater level of excellence is through the application of technology to teaching methods. The integration of technology into the learning experience can provide a cohesive thread which will upgrade the level of achievement.

South Carolina has set an exemplary record in the use of television as a supplement to traditional educational materials. Pioneering in the late 50s in the use of that medium, South Carolina educators have been successful in using ETV to achieve educational objectives.

We are on the edge of exciting new frontiers leading into the fantastic world of technology, and we must keep pace with progress in that realm if education is to lead, rather than follow, civilization.

But, we cannot overlook, nor underestimate, the importance of the teacher-pupil relationship in the learning process. The human touch provides inspiration, encouragement, and understanding, which we all need in order to develop our mental and physical capabilities.

Education is a complex universe made up of many worlds, each moving in its own sphere. The interrelated components have a contribution to make toward our common goal of excellence.

Teacher colleges move in one orbit, while administrators and classroom teachers function in another world; they are out there working in the trenches, so to speak, where the real world exists. Our colleges and universities, guided by state policies, must prepare school personnel for that real world.

According to Secretary Bell, the most sweeping challenge in education has to do with teacher competence. He has said that the states must change their policies that relate to the education, certification, promotion, reward, and retention of teachers. At the present time, only 16 states require applicants for teacher certification to be tested for competency. The South Carolina Legislature has just passed a law requiring teachers to pass the National Teachers' exam for certification.

Surrounding the colleges and neighborhood schools are parents and the community. Those satellites play a key role in the success or failure of a school. A recent study by the Southern Regional Education Board concluded that caring parents and an involved community contribute immeasurably to the success of a school. In fact, students are more highly motivated when parents and the community are involved in school activities.

Can we have excellence in education? Yes, if we make that our expectation and discipline ourselves toward that goal.

True education requires discipline, a fine sense of selection, discrimination between what is worth knowing and not worth knowing, an appreciation of the mastery of skills before frills.

Teachers are not social reformers charged with remaking society or finding solutions to social ills. Teachers are torch bearers; they enlighten the minds of their pupils with the wisdom of the ages, and that wisdom is made up of the components of concrete knowledge.

The primary purpose of education is to help each student master basic skills in language arts, mathematics, social studies, and science so that he is able to go on from there and develop his particular talent to his fullest potential. Anything less than that falls short of the mark of excellence.

Let us go forward toward the mark of your high calling and, together, achieve that degree of mastery in education deserving of the term excellence. Thank you for inviting me to share these thoughts with you. It has been my pleasure.

THE PUBLIC PURPOSES OF PRIVATE COLLEGES[1]

ALICE STONE ILCHMAN[2]

Dr. Alice Stone Ilchman was installed as the eighth president of Sarah Lawrence College in Bronxville, New York, on November 6, 1981. The school was founded in 1926 as a women's college, but in 1968 was opened to men, who currently represent nearly one quarter of the 850 students. As a relatively young college with fewer than six thousand alumni and a small endowment, the school is one of the more expensive of the nation's private colleges.

Dr. Ilchman was selected by Sarah Lawrence as the fourth woman to head the college from 200 candidates, after a search that lasted a year and a half. She taught for seven years at the University of California at Berkeley and in 1973 became dean of Wellesley College where, according to a former student, "she was probably the most popular person ever to hold that post." (Feron, *New York Times*, N. 7, '81, p 11) Dr. Ilchman received two presidential appointments in 1978, first as Assistant Secretary of State and then as the associate director for educational and cultural affairs of the new International Communication Agency.

Dr. Ilchman delivered her inaugural address to representatives of 39 colleges, learned societies, and cultural institutions and 2,000 other people under a huge tent on the main lawn of the campus.

In her address, she spoke of the uniqueness of the school, saying that "it is not easy to organize a ceremony such as this in an institution whose greatest tradition is to avoid tradition," for it "refuses to learn any song at all, let alone permit a seal of office, or even separate the faculty into rank." However, she forcibly reaffirmed the importance of private colleges such as Sarah Lawrence, saying:

> I wish to assert unequivocably that ... without private institutions our society would be the poorer. At the most immediate level, private colleges are important be-

---

[1] Delivered at the inauguration of the eighth president of Sarah Lawrence College, Bronxville, New York, on the lawn of the main campus on November 6, 1981.
[2] For biographical note, see Appendix.

cause they assure choice and variety in our educational system; and this pluralism in education helps to assure other arenas of life-affirming opportunities for choice.

Alice Stone Ilchman's speech: Colleagues, students, and friends of Sarah Lawrence College: Graciously you have gathered here to participate in the inauguration of the eighth president of this institution. That, at least, is the purpose of the occasion. Its function is more basic and fundamental. The function of today's events is to provide a witness to the special role private higher education plays in our times, in our lives and in our nation.

I should point out that it is not easy to organize a ceremony such as this in an institution whose greatest tradition is to avoid tradition; with the same passion which produced "Boola, Boola" and the "Dartmouth Fight Song," this institution refuses to learn any song at all, let alone permit a seal of office, or even separate the faculty into rank. The hoary tradition clasped by even the most recent institution, the academic procession with invited representatives, is a generous indulgence to a new president. No doubt, the faculty and students hope that she will soon be able to function without such conventional props.

Earlier this afternoon, we were fortunate in being able to explore together a subject that I believe to be of particular importance at this time. With liveliness and considerable insight we examined the public purposes of a private college such as Sarah Lawrence. I am grateful to those who participated in this discussion—grateful for their interest, grateful for their dedication, grateful for the obviously careful thought they gave to the subject, grateful for their willingness to share and to help enhance the understanding of others such as myself.

As our colleagues in that panel stressed to us, there has perhaps seldom been a time when a serious reexamination of the public purposes of private institutions such as ours seemed so pertinent, when the discussion of the relationship between the public and private sectors of our society was so vigorously debated.

What sort of institution is Sarah Lawrence? We are a small institution in a world in which size is frequently equated with efficiency. We are an elite institution in a world that has been seized with egalitarianism. We are an expensive institution in a world that finds it increasingly difficult to support its most basic needs. We are aggressively and proudly an institution of the liberal and performing arts in a world whose jobs and financial rewards go increasingly, it seems, to the technically trained.

In short, we are a rather obvious anomaly. That in itself should command our serious attention to the question of whether we are at least an important and relevant anomaly, an anomaly which does indeed serve some larger public purposes, an anomaly essential to the quality of our collective lives. I wish to assert unequivocally that we do indeed serve larger public purposes and that without private institutions our society would be the poorer.

At the most immediate level, private colleges such as Sarah Lawrence are important because they assure choice and variety in our educational system; and this pluralism in education helps to assure other arenas of life-affirming opportunities for choice. Diversity of affiliations, curricula, size and constituencies served have been a central and cherished characteristic of American education. Less constrained by public authorities, private colleges are important because they are often in a better position to innovate, to test new ideas or methods, to push out the boundaries of the conventional. A case in point is a Sarah Lawrence that has led the way in such pathbreaking efforts as continuing education, women's history, human genetics, and now in health advocacy. In these and other innovations, private institutions can set precedents that allow more constrained public institutions to follow suit.

The contribution to pluralism is fundamental. But I believe there are two other considerations that, at the present time, encompass and override even this. And it is on these two points that I wish to focus for a few minutes this afternoon.

First, I would suggest that one of the foremost public purposes of a private college such as Sarah Lawrence is to maintain an independent critique *vis-a-vis* public authority. We *are* different from a publicly-financed institution. We are *not* subject to the same system of short-leashed political account-ability which can, from time to time, prove so stifling to crea-tive thought and independent action. We are *not* quite so sus-ceptible to the constantly shifting, variable winds of public opinion. And because we are privileged to be different, be-cause we enjoy a certain protection from the whims of public authority, I would argue that we have both a right and a duty to exercise our independence aggressively to the broader public purpose.

Let me illustrate the point by commenting on three issues recently in the news that are of great concern to me, and per-haps to you, first as educators but more importantly as citi-zens. Our current administration has ordered a dramatic re-duction in federal government support for international educational and cultural exchanges, for basic research, and for student financial assistance. All three point to what I see as a disturbing problem in our national life, a problem on which the independent perspective of a private college is per-tinent.

Let me preface my comments by the recognition that our nation has been suffering from rather severe economic prob-lems. Most of us, no doubt, would support the efforts of the Administration and the Congress to restore our economy to a condition of low inflation, low unemployment and sound, sta-ble growth and see as necessary to these ends imposing re-straint on public expenditures.

Likewise, few of us would argue with any reasonable measures required to maintain our security as a nation.

But, born of our frustration, with the failure of past efforts to deal successfully with these problems, there is at large a yearning for simplicity and for solutions that imperil our long-run fundamental interests.

Take the case of international cultural and educational exchanges. These are programs that have benefited our na-tion, quietly but immeasurably, for some thirty-five years. They have given well over 100,000 foreigners, many of whom went on to become leaders of their respective societies, their first, their most comprehensive and often their only direct encounter with what we have to offer as a people, as a society and as a value system. Over thirty current heads of state or government, in addition to an untold number of cabinet and legislative members, have learned about the United States through these programs.

Similarly, these are programs that have also provided many thousands of Americans with a direct familiarity with other societies and cultures, with insights and understandings that are essential if we are to survive and compete successfully in an ever-shrinking, ever volatile world. These exchanges may fit us well for competition; but they also provide the basic framework for cooperation: where our public, intellectual and corporate leaders and those of other nations can develop the mutual understanding to provide common address to common problems.

These are programs that have been admired and emulated around the world. They bear names which are household words—Fulbright and Humphrey—and they support dozens of private initiatives toward international understanding. They are also programs whose cost constitutes a tiny 1/100 of one percent of the federal budget, and whose elimination could have no noticeable impact on balancing the budget or reducing inflation. This week Congress may acquiesce in the Executive effort to almost eliminate these programs.

The true measure of these programs can be taken from a variety of perspectives. They contribute to a better understanding among peoples, and therefore to a less dangerous world; they stimulate the sharing of ideas for human betterment across arbitrary national boundaries; they enhance the human and technical skills required to bring greater prosperity and stability to the third world. But even from the much narrower perspective of those whose world is more or less defined by the East-West conflict, these programs make nothing short of eminent good sense.

The paradox is stark. The current dominant rhetoric portrays our nation as engaged in a perilous struggle to maintain and preserve our way of life, a contest whose outcome is depicted as far from certain. We invest in ever more sophisticated and powerful weapons systems for precisely this struggle, hoping that they will deter but never actually have to be used.

Yet, every day around the world there is an equally important battle raging on a very different front—not with bullets and bombs, but through the instrument of education, through international visits and contacts, through films and books and articles, through direct, face-to-face conversations. This is a battle of ideas, a struggle of competing value systems, a competition for human minds and allegiances. It is a battle that we should win hands down, for it is played on our field.

When we as a nation have been admired and respected and been the object of emulation, it has been not for our military prowess but rather for our ideals and our values and the vitality of our way of life. But, however great our national advantage, we cannot hope to win the battle without the instruments to wage it. Foremost among these instruments are our international cultural and educational exchanges.

This is a time when our adversaries already far outstrip us in their financial commitment to this battle. This is a time when they are reaching out to more foreign students to educate them in *their* values and *their* system. This is a time when we are pulling back. Is it not in our interest to share broadly one of our greatest assets: American higher education? Is it not shortsighted to leave this crucial battlefield of ideas and values uncontested to our rivals?

A similar shortsightedness pertains to the threatened decline of federal support of research. In recent times, we have become increasingly concerned about our scientific and technological capabilities in comparison not only to the Soviet Union but to other advanced industrial nations as well. Hardly a day passes without another article in the press about our aging industrial plants, our declining competitiveness, our inability to maintain our leadership in technological innovation.

Yet, proposals now pending in Washington would, in a

manner similar to those affecting international educational
and cultural exchanges, imperil support for basic research.
There is a direct link between research, technology and increased productivity. As colleagues at the National Academy
of Sciences have recently declared, "The express goals of this
administration for a strong economy and improved national
security demand more rather than less investment in basic research." We must make ourselves heard on this score.

As a final example of short-term shortsightedness with
long-term implications, I refer to the proposed reduction in
student financial aid. Well over a million students will have
lost their federal financial assistance this year alone if the latest, and fourth, round of cuts is implemented. Many of these
students will not be able to continue their college educations
in the wake of this loss.

A well-educated populace surely is one of the most vital
elements of our national policy and of our national security. It
constitutes the major factor in our capacity for governing
ourselves and provides the essential foundation of our efforts
to compete and communicate effectively—economically,
diplomatically, morally. Are we prepared to run the risk of
limiting our talents only to those wealthy enough to afford
today's high, and rising, cost of a college education? I would
hope not.

Each of these examples has important elements in common. Each is a fundamental ingredient of our national security and economic health, properly understood. Each is a relatively minor federal expenditure. Each is an investment in the
future. Each involves a fragile structure which, while it can
be quickly destroyed, would take years to reconstruct. Each is
a logical outgrowth of our most fundamental values as a people. Each is under serious attack.

To repeat, I believe it is the privilege, indeed the duty of
private institutions such as Sarah Lawrence, institutions
which maintain a certain distance from public authority, to
recognize deficiencies such as these in public decision-making, and to speak out responsibly in an effort to make known
their independent perspectives.

The second public purpose which I wish to address has to do with educating people to make value choices.

What I find most disturbing about the multitude of social and economic problems that confront us today is not the problems themselves, but rather the attitude we have developed toward these problems. To a large degree we have come to look upon our situation as almost intractable. In contrast to our present sense of intractability, in the early 1960s we saw, at least in some quarters, a spirit of constructive hope, a spirit that could generate such achievements as the Peace Corps, the War on Poverty, the Alliance for Progress, the Civil Rights Acts. However one felt about these and other specific attempts to deal with the problems, they were at the very least born of hope, a belief in the notion that individual constructive acts can make a difference. Today, we are less hopeful, more disillusioned, more pessimistic, more frustrated.

As a result, we have diverted our attention and our energy in a variety of ways. Over the past decade or so, we have witnessed a kind of turning inward, the much-talked-about focus on the individual self. We have also watched the growth of a longing for simpler times. And we have seen an increasing emphasis on specialization.

None of these diversions I would suggest offers an acceptable lasting solution to our present condition. Our best hope, I would argue, lies in confronting the complexity of our times head on and dealing with it in all of its ambiguity.

Herein lies the most fundamental public purpose to be met by private colleges such as Sarah Lawrence. These colleges are dedicated to the training of human minds and spirits in such a way as to be able to tackle problems with the skills to analyze evidence, to exercise judgment, to tolerate uncertainty, and make moral commitments.

To have a sense of the ebbs and flows of history, to acquire some feeling for the languages and cultures of other peoples, to apprehend the beauty of a wide range of prose and poetry, to sample the processes and procedures of scientific inquiry, to engage the emotions in a work of music or dance or the theatre, to wander down the twisting corridors of philosophic speculation—these are the hallmarks of a classical liberal education. Such an education strives for the creation of some version of the worth of a whole person. This, of course, is precisely what Sarah Lawrence does. We make no claims to training our students for specific jobs or professions. In an individual's life cycle, jobs will come and jobs will change. So, too, with professions. So, too, with problems. These problems that consume us today, those that seem so overwhelming and irresolvable, will be transformed into different problems as yet unforeseen.

What is important then is that we prepare our students, not only to acquire specific bodies of knowledge, but, rather, to deal with the world that is changing at a rate faster than any of us can truly comprehend.

Central to such an education is an appreciation of context, a working awareness of the immense diversity and complexity of the human condition both in times past and throughout our world today. *It is the absence of context and perspective that leads people to make the kinds of short-sighted, narrow-minded, and ultimately self-defeating decisions to which I referred earlier.*

Another key to a liberal education is the ability to discriminate, to sort out not only the relevant facts in a given situation, but to determine what is relatively more important and what is relatively less so.

To a large degree, we were misled by the temporary, historically fleeting affluence and world dominance that we enjoyed in the period from 1945 to the first great economic shock in the winter of 1973–74. It was in this period that we came to believe, or at least to act, as if we could have everything, that we didn't have to make important choices, that the easy satisfaction of the full range of our economic and social desires was our historical destiny. Surely, by now, we know differently. Surely, by now, we appreciate that we must make choices, that we must decide what is really important to us. But if you are to do so, and particularly if we are to do so successfully, we must be anchored with a sense of deeply held values, with a notion of those things that are of fundamental importance to us, and those that are of secondary or tertiary concern. It is only from such a foundation of acknowledged values that we as individuals, or we as a nation, can make meaningful choices. This, too, the capacity to exercise critical judgment, lies at the heart of a liberal education.

What I believe I have been saying to you today is that a liberal education should leave us with a sense of just how connected we are to the rest of humanity. We all know, of course, that there is a sense in which we enter and leave this world in individual solitude. That cannot be denied. But some of us have perhaps forgotten, particularly in the inwardly focused decade just ended, of just how intricately our lives are intertwined with a larger society of humanity. Dedication to our own ends is diminished by the very privacy of those ends so that self-fulfillment is denied when it is directed only toward self.

What are the public purposes of a private college such as Sarah Lawrence? To recognize and use our "privateness" to the fullest. To preserve and protect the pluralism not only in American higher education but of American society. To continue to innovate, to test new ideas that may be too risky for institutions under the close scrutiny of public authority. To allow minds and spirits to grow in a humane setting. To observe and to analyze and to speak out uncowed by the intimidating power of public authority. But most of all to help people face, with some sense of competence, the chaotic, uncertain, ever-changing world it is our task to improve.

These are large public purposes. They are important public purposes. They are purposes which, it can be justly argued, are not met exclusively by small, private, independent institutions such as Sarah Lawrence. But they are purposes, I would contend, which institutions such as ours are in a unique position to serve. They are purposes basic to our reason for being. They are purposes which will be central to my tenure as president.

THE GODS OF THE COPYBOOK HEADINGS[1]

John R. Silber[2]

"The Gods of the Copybook Headings" was a speech delivered by John R. Silber at the 108th commencement of Boston University, on May 17, 1981. Its setting was Nickerson Field, the University's athletic stadium, and Silber was filling in for the scheduled speaker, the West German publisher Axel Springer, who became ill several days before the ceremony. The audience of approximately 15,000 was comprised of graduates, guests and relatives of graduates, faculty, students, and University staff. The weather typified the brilliance of high spring in New England.

Preceding the speech, honorary degrees were awarded to Lewis F. Kornfeld Jr., president of Radio Shack; the American tenor William Warfield; John Houseman, the actor and director; Margaret Bush Wilson, president of the NAACP; Michael Novak, the social theorist and philosopher; Talcott Banks, president of the Boston Symphony Orchestra; and Axel Springer *in absentia*.

John R. Silber became the seventh president of Boston University in 1971. In the decade that followed his appointment, the University's fiscal and academic bases were quickly transformed from a situation in which deficits were common to an uninterrupted series of modest surpluses. In addition, while this was being accomplished, the faculty was upgraded with approximately two hundred appointments of distinguished new faculty. Declines in both enrollment and average SAT scores were reversed: the latter is particularly noteworthy as it represented a continuing increase in average scores during a time when the national average was declining.

Silber is a national spokesman for higher education. He has articulated the case for independent higher education, and his Tuition Advance Fund proposal, which would allow students to draw advances to pay tuition charges that would be paid back gradually through the IRS, has attracted wide support.

"The Gods of the Copybook Headings," with its emphasis on the importance of the family, on early childhood education, and the primacy of morality, embodied many of the themes which

---

[1] Delivered at the 108th Commencement of Boston University at Nickerson Field on campus, on May 17, 1981.

[2] For biographical note, see Appendix.

Silber, a leading interpreter of Immanuel Kant, has stressed in past speeches and essays.

Dr. Silber has been described as "an articulate, pugnacious 54-year-old who sprinkles his conversation with quotations from Greek philosophy and English literature." (Butterfield, *New York Times*, N. 9, '81, p 10)

John Silber's speech: This is the eleventh time that I have celebrated commencement with students, faculty, staff, alumni, and friends at Boston University. As deeply as I regret the fact that Axel Springer cannot be with us today, I am pleased that you have in your programs a printed copy of his moving speech for your reading and reflection. In Dr. Springer's absence, I have been asked to speak in his place.

On March 4, 1825, only fourteen years before the founding of Boston University, John Quincy Adams came to the presidency of the United States. In his inaugural address he said:

Since the adoption of (our) social compact, (a generation) has passed away. It is the work of our forefathers. We now receive it as a precious inheritance from those to whom we are indebted for its establishment, doubly bound by examples they have left us and by the blessings which we have enjoyed as the fruits of their labor to transmit the same, unimpaired, to the succeeding generation.

John Quincy Adams was the first President of the United States to speak of the revolutionaries as belonging to a previous generation. Before him, each President had himself been one of the founders of the nation.

His position had a peculiar poignancy, but it is one in which all responsible individuals find themselves in every generation, and which affects most deeply young people like yourselves who are completing their education. You look in two directions, behind and ahead.

You look behind to your parents and mentors, to those who have been your teachers and who have passed on to you through many generations the legacy which 200 years ago was passed from John and Abigail Adams to John Quincy Adams and by him to his successors and eventually to us.

Those of you who stand in this graduating class look backward, not only to the education you have received at Boston University, but to your great inheritance as Americans.

But you also look forward. You stand between the generation that is moving from the scene and the generation that is yet unborn. You, in your turn, now have the responsibility to create a generation and to pass on to it the tradition that has been given to you. It will be your responsibility to be the parents—both physically and spiritually—of the next generation, to pass on to the next generation an inheritance as good, if possible, as the one you have received, just as it has been our responsibility to pass that precious inheritance on to you.

As you commence your adult lives with these responsibilities, I suggest that you seek guidance from the education that earlier parents provided their children. In the provision of elementary and secondary education I am not sure that my generation has done as well as the generation that preceded it. I received a far better education in the public schools of San Antonio, Texas, than those schools provide their students today. I am convinced that the schools in Boston at this time are not equal to the schools in Boston fifty years ago, certainly not equal to those 100 years ago.

We should acquaint ourselves with earlier educational standards and expectations, so that we do not diminish the richness of our inheritance, but pass that treasure on to the next generation faithfully and undiminished.

The first objective of early education should be training in the reality principle. It has been argued that the child who grows up with television, finding that he can alter the reality of the screen by changing channels, believes that he can as easily alter the world itself, a point made brilliantly by Peter Sellers in the film "Being There." In a world in which the very young are given such misleading intimations of omnipotence, concern for reality is more important than ever.

The child's confrontation with reality, a hundred years ago, began with the realization of death, which might come through the death of a sibling, a friend, or a parent, aunt, uncle or grandparent, any of which was far more likely to be experienced by the young. Today, in contrast, the death of a child is so rare a misfortune as to be thought nearly unbearable, and increases in the lifespan have significantly postponed the time at which most children experience the death of an elder.

Learning about the fact of death is a most shocking contact with reality. Sound education absolutely depends on it, because it is the condition on which our full humanity depends. Education should expose us to what is true, to a confrontation with what is real. A true education, therefore, must provide an acquaintance with death and with the conditions by which people can achieve happiness in the awareness of death. It must explain, for example, the essential role of virtue in the attainment of happiness: it must explain that virtue establishes one's worthiness to be happy. These are aspects of reality that must be introduced into the education of a child, if the child is to develop fully.

Long before a child went to school in 19th-century America, or even early 20th-century America, he learned these things. This confrontation with reality had been provided for several hundred years through *Mother Goose* rhymes. In *Mother Goose,* we find important moral lessons that were thought to be far too important to be kept from the child until he entered school at age six. The child of three or four learned to repeat: "If wishes were horses, beggars would ride." The child was warned to remember the reality principle, and not to be misled by the attractions of wishful thinking.

Recently I reviewed some early books used to teach reading and writing—pre-primers and primers used in the first grade and even earlier by parents who taught their own children at home. These books had a rhyme for every letter in the alphabet, for their authors capitalized on the delight that children take in verse. Let me read a few of them from the *New England Primer,* widely used in our local schools.

A. Adam and Eve their God did grieve.
B. Life to mend this book attend. (This was accompanied by a picture of the Bible.)

C. The cat doth play and later slay. (Cats, you see, were not just pets. They tormented, killed, and ate mice and children were not protected from that grisly fact.)

D. A dog will bite a thief at night. (This was an admonition to dogs and thieves alike.)

F. The idle fool is whipped at school. (A self-explanatory point.)

H. Wrought by hand great works do stand.

J. Job felt the rod yet blessed his God.

Q. Queens and Kings must lie in the dust. (A child who has not yet gone to school is thus reminded that Queens and Kings are mortal.)

T. Time cuts down the great and small. (In case the child missed the point earlier or thought it was restricted to Kings and Queens, the point is generalized: all people must die.)

X. Xerxes the Great shared the common fate. (Now the child, who has not learned to read and write, has been told this fact three times.)

This is the way Americans of earlier generations taught the alphabet. This book addresses the child at a far more dignified level than such contemporary efforts as, "Spot and Jane run and play. Run Spot run. Catch Jane catch. Dick and Jane are friends." This book was written in a period before condescension toward children had been developed into a dogma.

Reality provides the conditions on which pleasure can or cannot be achieved, and provides the moral conditions on which pleasure should or should not be achieved. This value-freighted reality reveals the conditions that must be met or avoided if there is to be any gratification at any time. The child learned that wishes were not horses because before he learned to read he was taught through these verses that if they were horses beggars would be riding, and every child knew that beggars went on foot. Thus *Mother Goose* taught the child that there's no such thing as a free lunch. Unfortunately, many politicians in Massachusetts and in Washington have never read *Mother Goose*.

This was the normal education of the young child before he went to school. It taught him the alphabet and prepared him to read. It also prepared him for something much more important than reading. It prepared him for life.

Consider, moreover, how children learned to write, a skill on the endangered species list in contemporary America. They did it through the use of copybooks, manuals with beautifully handwritten sentences—copybook headings— printed at the top of each page. The child was expected to imitate the excellent writing of the headings by copying them many times on the lined spaces below, until he had learned to write all those beautiful and wondrous words and by doing so he had learned the headings by heart.

Now, what did these copybook headings say? I quote from The *Art of Penmanship,* one of the most widely used copybooks of the period: "Religion conduces to our present as well as our future happiness." This sentence was in the copybook of a child so young that he was just beginning to learn to write. And another, "Persevere in accomplishing a complete education." "Persevere in accomplishing a complete education." "Persevere in accomplishing a complete education." And on and on until the word "persevere" was learned by heart, and the meaning of perseverance learned by persevering long enough to write it twenty times.

The educators who prepared that copybook knew that children are naturally fascinated and excited by grown-up words. The educators of that period understood the attraction and the power of language. In these copybooks words appear as treasures, language as a treasure-house, and education as the key. Let me read a few more of these copybook headings.

Quarrelsome persons are always dangerous companions.
Employment prevents vice.
Great men were good boys. (This thought somehow managed to survive the copybooks—at least in one corner of America. When I was growing up, the wall of the San Antonio YMCA boasted a large sign which said: "Don't wait to be a man to be great! Be a great boy.")
Praise follows exertion.

Trifles alienate friends.

X begins no English word. (Presumably this was before xylo-phones.)

Build your hopes of fame on virtue.

Death to the good brings joy instead of terror.

Zinc is a white semi-metal useful in galvanism. (If not edifying, this heading was at least semi-informative.)

One may perhaps understand better why the abolitionist movement began in Boston when one reads the copybook headings that shaped the minds of Boston children. "Justice is a common right." "Magnanimity ennobles." "Overcome all prejudice." "Justice will pursue the vicious." "Zeal for justice is worthy of praise." If there is to be an effective moral edu-cation, the education must begin in early childhood. The child's education started when he began learning the lan-guage. These copybook headings were the efforts of an earlier generation to pass on their moral heritage to their children, to acquaint their children with nature—not merely physical but moral and spiritual. By introducing moral and spiritual reality into the education of the child they expressed their concern to educate the child in all dimensions of reality, to prepare children, in short, for a true and complete human existence.

It was not enough to teach penmanship merely as beauti-ful writing. It was important to have something to write *about,* to have content in all the curriculum, a content that was the distillation of a high culture. It presented as apho-risms the things that thoughtful, understanding people would be expected to know about the nature of the world, about the nature of society, about the nature of the universe, and about themselves. The full meaning and justification of these apho-risms were provided in later stages in the curriculum in the works of Plato, Aristotle, Aquinas, Spinoza, Kant, and many others.

But it never crossed the mind of an 18th-century or a 19th-century parent or teacher that his principal responsibil-ity was to be a pal to his children, or to try to make life easy, comfortable, convenient, or maximally pleasurable. Rather it was his duty to prepare the child, through exposure to reality, for the uncertainty of human life and the ever-present possibility of death. The child was led to the realization that virtue and achievement count, and that, since death cannot be avoided, he prepares for death by living well. It was fine to welcome pleasure when it came, but the child had to recognize the folly of basing his life on mere pleasure-seeking.

If we are to recapture this wisdom, we must go back to the copybooks and primers of the 18th and 19th centuries. I do not mean that we should literally reintroduce them into the curriculum. But we must reintroduce their subject-matter, we must return to reality. And that requires us to look to the past because the past necessarily shapes the future. If our future is to be as strong, as good, as fine, and as just as our past has been, we must reassert what was best in a more distant past out of which that more recent past came to be.

A prophetic poem on this subject was written by Rudyard Kipling over sixty years ago: "The Gods of the Copybook Headings." Let me read it to you: the poet speaks as the voice of mankind.

As I pass through my incarnations in every age and race,
I make my proper prostrations to the Gods of the Market-Place.
Peering through reverent fingers I watch them flourish and fall,
And the Gods of the Copybook Headings, I notice, outlast them all.

We were living in trees when they met us. They showed us each in turn
That Water would certainly wet us, as Fire would certainly burn;
But we found them lacking in Uplift, Vision, and Breadth of Mind.
So we left them to teach the Gorillas while we followed the March of Mankind.

We moved as the Spirit listed. *They* never altered their pace,
Being neither cloud nor wind-borne like the Gods of the Market-Place;
But they always caught up with our progress, and presently word would come
That a tribe had been wiped off its icefield, or the lights had gone out in Rome.

With the Hopes that our World is built on they were utterly out of touch,
They denied that the Moon was Stilton; they denied she was even Dutch.

They denied that Wishes were Horses; they denied that a Pig had
    Wings.
So we worshipped the Gods of the Market Who promised these
    beautiful things.

When the Cambrian measures were forming. They promised per-
    petual peace.
They swore, if we gave them our weapons, that the wars of the
    tribes would cease.
But when we disarmed They sold us and delivered us bound to our
    foe,
And the Gods of the Copybook Headings said: *'Stick to the Devil
    you know.'*

On the first Feminian Sandstones we were promised the Fuller
    Life
(Which started by loving our neighbour and ended by loving his
    wife)
Till our women had no more children and the men lost reason and
    faith,
And the Gods of the Copybook Headings said: *'The Wages of Sin is
    Death.'*

In the Carboniferous Epoch we were promised abundance for all,
By robbing selected Peter to pay for collective Paul;
But, though we had plenty of money, there was nothing our money
    could buy,
And the Gods of the Copybook Headings said: *'If you don't work
    you die.'*

Then the Gods of the Market tumbled, and their smooth-tongued
    wizards withdrew,
And the hearts of the meanest were humbled and began to believe
    it was true
That All is not Gold that Glitters, and Two and Two make Four—
And the Gods of the Copybook Headings limped up to explain it
    once more.

As it will be in the future, it was at the birth of Man—
There are only four things certain since Social Progress began—
That the Dog returns to his Vomit and the Sow returns to her
    Mire,
And the burnt Fool's bandaged finger goes wabbling back to the
    Fire;

And that after this is accomplished, and the brave new world
  begins
When all men are paid for existing and no man must pay for his
  sins,
As surely as Water will wet us, as surely as Fire will burn,
The Gods of the Copybook Headings with terror and slaughter return.

If we have the courage to face reality, we will know and
we will proclaim these harrowing truths. That the degenerate
society consumed in pleasure seeking will not survive. "The
wages of sin is death." That the society that will not defend its
freedom will lose it. "Stick to the Devil you know." That a
society that consumes more than it produces will go bank-
rupt. "If you don't work, you die." We, members of the graduating class, faculty, parents—all of us—we will ill serve ourselves and our children by preparing ourselves and them for a
life of freedom and easy pleasure that may never come and
most certainly will never last. We had better prepare ourselves and them for reality: a reality that is infused with moral
laws as surely as it is infused with physical laws; a reality in
which there is no consumption without production, no freedom without defense, no self-fulfillment and no self-government without self-disciplined persons who govern themselves, persons who are capable of subordinating their desires
long enough to achieve that conditions on which freedom and
survival, and even pleasure, depend.

It is often said, and said mistakenly, that students at grad-
uation go out into the real world. That is an expression of es-
capism. It suggests that we were avoiding the real world all
the time we were in school and in college. No world is more
real than the world of ideas in which students are, or should
be, immersed from kindergarten through college. And we had
better take hold of our educational program and see to it that
reality is packed into the curriculum so that our graduates
will confront reality with the ideas of the copybook headings
in mind. They will then find themselves in the same world
that they learned about in school and in college, and will be
guided by ideas and principles that can anchor their lives, and

can give meaning, direction, and support. That should be our legacy to them.

These ideas must prepare them for the disappointment which is an essential part of the joy of living. All of us must live with disappointment, accept limitations and imperfections. We live in a world of becoming and change. Inevitably you will sometimes be disappointed with friends. You will sometimes be disappointed in marriage, disappointed in institutions, and sometimes disappointed in yourselves. Thus if you are to retain your joy in life you must find much of that joy in spite of disappointment, for the joy of life consists largely in the joy of savoring the struggle, whether it ends in success or in failure. Your ability to go through life successfully will depend largely upon your traveling with courage and a good sense of humor, for both are conditions of survival. It is for this reason that I stress the importance of living with reality and therefore with disappointment.

The difficulties of life did not destroy John Adams' parents, or John Quincy Adams' parents. They did not destroy your teacher's parents or your parents. They need not destroy you. Hence there is room for hope. There is hope for fulfillment in your own lives and in the lives of your posterity.

When I look to the future of our country over the next twenty-five years, I find it very difficult to be hopeful in the conventional understanding of that word. But it is easy to be hopeful at a more profound level. The difficult years that lie before us may turn out to be far happier than the twenty-five years through which we have come. For the ancients knew that happiness is more often achieved in adversity than in luxury and affluence. Juvenal rightly said, "Luxury is more ruthless than war."

We now face the disappointments that follow affluence. And as affluence begins to wind down and the struggle for survival increases, and as we discover our ability to cope with disappointments, with limitations, with greater privations than most of us have ever known, we shall find at the same time increasing opportunities for personal achievement, fulfillment, and happiness.

We must quickly come to terms with our unavoidable imperfections and with the unavoidable imperfections of others and of our institutions. We must find it possible to live happily in an imperfect world with self-confidence and joy, for there is a stern reality to be faced and much hard work to be done. We must join with one another to build a more basic foundation than pleasure, a foundation of enduring happiness that comes through triumph over one's self in a world not of our own making by achieving a disciplined and moral relation to reality. We must find courage, personal renewal, and, ultimately, happiness by regaining a sense of ourselves as a free people in a common cause on behalf of our free nation, prepared to do, and prepared to do without, whatever is necessary in order to preserve what is best in the American way of life. (The phrase may be shopworn but the reality behind the phrase is still our last, best hope.)

Rebuild our defenses, balance our budget, achieve energy independence, rid our cities of crime? Of course! Educate a new generation for reality, for responsible productivity rather than irresponsible consumption? Of course! Regain our sense of direction as a nation, a sense of direction as individuals who seek not pleasure but happiness? Yes, that too! All this or nothing. For we will either learn the lessons of the Copybook Headings and respond creatively and responsibly to those lessons or we will succumb to the consequences of ignoring them.

I am convinced that the graduating class of Boston University and other graduating classes all over the United States, this spring of 1981, are a worthy generation of young Americans, who are prepared for a return to reality and for a courageous moral existence. I am confident that you will savor and treasure your inheritance, that you will contribute substantially to it, and that you will transmit that inheritance unimpaired and perhaps enhanced to succeeding generations.

As John Quincy Adams said, "Think of your forefathers; think of your posterity." That is to say: think of yourselves.

THE PRESS AND THE PUBLIC

ACCEPTANCE OF THE ELIJAH PARISH LOVEJOY AWARD[1]

A. M. ROSENTHAL[2]

President William R. Cotter of Colby College, Waterville, Maine, welcomed approximately 150 persons to the annual Elijah P. Lovejoy convocation at 8 P.M. on November 9, 1981, in the Robins, Hurd, Smith rooms of the Roberts Union building. The audience included broadcast and print journalists, students, faculty, and staff. President Cotter began the program by saying,

> Tonight's convocation honors the memory of Elijah Parish Lovejoy, a Colby graduate of 1826, America's first martyr to freedom of the press who died bravely while defending his printing press against a mob that was violently opposed to his persistent writing against slavery in his abolitionist Illinois newspaper, the *Alton Observer*. By this annual observance, we also honor, in Lovejoy's memory, those men and women reporters, writers, editors, and publishers who have continued the tradition of fearlessness and courage and who stand for free exchange of ideas and who refuse to forsake their editorial principles.

He then introduced members of the selection committee who were present at the presentation ceremonies, including some distinguished journalists. He also read the citation honoring A. M. Rosenthal, executive editor of the *New York Times*, as the 29th recipient of the Lovejoy award. It praised the journalist for devoting his life to enhancing freedom for everyone:

> You have brought into focus and into print some of the most difficult stories of our time including publication of the Pentagon Papers and documentation of the decision to admit the Shah of Iran into the United States. Son of a farmer born in Byelorussia you have demon-

---

[1] Delivered at a convocation at Colby College, in the Robins, Hurd, Smith rooms of the Roberts Union building, Waterville, Maine, at 8 P.M. on November 9, 1981.
[2] For biographical note, see Appendix.

strated an inspiring reverence for freedom. Now in your
thirty-eighth year with the *New York Times*, and executive editor since 1977, you more than any other single
American, define what is worthy of public attention and
debate. We are secure in your stewardship of that awesome responsibility. You have been described as a tough,
intelligent, endlessly questioning reporter. For your
forthrightness in covering the news during two years in
heavily censored Poland, you were expelled. In 1960 you
were selected for the Pulitzer Prize for your reporting
during that era.

In the nearby rural community of Albion, Maine,
Elijah Parish Lovejoy was born 179 years ago today. In
an editorial for the first issue of the *St. Louis Observer*,
Lovejoy in 1833 pledged his paper 'to divine truth in all
its severity.' On this special occasion coinciding with the
birthday of that respected martyr, his college takes pride
in honoring you as the twenty-ninth Lovejoy Fellow for
your like willingness to defend freedom of the press regardless of costs of consequences.

In addition to awarding the Lovejoy award to Rosenthal, the
school conferred upon him the degree of Doctor of Laws *honoris
causa.*

While Colby College is a relatively small private school with
an enrollment of 1,600, the Lovejoy award is a highly prestigious
prize. Since it was established in 1952, its recipients have included
many of the most respected journalists in the country, including
Ralph McGill, Erwin Canham, Katharine Graham, Arthur Hays
Sulzberger, Vermont Royster, and James Reston.

Before becoming executive editor of the *New York Times*, Rosenthal was a reporter and foreign correspondent for many years.
In addition to covering Poland, he reported from Japan, India,
Africa, Western Europe, and diplomatic events in the United Nations, receiving other major journalistic awards for his work.

In his speech of acceptance, Rosenthal claimed that the nation's free press was under attack by legislators and judges and he
warned his audience of the dangers of recent court decisions and
Congressional legislation.

A. M. Rosenthal's speech: Let me tell you a little true story
about how a reporter I knew operated. Every day he would
go out and cover his beat the best way he knew and the *only*

way he knew: by talking to people in the town about what
concerned them, about the cost of living, about the feel of
life, about what they thought about their leaders, about politics.

Every night that reporter went home, wrote a story, and
then carefully burned his notes or flushed them down the toi-
let. It was a pity, because he knew he might forget what he
couldn't write that day if he burned his notes. But he also
knew the police had permission to search his files any time.

A lot of people did not want to talk to the reporter because they felt he might reveal their names on purpose or
through a slip of the typewriter. They were defenseless people and they were afraid.

The reporter never urged them to talk because he understood their fear. Others, however, did talk to the reporter,
precisely because they felt powerless and wanted somebody
to tell the truths they knew. They accepted his word that he
would suffer imprisonment before telling their names.

The government became very annoyed at this reporter.
They questioned him directly about his sources and, of
course, he did not respond.

They bugged his home and followed him wherever he
went and they searched his office and tracked his phone calls.
Finally, the government got really angry and said, you can't
write about us any more, you can't have access, go away. But
some of the people about whom he had written and whose
names he had never revealed kissed him when he went away,
and gave him roses, and everybody said he was a hero, and
later he was loaded with honors.

I was the reporter and the beat I covered was Communist
Poland. That was the first time I had to operate worrying
about the police and courts and the first time I had to burn
notes and think about going to jail. I thought it would be the
last, because I resolved never again to work in a totalitarian
society.

Now it is twenty years later and I am the editor of the
same newspaper for which I was a reporter in Poland. I spend
my time dealing with news and with staff matters, but there is

one subject that now takes up a considerable amount of my time and thoughts and that has to do with whether reporters should burn their notes, whether they are going to go to jail, what are the possibilities of a sudden police search, whether people who once talked to us will talk any more, whether other papers can be fined out of existence, whether the police will secretly commandeer our phone records to find our sources of information, whether we will be allowed to cover the administration of justice, how to get the police to reveal necessary information.

New York, not Warsaw.

I do not tell you all this to imply that we have gone totalitarian or that the Republic will fall. But I do tell you that the *process* essential to a free press, one of the institutions that will help guarantee that we do *not* go totalitarian, that the Republic will *not* fall, is under attack, and not from our enemies or the enemies of freedom. That we could handle. No, it is under attack from some of the very people whose professions have helped create and strengthen a free press, some of the lawyers and judges of our country, honorable men and women who traditionally have been the philosophic allies of the free press. And it is under attack from federal legislators and politicians who certainly do not see themselves as enemies of a free press. They just think the American press is a little too free for their tastes.

They want to prevent the press from printing certain kinds of information. They say that obviously this does not affect such respected newspapers as the *Times* or the *Washington Post* or the *Boston Globe.* All they're aiming at, they say, is certain nasty fringe publications. Now I happen to agree that some of their targets are indeed nasty and fringe, but it is precisely the fringes, not just the center, that the First Amendment was designed to protect.

Simply see what has happened in the past few years. A dozen or so reporters and editors have been sent to jail for no other crime than trying to protect their sources, exactly what I did in Poland every day and for which Americans praised me. Others are now under orders to reveal sources or face jail.

The courts have permitted newsrooms to be searched. Thousands of memoranda and files have been subpoenaed in different actions around the country. One large newspaper, our own, has been fined hundreds of thousands of dollars. Now every small newspaper lives under the threat of being fined into bankruptcy at the decision of a judge. Laws erected by state governments to protect the reporter's right to work freely have been destroyed by some courts.

Many judges have decided that reporters can be barred from essential parts of the court process, pretrial hearings, which constitute so important a part of the administration of justice. Other courts have placed severe restraints on participants in the judicial process, preventing press and public from finding out what is going on. A wall of judicial protection has been built around information held by the police behind which they can operate in relative secrecy.

In more and more cases, courts have upheld the principle of prior restraint, that is preventing the press from publishing what it feels *should* be published. Until a few years ago this was unthinkable.

And in case after case, by demanding notes and files and sending reporters to jail for not revealing sources, courts in effect have ruled that they have the power to enforce publication of what reporters and editors feel should *not* be published, because the information is either confidential or simply inaccurate, untrustworthy, or damaging to innocent people, just raw material.

In totality courts now have ruled themselves overseers of essential decision-making processes of the free press that the First Amendment was designed to safeguard from government encroachment—what to publish, when to publish, how to operate, what to think.

To understand why all this is so important to the press and the public, it is necessary to understand not only the law, but the nature of news and how it is gathered. And newspaper people have not succeeded in giving the public a real understanding of the news process.

Virtually all the news that is printed in newspapers or

broadcast on TV is official news. That is, it is information disseminated by one governmental or business or professional
source or another.

A President makes a speech, a legislator introduces a bill,
a company issues an earnings statement, an investigative
body issues a report, a consumer group demands action, a
union strikes, a government department asks for money, a
civil rights group protests discrimination. It is news that the
prime mover or central subject usually wants printed. Now,
this kind of news is extremely important and essential to an
informed citizenry.

In totalitarian societies, most of what we would consider
official news is secret. In our country our leading institutions
and figures disseminate news because it is in their interest to
do so and their interest often includes the pressures and need
to inform the public and engage in a public dialogue. That is
part of the contract of freedom.

But it is still official news.

There is another kind of news—news that institutions or
leaders or professions or organizations do not want made
public.

It can be as big as the Pentagon Papers or Watergate or
CIA violations or as small as minor chicanery within a city
council, questionable business ethics in a manufacturing company, or even conflict of interest in a newspaper.

Most often this information is held by dissidents, people
who feel they cannot afford to be identified with its publication. Sometimes they volunteer the information; sometimes
the reporter comes across it in the course of inquiry or because of a trusted relationship with the source. A dissident
need not be a radical or a shadowy operator with a hot story
to tell. A dissident can be an ambassador who thinks administration policy is wrong and wants it known, but not at the
price of his own immediate retirement.

A four-star general can dissent with the chief of staff and a
clerk who sees waste can dissent with his government department chief.

What binds all dissidents together is the fact that they

hold information that is of public interest but which, either out of self interest or fear, they will not make public if they are to become known as the source—that is, unless they are guaranteed confidentiality. Confidentiality is a last resort for a good reporter. She or he makes every effort to name sources, because the source is an important part of information and lends strength to the story. The so-called anonymous source is only a last resort.

The press is usually portrayed as some huge, all-powerful machine strip-mining the defenseless government of its secrets.

The fact is that only a small part of any newspaper or television program, daily or over the year, contains information uncomfortable to government or institutions—too small a part. But without press confidentiality, the dissident information would vanish and the press would become a handout press.

I do not think there is a plot against the press on the part of the courts. I *do* think that there is a resentment against the press that comes from many things. I do feel that most of that resentment comes from the virtues rather than the failures of the press, the unpleasant virtues of telling the people the truth about Vietnam, Watergate, corruption in government or in business, the aggressiveness and cantankerousness which are part of our makeup and function.

We annoy the hell out of people. And we have our faults, by God, we have our faults. There are scores of publications I wouldn't read, let alone work for. And there are a few for which I have loathing and contempt.

But there is a difference between resenting the press or even loathing it and trying to control it.

The First Amendment was written not to protect the press from the admiration of government but from the loathing of government, all branches of government.

Courts and the press are involved, it seems to me, in two philosophic differences. One is that some judges feel that it is incumbent upon them to protect what the government says for the national security of the United States. National security usually turns out to be a matter of political or diplomatic interest or plain embarrassment. The price of prior restraint, a fancy way of saying judicial censorship, strikes me as a very expensive price indeed to pay to save government face.

Remember what the government said would happen if we published the Pentagon Papers? National calamity, revelation of state secrets, disaster upon disaster. The government position was a fraud and the government, I believe, knew it.

Here is a quote that might interest you: "One shudders to think of what our future would be like if the *New York Times* had not exposed a policy of mistakes and misdeeds and published the Pentagon Papers." That quotation comes from the then Vice President of the United States, Walter Mondale, about a year ago in Kansas City, about ten years after we published the Pentagon Papers.

More important to most judges and lawyers is the issue of access and confidentiality in relation to a fair trial. An ambiguous decision by the Supreme Court on court closing, called *Gannett v. De Pasquale*, created a great deal of confusion, and for a while judges were closing trials right and left. Later, the *Richmond Newspapers v. Virginia* decision clarified that somewhat, but still allowed judges to close pre-trial hearings.

That may not sound like much except when you realize that about eighty-nine percent of all indictments are settled before the case ever comes to a full trial. Without access to pre-trial hearings, the press and the public lose access to the heart of the whole judicial process.

I do not believe that the issue is one of a fair trial versus a free press and I do not believe that the First and Sixth Amendments need ever be in true conflict. Let me read to you what Hans Linde, a Justice of the Oregon State Supreme Court had to say:

The supposed conflict between the constitutional right to a fair trial and a free press rests on a simple fallacy. There are often genuine conflicts among competing objectives and individual interests, and I do not minimize their importance. We can even speak of competing rights, but not of conflicting constitutional rights. For what is a constitutional right? It is a claim that runs against the government—usually not a claim that the government do something *for* you or me, but that it refrain from doing something *to* us. The Constitution prescribes how government is to behave and how not. The Constitution does not make rules for private persons, unless they act on behalf or in lieu of a government. Only a government can violate a constitutional command.

If a judge believes that the actions of the press may violate a defendant's rights, the remedy is not to wipe out the First Amendment by barring the press or eliminating its requirements for confidentiality and access, but simply by using his powers to strengthen the Sixth Amendment—by control of the courthouse, by continuation or change of venues, by sequestration of jurors and witnesses, by instructions to jurors—and even by freeing defendants. Surely better that a guilty man go free than the First Amendment be repealed.

The most controversial of the incidents involving conflict between a reporter and the courts was the Farber case. Millions of words have been written about it by now, but I will go into it only briefly.

On May 17, 1978, a subpoena was issued to the *New York Times* and its reporter Myron Farber for all notes, all records, all memoranda, all correspondence, all recordings of all interviews with all witnesses for the prosecution and all witnesses for the defense in a murder trial taking place in New Jersey.

The subpoena called for the production of more than 5,000 documents. That is an estimate. No justification was presented other than a single affidavit by the defense lawyer saying that it was his belief that something in the files would be helpful to the defense.

No attempt was made to show that even a single document in those thousands was relevant. There was no attempt to show that anything was critical to the defense. There was no attempt to show that the information could not have been obtained through other sources. It seemed, purely and simply, a fishing expedition—a diversion on the part of the attorney.

The *Times*, Mr. Farber, and their attorneys tried repeatedly and unsuccessfully just to obtain a hearing on the relevancy or materiality of the documents. We never got that hearing nor was the shield law which specifically protected reporters in such cases respected in any way by the courts.

What we had here was a plain attempt to divert attention from the heart of the case by making a reporter and his newspaper the defendants, a growing trend among lawyers. We never said that we would not under any circumstances turn over any of the notes. What we did insist upon was what we saw as our constitutional right to a hearing to demonstrate whether there was any relevancy or materiality in the documents. We never received such a hearing and, for insisting upon our constitutional rights, the *Times* was fined $287,000 and Mr. Farber spent 40 days in jail. Later courts upheld our basic position that we were entitled to a hearing but it did not apply to us.

As Judge Harold Medina once put it, any judge who knows his business and who has a stiff backbone can afford a fair trial without any invasion of the freedom of the press.

In that speech of his, Judge Medina laid it pretty heavily on judges who he thought violated the First Amendment. He also laid it pretty heavily on reporters and editors and publishers who were too quick to compromise. He gave them a piece of advice: "Fight like hell every inch of the way."

Well, we are fighting and it seems that almost every time we turn around there is a new battle to be fought.

One had to do with the seizure of the telephone records of our Atlanta bureau by the Department of Justice. They were not investigating us; they were investigating the Ku Klux Klan, which we also had been investigating, without informing us or giving us a chance to fight. Southern Bell bowed to a subpoena of the Department of Justice and turned over all the records from our Atlanta bureau and from the home of our bureau chief. The purpose of the subpoena was to find out who our reporters were talking to.

This clandestine investigation of a reporter's work is a clear violation of the spirit of the First Amendment. I'm happy to say that that particular threat has been considerably eased. Because of complaints from the press and the bar, the Justice Department issued new guidelines that made unnotified seizure much less likely. Right now a new quite important threat confronts the press and will be fought out in the courts. Congress has adopted legislation that would make it a crime for newspapers to print the names of United States intelligence agents, past or present, if the newspapers had reason to believe that such printing would affect United States intelligence operations.

Now that bill is not aimed against the *New York Times* or the *Washington Post* or the *Boston Globe.* It is supposed to be aimed against the nasty fringes. There are a couple of publications, which indeed I consider reprehensible, that make a practice of identifying United States intelligence agents. Usually those names are no secret at all to foreign intelligence groups, but they could indeed cause trouble.

Papers like the *New York Times* do not generally print the names of intelligence agents. In fact, we avoid it unless we think there's a strong public interest in doing so.

This bill strikes virtually every First Amendment lawyer as clearly unconstitutional because it would amount to legislation forbidding certain types of information, even in public, from being printed in the press.

It is not simply a theoretical matter, however important that is. The fact is if that legislation had existed, it might, for instance, have been impossible to print a large part of the Watergate story because some of the people who participated in it were indeed former CIA agents and even had connections with the CIA at the time.

It would have been totally impossible for the *New York Times,* for one, to conduct its current investigation of the transfer of secret communications material and weapons to the Libyans, because the people at the heart of this odious operation so damaging to the interests and honor of the United States, are former CIA agents and there is every reason to suspect that people now in the CIA had knowledge of the whole sickening betrayal of American interests. Two *Times* reporters have devoted their full time for months traveling all around the world, tracking down this network of agents and former agents engaged in selling American interests to the Libyans. If this legislation had been in existence, that investigation would probably not have been possible. The sad but important truth that the intelligence "old school tie" seems to have been the connecting link in this operation—to strengthen a dictator called a madman by our own leaders and to strengthen him at the expense of the United States—would have been kept from the public.

The press is not asking for privilege. That word implies some special gift to be bestowed upon the press or withheld from the press at somebody's discretion, a judge's or a legislator's or a policeman's. No, we are not talking about the privilege of the press, but the right and ability and duty of the press to function in any meaningful sense.

Yes, this all concerns editors, reporters, and publishers, but I beseech you to consider that this concerns each of you as citizens of a country based on freedom of thought and expression.

Every individual American has to ask herself or himself some questions:

Do you want a society in which newspapers have to operate under the fear of being fined to death?

Do you want a society in which newspaper offices can be searched without advance hearings?

Do you want a society in which the public does not know what is taking place in vital parts of the court processes?

Do you want a society in which the police process is made virtually secret?

Do you want a society that is the totality of all these things?

Please think about it. If your answer is "No, I don't want that kind of society," then fight like hell every inch of the way.

SOME FLAWS IN THE GOLDEN AGE OF JOURNALISM[1]

WILLIAM A. LEONARD[2]

The trouble with many journalists today, one of the nation's top broadcast news executives suggested to an audience on June 5, 1981, is that they have an inflated view of their own importance. William A. Leonard, president of CBS News, said, "There is a tendency among us all to use freedom of the press as though it were some sign of high rank, some badge of privilege which confers special liberties upon its possessors."

Mr. Leonard made his remarks in a keynote address at the annual convention of the Association of Press Broadcasters, Inc. in the Hilton Hotel, Washington, D.C. The Association has a membership of approximately 4,000 radio and television stations who also belong to Associated Press. Its goal is to advance journalism by making available an accurate and impartial record of the news through the media of radio and television. The audience was made up of 400 station owners, general managers, and news directors assembled in a hotel meeting room.

While Leonard noted that through technology journalism had made great strides in recent years in its ability to convey a much greater amount of information clearly and accurately to the public, he said:

> I am troubled by the fact that no matter how much information we give the people, and how often we give it to them, they don't seem to pay any more attention to it than they ever did. There are more facts floating around now than ever, thanks to us, but it is by no means apparent that the public is any better informed.

He recommended that journalists place more emphasis on delivery of the news—good reporting, good writing, and good editing. "My advice," he said, "is that we worry less about the new technology and more about the old English language and that we try to improve our bedside manners."

[1] Keynote speech delivered at the annual convention of Associated Press Broadcasters, Inc., on June 5, 1981, at the Hilton Hotel, Washington, D.C. Title supplied by the editor.

[2] For biographical note, see Appendix.

William Leonard's speech: There is always a danger in having as a speaker a veteran newsman who is nearing retirement . . . because his tendency is to review every story he has covered beginning with World War II. I'll spare you that today. But I do want to take a look at some of the recent changes that have taken place in our profession, and suggest some things we should be thinking of in the future, as well as a few thoughts about where we are strong and where we are weak.

Journalism in its broadest sense—the practice of communications—is expanding and exploding in ways that we can hardly even comprehend. As a nation, we are widely, even wildly, informed. Some people call it "electronification," others call it the information age. Whatever the term, we are seeing an avalanche of knowledge and data which dwarfs anything that past ages and past journalists could imagine. We are surrounded by information, we are bombarded by news, we are engulfed in entertainment. Stores and elevators have cameras, cars have cassettes, homes have videotape recorders. And as you've noticed on city streets these days, it appears that most people under 25 are walking around with wires coming out of their ears. When I look at the technical progress of our business, it is with a mixture of wonder and dismay.

Just consider one industry, television. With microwave facilities we can now set up and transmit from virtually any part of this city in minutes; as the country becomes more and more wired we are able with the help of our affiliates to do the same from almost any other part of the country within hours. We will soon have those microwave facilities in suitcases carried by camera crews, to be set up anywhere geography allows. Satellites give us the same instant capabilities from most other parts of the world.

The mushrooming of cable facilities, meanwhile, has opened up entire new dimensions of news and information. You can watch a Broadway musical or a sporting event, or a pornographic movie, or the House of Representatives . . . but I repeat myself. Next will be low-power neighborhood television—it will eliminate the back fence as the center of gossip, and it may fulfill Andy Warhol's prophecy of the day when everybody will be a celebrity for 15 minutes.

The revolution is not confined to the electronic industry—print journalism is beginning to feel the wave too. Computer terminals have invaded newspaper city rooms. Now instead of the green eyeshade, it's the green computer screen. I've talked to some diehard reporters who even shunned electric typewriters, but they tell me that they use the new word processors and they like them. The story is going around that a city editor put one of the word processors on obits and it threatened to resign. But all this is just the beginning of the revolution for print journalism. It is now technically possible, for instance, to bring newspapers and magazines into the home, both on television and by printouts. That includes not only news copy but ads as well—which has prompted on the part of publishers a sudden interest in the field of telecommunications which had never been detected in publishers before. All these advances, all this wizardry, represents the technology which already exists. To think what could be in store for the future is astonishing.

Side by side with these developments has come an opening up of government and other public bodies which is quite beyond what we could have hoped for even a decade ago. In the U.S. Congress, House and Senate Committee Sessions—even Executive Sessions—are now open to news coverage. The House itself is on closed-circuit television. And the Senate is also considering opening up its sessions to television cameras. Sunshine laws have brought increasing openness to numerous government bodies around the country. Some courts are open now to cameras. And the Freedom of Information Act has released to public scrutiny a whole new realm of documents.

Beyond giving us in the news business more raw material than ever to work with, these advances have done something else that is significant—they have narrowed the distance between electronic and print journalism. Radio and television depend on print journalism for many things, and now print depends on radio and television for many things as well. Both rely more and more on each other for putting news sources on the public record, and both draw on each other's talent for questioning these sources. And once the print media comes into the home through the television set, the questions of government regulation which radio and television have always lived with will become important to print journalists as well. Electronic and print journalism, which used to be sharply divided, both technically and emotionally, are coming closer together. And that, I think, is a happy development.

These changes I have cited are mostly technical ones, brought on by advances in science and development. Another change occurs to me. I am referring to the new status that our business seems to have acquired.

The news business has become somewhat more respectable. It has become, in fact, almost fashionable. Not so long ago the reporter's trade was often considered, as the phrase goes, "of no redeeming social value." Some people thought the press was a necessary evil; some even thought it was an unnecessary evil. Working press used the tradesmen's entrance, and the caricature of the reporter always included the pork-pie hat with the press card in the brim. I know—I still have that hat in my closet, in case things turn around again.

Once in a while in those days Spencer Tracy or Jimmy Stewart made reporting look like a dashing and altogether top-drawer career. There were always giants in our field of course. James Gordon Bennett could open up the African continent, or William Randolph Hearst could orchestrate a war, or Walter Lippmann could shape government policy with a quiet conversation. *Working* press stood on the sidewalk.

But you can't keep good newsmen down forever. Through various circumstances, journalism in very recent years has in many ways traded its rough-and-tumble image for a far more urbane kind of glamor . . . and its raw force for a far more sophisticated kind of influence.

Radio and television certainly had a hand in this transformation. So too did the manner in which the Watergate story worked to cast the press in the heroic mold. Whatever the reasons, journalism has acquired a certain celebrity status, and some journalists have become stars. Where once the reward for the prize-winning series was a small raise and a better beat, now it is often a book contract and movie rights and a lecture tour. And even where success is not so dramatic . . . how can a cocktail party or a dinner be fashionable these days without a few of the area's reigning journalists—as guests, I mean, not just to take down the *names* of the guests?

This new prestige has had a number of effects on our business. For one thing, it has raised our standard of living. It has broadened our opportunities for speech-making. And, perhaps most important for the future, it has quickened a greater interest in journalism than we have ever seen, especially among the young. Our profession is now attracting as never before very talented, very dedicated, very industrious men and women. In the past ten years, for example, the number of college students earning degrees in journalism has jumped 26 percent. Where once the editor looked with suspicion at the job applicant who flourished an undergraduate degree, now he looks with suspicion at the applicant who has *only* an undergraduate degree. Journalism today has a wealth of talent to choose from, an abundance of young energy and ability and enthusiasm.

All of these bright developments have come, I believe, without our sacrificing any of the essential skills and the high ideals in which we take pride. I can't help but think how far our profession has come in the last century. A hundred years ago the news business was still in many ways an organized form of pamphleteering. What information people were given on public affairs was as often as not politically generated, and often untrustworthy. Today the American people not only have more information than they have ever had before, but they have it in a more level and unbiased form as well.

So it would seem that we are in a kind of golden age of journalism. We have at our fingertips more ways of gathering and transmitting information than we have ever had. Our profession has a sophistication and luster which is new and flattering. We are making a better living than our predecessors. We are attracting countless numbers of talented young people.

It's a rosy picture. But I wouldn't be a newsman if I couldn't find a few things wrong with it, and I can.

For instance, I am troubled by the fact that no matter how much information we give people, and how often we give it to them, they don't seem to pay any more attention to it than they ever did. There are more facts floating around now than ever, thanks to us. But it is by no means apparent that the public is any better informed in what we consider areas of importance ... or whether they care much either. Consider national elections. Last year the networks alone spent seventy-five million dollars covering the presidential campaigns. The political parties spent one *hundred* and seventy-five million. And what do the voting statistics show? Less than 54 percent of the eligible voters went to the polls, which was less than the percentage in the previous presidential election, which was less than the percentage in the presidential election before that. Without the benefit of our superior technology, the island of Malta has a voting percentage of more than 90, and in Iceland more than 80 percent of the citizens vote. Elections in America are attracting more and more reporters and fewer and fewer voters. The emphasis we put on them seems to mean nothing to the people we are talking to.

It's not much different in other areas of public knowledge. Various surveys show that the average American has little awareness of national or world affairs and an imprecise understanding of what we consider current events. People don't know their own congressmen, they don't know their state legislators, they don't know how the judicial system works, they don't know the Bill of Rights. The things we place the most emphasis on are the very things they ignore. We keep telling people that something is important and they keep telling us to go soak our heads.

We get the same low marks on the question of public confidence. Survey after survey shows that the public doesn't trust the press. We usually rank higher than other targets, like congressmen and lawyers. But that is cold comfort, because neither of these groups ranks very high.

I am not suggesting that it is our mission to win popularity contests, any more than it is our duty to get out the vote or to educate the population. But nonetheless, it is disconcerting and disappointing to me to realize that our trade, which has such a continuous and intimate relationship with the American people, evokes such a mixture of apathy and distrust. We could blame our listeners and our readers, and no doubt we sometimes do. But it is hard to escape the conclusion that the fault is partly ours, that something about the way we do our work either turns people off or ticks them off, or both.

Does that mean we are not doing our job well enough? Or does it mean we're doing it too well? I think the answer is a little bit of both.

For one thing, we often assume that everyone is as interested in the news as we are. I think, for example, that our saturation coverage may be part of the reason why so many people don't vote. Politics has become so complicated. It used to be that when you wanted to know who to vote for, your precinct captain told you who was the good guy, then you went for him. And 50 percent of the time you were right. Now you must ponder the candidates' families, and their finances, and how they come across in their commercials, and whether they look the way their image-makers want them to look, and whether you like the image-makers when they do *their* interviews. With many people it is all too much.

In covering a major story, sometimes it seems we don't just report it, we throw it to the ground and smother it. But telling it all and telling often isn't the same thing as telling it well. Satellites and fiber optics and 80 channels of television and 36-hour-a-day newscasts don't by themselves improve the quality of reporting one bit, any more than instant replay ever made a tackle or caught a pass or took a team to the Super Bowl.

In many of the areas that we cover we are constantly flirting with the danger of overloading our audience, leading them to distraction or despair. I do not pretend to have the answer to how to provide all the information we think people should have and yet do it in a way that they are willing to absorb it. But I know it is not just a matter of throwing facts and hoping some of them stick. E. B. White, in *The Elements Of Style,* says: ". . . sympathize with the reader's plight . . . most readers are in trouble about half the time." We can help out the reader or the listener best by sharpening the elements of our profession—good reporting, good writing, good editing. These simple but demanding skills are the best things we can offer our readers and our listeners. The more these things become overwhelmed by mountains of information and by wonders of technology, the more we all suffer.

And while we are trying to make the news clear to our audience, there is something else we should try to make clear, and that is ourselves. I think we fail as an institution in not telling people what we are all about, and I believe our failure grows more apparent and more damaging with the passage of time. I'm not talking about public relations, except in the broadest sense. I'm talking about dealing with the public in a straightforward way, without special pleading and without an attitude of special privilege.

It's my guess that one of the principal reasons people give the news business such a low ranking in the polls is that they think we are too self-important, too remote and too arrogant. There is a tendency among us all to use freedom of the press as though it were some sign of high rank, some badge of privilege which confers special liberties upon its possessors. As someone said unkindly about a well-known editor recently, "He's full of the First Amendment—and that ain't all."

All of us here believe, with true passion, in the freedom of the press. But must we always seem so anxious to climb on that high horse? To us First Amendment is a cherished weapon to be used in defense of the people's right to know. But I think to the uninitiated, it often appears that we use the First Amendment the way a maiden uses a crucifix against a vampire, and I don't think people like that.

What we fail to make clear is that we are accorded a few

special privileges because we are surrogates for the people, because we are acting in their stead to keep them informed about their government and their community. I think we spend too much time telling people about our rights and not enough time explaining why we have them . . . and making it clear through our good faith that we know our readers and our listeners share in whatever special place we may hold.

We in the news business are always in a very delicate relationship with the people. We are frequently telling them things they don't want to hear, we are often exploding their myths and invading their lives. No wonder people sometime feel that we are distant and superior. When we are criticized, for sins real or imagined, we have a pat response: "We don't make the news, we just report it." That response seems logical to us. But to people who feel they have a grievance with us, it must seem both distainful and smug. They know that we don't just report the news—they know we find it and shape it and package it and decide just what is put in and what is left out, where it starts and where it stops. That is our job. It is a heavy responsibility, and we would be wise to remember how quickly people will take us to task when they feel we are abusing it.

A doctor may be able to tell a patient "this is going to hurt a little, but it will do you good" and get away with it. Centuries of experience have taught the medicine men how to get across those unpleasant truths and make the patient like it. I guess that's called bedside manner.

My advice is that we worry less about the new technology and more about the old English language; that while we search for those grains of truth, we look on ourselves with a grain of salt; and that we try to improve our bedside manners.

THE STATE OF BLACK AMERICA[1]

John E. Jacob[2]

President Reagan's first year in office was a year of "betrayal of basic civil rights protections," the president of the National Urban League said on Jaunary 18, 1982. John E. Jacob, in his first major news conference since he took over leadership of the civil rights group from Vernon E. Jordan Jr., made this assertion in a short address delivered when the organization released its 1982 edition of the league's annual "State of Black America" report.

"For black America, 1981 was a year of economic depression, savage cuts in survival programs for the poor and the betrayal of basic civil rights protections," Mr. Jacob said, contending that "This time around the social safety net is in shreds." "Cuts in federal social programs did not just trim the fat" but, according to Jacob, "they slashed down to the bone. And those cuts were concentrated in programs in which blacks were a third to a half of all beneficiaries." "We must be very clear about what happened in 1981," Jacob asserted, "The rich got tax cuts, the Pentagon got a blank check; but poor people lost jobs, training opportunities, food assistance, health care, and much else."

Jacob delivered his speech in the Blackburn Student Center at Howard University in Washington, D.C., at 11 A.M. to an audience of approximately 400. The occasion was a press conference, so the principal concentration was on the media. However, Howard University students had been invited and they and a number of their instructors were in attendance.

The media paid particular attention to the address since it was the first important statement by the new leader of the Urban League, who had replaced the charismatic Vernon Jordan, leader of the organization for ten years previously. Following his address, Jacob appeared the same night on the MacNeil-Lehrer Report television program and the following morning on ABC television's "Good Morning America." The address was widely covered by national and local television, as well as the print media.

---

[1] Delivered at the Blackburn Student Center, Howard University, Washington, D.C., at 11 A.M. on January 18, 1982.
[2] For biographical note, see Appendix.

John Jacob's speech: Today the National Urban League releases its seventh annual State of Black America report.

Never in that time has the State of Black America been more vulnerable. Never in that time have black people so strongly felt themselves under siege. Never in that time have black economic and civil rights gains been under such powerful attack. Never in that time have so many black people been so alienated from their government.

This is an unhealthy and dangerous situation. It is something the government must act to dispel. It is a situation created by this administration's actions, and only this administration can reverse it.

In 1981, the black community was hit by economic and political disasters of the first magnitude. For black Americans, 1981 was a year of economic depression, savage cuts in survival programs for the poor, and the betrayal of basic civil rights protections.

Let me briefly summarize some of those elements. Black unemployment is at record levels—sixteen percent by the understated official statistics that don't include discouraged workers or involuntary part-timers. Teenage black unemployment went through the roof in 1981. We are in the seventh postwar national recession, so those numbers will get worse. After each recession, black jobless rates stay higher than they were.

This time around the social safety net is in shreds. Cuts in federal social programs did not just trim the fat, they slashed deep into bone. And those cuts were concentrated in programs in which blacks were a third to a half of all beneficiaries.

We must be very clear about what happened in 1981: the rich got tax cuts, the Pentagon got a blank check; but poor people lost jobs, training opportunities, food assistance, health care, and much else.

We didn't go through some sort of abstract budget adjustment process. We went through a series of earthquakes that left disproportionate numbers of black people with fewer resources and drove them deeper into poverty. Especially in the context of those economic disasters, the attack on civil rights is downright immoral. This nation did not go through a long, painful process of desegregating society only to have it *reseg-regated* in the 1980s.

In 1981, an administration from which blacks and minorities are virtually absent, took a number of negative steps on civil rights. From its backtracking on desegregating schools to its de-emphasis of civil rights enforcement to its attacks on affirmative action, the administration created a feeling among many blacks that they were forgotten people.

Perhaps the most blatant of those anti-civil rights policies was the unconscionable decision to reward racism by granting tax-exempt status to schools that discriminate. The President's later statement that we would ask Congress to pass a law authorizing the IRS (Internal Revenue Service) to refuse exempt status to such schools does not change the issue. The IRS had the authority. The courts said it had the authority. The administration's claim that this is simply a procedural issue about legal authority does not hold water. Its actions provided aid and comfort to the racists in our midst.

Taken together, these and other steps can only be interpreted as attempts to dismantle the process of desegregating America. They raise the grim prospects of a return to a past that denied basic human rights and tolerated racial discrimination. They account for the bitter feelings of alienation and isolation, not only among many black Americans, but among all who don't want the clock turned back to a meaner, nastier period.

What about 1982? Past experience indicates black workers will not recapture their losses in a general economic recovery. The administration, faced with enormous deficits, will try to cut what remains of important programs that help poor people. Attempts to bury affirmative action and civil rights enforcement are likely to accelerate.

But there is also greater hope in 1982 that these calamities can be prevented. The steamroller of the administration's radical approach to national problems has stalled. A year's experience has shown that supply side economics is indeed what

David Stockman said it was, nothing more than old-fashioned "trickle down." The fight against inflation used the old, discredited tools of the past—tight money and high unemployment. The promised economic growth turned to deep recession. The New Federalism just dumped problems on to the states, problems they know they can't handle.

So I sense a new realism today, especially among congressmen who recognize the political risks involved in policies that put their constituents out of work, increase pressures on local governments in their districts, and outrage the moral sensibilities of Americans who believe in fairness.

Two key tests of that new realism are now shaping up. The first is the framing of the 1983 budget. We call on congressional leaders of both parties to inform the administration that further cuts in poor people's programs are unacceptable. The budget deficit caused by the administration's tax cuts and defense spending increases can be closed by scaling down the defense budget and by closing tax loopholes for special interests.

A second key test is the Senate battle over extension of the Voting Rights Act. We call on the President to abandon his opposition to the House bill. The Senate should swiftly pass this vital protection of the right to vote, a right denied many black people until 1965.

We also call on the President to order his Justice Department to call a cease-fire in its war on affirmative action. To equate affirmative action with restrictive quotas is nothing less than a big lie. As practiced by both the public and private sectors and consistently endorsed by the courts, affirmative action is nothing less than fair play—removing race and gender as obstacles to hiring and promoting qualified people. As the National Urban League says in our new national advertising program, "everybody deserves a chance to make it on their own."

Nineteen eighty-two offers major challenges to all Americans. To all who are concerned with the terrible pressures placed on poor people, it is a time to take off the gloves and come out swinging against further attempts to weaken the weak. We must build coalitions to protect the interests of the forgotten and neglected.

To the administration and to political leaders of both parties, 1982 offers the challenge of replacing failed policies and noting the increased political risk attached to staying on the road of recession.

The private sector in 1982 is challenged to make our system work for all Americans and to reaffirm support for affirmative action and social responsibility.

And black Americans in 1982 are challenged to marshall community and political strengths. While we build external coalitions we must also mobilize black communities to deal with their problems at the neighborhood level. That's a job not only for civil rights and social service agencies, but for every community organization and every individual.

Nineteen eighty-two, then, will be a year of challenge and struggle; a year in which black people must channel their alienation and bitterness to positive efforts for change. It is a year in which all Americans must strive to recapture the faltering ideals of equal opportunity and equal rights. It is a year in which a nation concerned with the loss of rights in Poland must also become concerned with the threat to civil rights here at home.

SOLIDARITY, INDISPENSABLE KEY TO THE FUTURE[1]

Lane Kirkland[2]

The AFL–CIO (American Federation of Labor-Congress of Industrial Organizations) held its 14th biennial convention in New York City in mid-November, 1981. The observance marked the 100th anniversary of the labor movement in this country. The meeting was regarded as critical for the 102-union federation and its 15 million members because of the outcome of the previous year's election. At that time, syndicated columnist Nick Thimmesch described the unions' situation as follows: "I am not going to declare that the 1980 elections marked the year that the American labor union went into permanent decline, . . . or its greatest shock. But . . . I believe it is fair to say that organized labor admits it took a drubbing. . . ." (*Representative American Speeches,* 1980–1981, p 160)

In an effort to recoup its losses, unite its members, and regain the initiative, the AFL–CIO and 200 other organizations arranged a march in Washington, D.C., on September 19, 1981. The protest, named Solidarity Day after the Polish labor uprising which had led to martial law, was designed to draw attention to the problems of the American worker. The demonstration was generally judged to have been successful, with more than a quarter million participants and posed to labor leaders the question, "What can we do to top this?"

The answer was to politicize the union's convention. Traditionally the President of the United States is invited to address the conclave, but no invitation was sent to Ronald Reagan, but House Speaker Thomas P. O'Neill, Senator Edward Kennedy, and former Vice-President Walter Mondale—all Democrats—were invited to address the delegates.

AFL–CIO president Lane Kirkland contributed to the polarization of the delegates along party lines with a surprisingly slashing attack on the Administration in his inspired keynote address.

[1] Delivered at the 14th biennial convention of the American Federation of Labor-Congress of Industrial Organizations on the morning of November 16, 1981, in the Imperial Ballroom of the Sheraton Centre Hotel in New York City.
[2] For biographical note, see Appendix.

Prior to the convention, Kirkland had the reputation of being a "deadpan, plodding, scholarly" speaker (Brown, *Washington Post*, N. 15, '81) whose speeches were characterized by "long complex sentences in which thoughts interrupt thoughts," and "carefully reasoned, ardent defenses of working people." (Serrin, *New York Times*, S. 19, '81) Following the speech, John Herling wrote:

> It can almost be said that the AFL–CIO was born again in its convention here. The stage was set for the definitive coming out of Lane Kirkland as the accepted leader of American labor. . . . At the outset of the convention the 850 delegates . . . were in an expectant mood. When they settled back for Kirkland's keynote address, they were awaiting the delivery of a well-organized, even learned, speech, as befits a historic occasion. What they didn't expect was what they got: a stellar performance—brilliant, slashing, funny, sarcastic, high-spirited, earnest, dedicated. There followed a statement of such quality and derring-to as had not been heard in similar surroundings since the 1935 AFL convention in Atlantic City, where John L. Lewis denounced the established labor leadership of the day. . . . Kirkland was standing up to the President of the United States. (*New Republic*, D. 16, '81)

Other reporters called the speech "the most impassioned yet coherent attack on Reaganomics yet delivered from any podium," (Coakley, *Chicago Tribune*, N. 22, '81) "the most forceful speech since his election as AFL–CIO president," (Lipp, *New York Times*, N. 17, '81) and "indubitably the best oratorical effort of his career, as much because of the uncharacteristic vigor of his delivery as the sparkle of his always redoubtable wit." (Raskin, *The New Leader*, N. 30, '81) The speech was also described as "fiery," "unusually vitriolic," "laced with sarcasm," "a scathing attack," and "a call to arms by labor against (the) national government." Columnists Jack Germond and Jules Witcover observed, "Never in memory of old labor skates has an AFL–CIO chieftain excoriated an occupant of the White House the way Kirkland oratorically clobbered Reagan in his keynote speech." (Baton Rouge *Advocate*, N. 22, '81)

Kirkland delivered his speech at mid-morning in the Imperial Ballroom of the Sheraton Centre Hotel in New York City to 836 union delegates, around 800 representatives of the media, and 95 foreign trade unionists. An invocation and remarks by New York Mayor Edward Koch, New York Governor Hugh Carey, and Senator Patrick Moynihan preceded Kirkland's speech.

During the speech, the audience cheered Kirkland and "repeatedly laughed at his jibes at the Reagan administration." (Moody, *Pittsburgh Post Gazette*, N. 17, '81) During the address, he was interrupted a dozen times by applause and laughter and given a two-minute standing ovation following its conclusion.

Lane Kirkland's speech: Reverend clergy, distinguished guests, members of the Executive Council, delegates, brothers and sisters, two years ago, George Meany left us this charge:

> . . . the labor movement cannot be content with defending the status quo, or reliving past glories. We must constantly look to the future, develop new leadership, adapt policies to changing conditions and new technologies, but—always, always—with unswerving loyalty to the mission of the trade union movement as the instrument for improving and enhancing the working and living conditions of those who work for wages.

Yesterday, November 15, 1981, we made the crossing into our second century as a confederated trade union movement. We are here, at the conclusion of our first hundred years, not just to honor the past, but to prepare ourselves to serve the future.

There is an old church anthem which instructs us as follows: "New occasions teach new duties. Time makes ancient good uncouth." That is not a call to pursue novelty for its own sake, nor to bend and trim to the shifting winds. It is a message, rather, of the need to acknowledge essential change and to respond to its requirements.

We are here in strength and vigor because those who went before us and built this great instrument of progress did indeed adapt its role and structure to the needs and demands of their times. The makeup of this body bears little resemblance to the Horse Collar Workers, the Architectural Cornice Makers, the Box Sawyers and Nailers, and the Umbrella and Walking Stick Makers who gathered into the Federation a hundred years ago. This body will bear as little resemblance to those who assemble under our banner a hundred years hence.

Throughout its history, labor has reflected all the trends and events—sometimes harmful, sometimes enriching—of its times, at home and abroad. Like our nation, we have been enriched by refugees from strife and tyranny in other lands. Like our nation, we have been compelled to grapple with the consequences of vast technological, social, and economic changes that have taxed our wits and capacities.

At times we have lagged behind the path of the curve of change; at times we have surged ahead. Too often to recount, we have been written off and left for dead by the fashion-mongers of the day, only to see them come and go while we remained steadfast on the field of action. Through it all, we have never abdicated our role of leadership in the struggle for human freedom and human progress and we shall not do so now.

Conversely, we are often taken to task because we do not confine our role to the most narrow interests of the dues-paying members, but assume responsibility for the broadest range of human concerns. Seafarers understand their duty, not only to their immediate shipmates, but to all castaways and drifting souls at sea. Last summer, the SS President McKinley was steaming through a stormy night in the China Sea. She came upon a small boat in distress and rescued ten persons fleeing from tyranny on the mainland. When the captain was asked why he felt obliged to risk his ship to rescue these forlorn refugees, he responded:

Shall we ship's masters just leave refugees or seamen or others to drift hopelessly at sea until their ultimate death because they have no passports or seaman's papers?

Our answer, like his, must be "no."

We are honored to have as our guests most of the leaders of the trade union centers of the free world and we welcome them as comrades-in-arms. We share their problems and concerns. I pledge to them, in your name, our cooperation and commitment in our common universal struggle for the rights of working men and women, for bread and freedom, everywhere. To that end, with the support of this convention, we shall apply for re-affiliation, effective January 1, 1982, with the International Confederation of Free Trade Unions.

You have before you the comprehensive Report of the Executive Council which details the work of the federation since our last convention. It will tell you all that you might want to know about that work and probably more. Without trying to retrace all of that ground, let me note some of the ways in which we have sought to address the challenge of the times in keeping with our historic mandate.

We have a permanent mandate to seek and preserve unity within the family of labor, and we rejoice in the re-affiliation of a great union, the United Automobile Workers. We warmly welcome its delegates here, as we welcomed its President, Brother Doug Fraser, to the Executive Council last August. We welcome, above all, the addition to our ranks of the force and vigor of the UAW's role and voice in the fight for social and economic justice.

This old church will remain wide open at all hours. Our mission will not be completed until all of labor's flock is brought within the fold, to work and move together in solidarity. We have an enduring mandate to bring all working people the message of trade unionism and we have pursued that instruction. The officers and members of the Executive Council of this federation are deeply committed to the proposition that there is no matter of more constant urgency than to organize the unorganized.

The past two years have witnessed important breakthroughs against major strongholds of resistance by the Steelworkers, the Amalgamated Clothing and Textile Workers, the Food and Commercial Workers, the Teachers, AFSCME, CWA, and other affiliates, in testimony to the quality of their leadership and dedication. We have initiated an ambitious campaign in the Southwest, with the Houston Cooperative Organizing Program, and we intend to see it through to a solid result.

The strides we have made have been masked in part by offsetting historical factors. A deep recession; the decay of the nation's industrial base, infrastructure, and urban services; the export of jobs; and profound occupational, geographic, and demographic shifts in the work force, have taken their toll.

In the face of these trends, the fact that the labor movement at large has more than held its own and continued to grow is a remarkable achievement. It is evidence, not of weakness, but of inherent strength and vigor. It is a tribute to the capacity of modern labor to respond, to adapt, and to move with the times into new areas of service and growth.

I assure you now that the AFL–CIO stands ready to explore any method of approach and to offer any service that you, the affiliates, desire or will allow in pursuit of our common mandate to organize the unorganized. We have an age-old mandate to educate and agitate and we have over these past months sought to do it justice.

Democratic trade union education is a two-way street and we ignore that at our peril. All channels of information-communication and participation must be open and active throughout and at both ends or they fail altogether.

We can survive adverse public opinion because—being so often the agents of controversy in the pursuit of our duty—we always have. Samuel Gompers summed it up, in 1913, when he wrote:

> Until all elements exert proportional influence in determining public opinion, until all individuals that make up the public become genuinely and unselfishly desirous of continuously striving for justice to all mankind, public opinion will not become an infallible dispenser of justice.

But we cannot long survive the erosion of support for programs and policies on the part of the membership. Without cultivation and conservation, erosion must surely follow.

Last spring, through a series of regional conferences extending over several weeks, the officers and department heads of the Federation met with state and local trade union leaders for face-to-face discussions on any and all issues, no holds barred. We committed ourselves to bring the ideas and opinions that emerged from those two-way conversations to the attention of the Executive Council, and we have fulfilled that commitment. Some of the steps we have since taken, as well as some that will be proposed to this convention, are the product of those meetings. We found them of such value that we shall repeat them next year and in the future. I strongly commend such a practice to every constituent organization.

From those sessions emerged the concept of Solidarity Day and the conviction that the spirit required for its success was there, waiting for an opportunity of expression. On that day, there gathered in Washington the greatest protest demonstration in our history. Over 400,000 members of the main stream of the trade union movement and their allies spoke with one great voice against the course of their government and for the human values we represent. My only regret is that many thousands more who wished to come had to be turned away because all available means of transport were exhausted. I am convinced that every member who assembled in Washington on Solidarity Day went home a better trade unionist, more ready, willing, and able to speak and work for the cause.

What can we fairly say now of these engaging, amiable, and persuasive men of power in Washington, whose measures drew our forces there in protest?

The President, we are told, is the Great Communicator; but so were many other heads of state in history whose policies left suffering and distress in their wake. Herbert Hoover was known as the Great Engineer, but wreckage was his legacy. Communication is scarcely enough, particularly for a President of the United States. Though he "speaks with the tongues of men and of angels, and has not charity," he is "but sounding brass and tinkling cymbals." He has shown a cold heart and a hard fist, but, where, indeed, is the rest of him?

It is one thing to use the full force of government to break a small union of hard-pressed public employees. That, I suppose, does express the harshest construction of the law and is, perhaps, popular. But is it then just and fitting to go out upon the field and shoot its wounded?

As for his brilliant and tireless team, drawn from the service of avarice, they promised us a boom and brought us a bust. They have drained the public purse to lavish welfare on the greedy rich, in the name of "incentive." They have stripped the poor and jobless of welfare, food stamps and unemployment insurance, also in the name of "incentive." That is known as the carrot-and-stick policy: for the rich, the carrot; for the poor, the stick.

What is the net result so far of their genius and masterful command of the Congress? Eight and one-half million workers are now unemployed, the largest number since 1939. Unemployment among blacks and other minorities has reached fifteen and one-half percent; eleven percent of all blue collar workers are unemployed. Unemployment has increased by one million in the last three months alone. The real earnings of workers are down 4.4 percent in the last year. Bankruptcies are up forty percent. The housing, automobile and related industries are being strangled by sky-high interest rates.

Mr. Paul Volcker, high priest of monetarism at the Federal Reserve Board, is a very kind and engaging man—until he goes to work in the morning. Then something happens. For the past few weeks, in public and private discourse, he has been blaming the terrible harm that his policies have already done the nation's economy on next year's wage bargains. To grapple for such a flimsy alibi is a sure sign of the final bankruptcy of monetary doctrine. It calls to mind an old, old ditty:

> It's the same the whole world over,
> It's the poor that get the blame,
> It's the rich that get the gravy.
> Ain't it a bleeding shame?

What can we who opposed the domestic policies of this Administration from the beginning now say that is one-half as devastating as the recorded fleeting spasms of honesty of its leading hatchet-man, Mr. David Stockman? What provoked his candor one can only guess. But you don't have to be an old sailor to know what it means when the smartest rat on board heads for the hawse pipe. Lest you feel a twinge of human sympathy for his public embarrassment, let me remind you that this is the man who once coldly declared that no one is entitled to anything from one's government. He even now boasts, as his proudest achievement, of the destruction of public service employment and trade adjustment assistance.

He was the original interior decorator of this economic

house of ill repute. Now that the sirens are sounding and the
bust is due, he has his story ready. He was only the piano
player in the parlor. He never knew what was going on up-
stairs.

The aftermath also tells us a lot about this Administration.
Was he chastised by the President for cooking the books, rig-
ging the computer, over-feeding the tax hogs, conning the
Congress and duping the public? No—he was taken to the
White House woodshed for, at long last, telling the truth. So
far have we come from young George Washington and the
cherry tree. Now, after his scolding, he tells us that it was all a
foolish mistake, that he was only guilty of being the south end
of a north bound Trojan horse.

It is hard to decide which is worse about the social and
economic policies of this Administration—the array or the
disarray. If this is the direction of the New Beginning that
President Reagan promised, God save us from the End.

When we turn to consider the course of our foreign and
defense affairs we find the same pattern repeated.

We were promised a more vigorous and consistent role of
American leadership and a more coherent and sustained approach to the revival of our forces in freedom's defense. We
welcomed that prospect, for labor has always believed that
our values are worthy of a strong defense in the face of external danger. But what is the objective record, stripped of the
fog of rhetoric?

We have, in the past year, witnessed the following:

The growing dismay and division of our allies;

The feeding of our deadliest adversaries on easy credit,
making lighter their growing burden of lethal arms;

The appeasement of the Saudi-financial-industrial complex with gifts of costly and exotic weapons, paid for in higher
oil prices, by the American consumer;

The destruction of domestic support for necessary defense
expenditures through the exemption of the rich and the
drafting of the poor in the service of its cost, and they have
the nerve to call previous administrations soft.

On the vital issue of human rights, they have sought to pose a fine choice between lice who are totalitarian and lice who are authoritarian. We reject such a choice and we call instead for a freedom of association everywhere as the keystone of a genuine human rights policy.

On that record, as regards this Administration's team of foreign and defense policy-makers, one need say no more than did the Duke of Wellington when he observed his own troops in a state of disarray: "I don't know if they frighten the enemy—But Gad, sir, they frighten me!"

We shall endure and survive all these afflictions, as we have so many others during the ebb and flow of the changing tides and the entrances and exits of great communicators, great engineers, and other flickering lights and shooting stars. Our fortunes depend, not on the stars, but upon ourselves.

As we approach a new election year, we must prepare now for the next battle in our long campaign. Tools and tactics may change, people may come and go, but one element remains essential to our prospects. That is, as always, true and lasting solidarity. Solidarity yields to the common wealth, to build the store of strength that each of our parts will surely need to draw upon, late or soon. Solidarity requires, not blind submission to command, but the free and timely exchange of views in search of consensus. Once that is gotten, it then requires of all the character and forbearance to defer one's own pride or preference to the general good.

The officers of this Federation will seek the advice, consult the wisdom, and promote the expression of the views of all quarters of this movement, so that its great and rich variety may be fairly and fully summoned to our common struggle. When we gain a goal together, there will be enough honor and recognition to go around to each organization that makes up this body. None will be slighted or deprived of its due.

As we go forth into our second century, solidarity remains the indispensable key to the future.

And now to work.

OF HEROES

IN MEMORY OF FRANKLIN D. ROOSEVELT[1]

Arthur M. Schlesinger Jr.[2]
Jennings Randolph[2]
Claude D. Pepper[2]

Joint sessions of the Congress of the United States are rare and stately rituals and it is seldom indeed that they occur twice within a few days. However, on January 26, 1982, President Ronald Reagan appeared on Capitol Hill to deliver his State of the Union address (see p 9) and two days later, on Thursday, January 28, 1982, the Senate and House of Representatives met in joint session to commemorate the 100th anniversary of the birth of Franklin Delano Roosevelt, 32nd President of the United States and the only president to be elected to four consecutive terms.[*] The coincidence of Franklin D. Roosevelt's centenary and Ronald Reagan's first year in office was not without its ironies and contradictions since Reagan, who tends to quote Roosevelt, a hero of his youth, is generally regarded by some liberals as a conservative determined to undermine a good part of the Roosevelt heritage.

The media observed the Roosevelt centenary with feature articles, reports, and newscasts; two national television networks carried special programs on Roosevelt; and in Washington, D.C., ten museums and galleries mounted exhibitions honoring the former president.

The joint Congressional ceremony in the House of Representatives began with a concert by the United States Army Band, after which the honored guests, sons James and Elliott Roosevelt, Mrs. John Roosevelt, grandchildren, and great grandchildren of the late President, entered and were seated. They were followed by Vice President George Bush; members of the Senate; ambassadors, ministers, and charges d'affaires of several foreign governments; and Cabinet members.

A color guard carried the flag into the chamber and the U.S. Naval Academy Midshipmen's Glee Club sang the national anthem. After an invocation by the chaplain, Speaker of the House

---

[1] All three speeches were delivered in the House of Representatives at a joint session of the United States Senate and House of Representatives at 11 A.M., January 28, 1982, in Washington, D.C.

[2] For biographical note, see Appendix.

[*] Roosevelt's actual birthday was January 30, 1882.

Thomas P. ("Tip") O'Neill welcomed the members of the Roosevelt family, asking them to rise and they were greeted with applause. He also welcomed former associates of the late President, Grace Tully, Benjamin Cohen, and James Rowe, and Governor Hugh Carey of New York.

After a medley of songs by the Naval Academy glee club, O'Neill introduced the first speaker, Dr. Arthur M. Schlesinger Jr. and opera singer Leontyne Price sang "America the Beautiful" and "The Battle Hymn of the Republic." Senator Jennings Randolph of West Virginia, and Representative Claude Pepper of Florida followed Schlesinger, both of whom delivered eulogies of their own. Then, Mrs. Averell Harriman, substituting for her husband, who had been a close associate of Roosevelt but that day had laryngitis, read her husband's reminiscences and tribute.

After being introduced by the Speaker, James Roosevelt prefaced his response as follows: "You will forgive me if I am a little moved by this whole very historic occasion. This joint meeting of Congress here in the Capitol of the United States in a place my father often spoke from is a fitting and wonderful tribute to him." The late President's son, in his short address, explained his father's philosophy of government, and accompanied his remarks with recorded excerpts from his speeches.

The ceremony ended at 12:28 P.M. after a benediction by the Chaplain of the Senate and the singing of "God Bless America" by the Midshipmen's Glee Club.

Arthur Schlesinger's speech: Mr. Speaker, Mr. President, Members of Congress, friends, it is a high honor for me to share with three such doughty warriors for liberty and justice as Averell Harriman, Claude Pepper, and Jennings Randolph the opportunity to address this most eminent legislative body in the world.

It is, indeed, a most special occasion that brings us together. We have heard all our lives about the first hundred days of Franklin Delano Roosevelt. We gather today to celebrate his first hundred years.

This is not a partisan occasion. Franklin Roosevelt, as he liked to say, was an old campaigner who loved a good fight; but he was not a strict party man. He cast his first presidential vote for a progressive Republican—after his own party had nominated a conservative Democrat. As President himself in 1933, he appointed two Republicans to his Cabinet. Seven years later, under the shadow of war, he appointed two more.

"People tell me," he observed at a Democratic party dinner in 1940, "that I hold to party ties less tenaciously than most of my predecessors in the Presidency, that I have too many people in my administration who are not active party Democrats. I admit the soft impeachment."

A few months before his death he was exploring the possibility of a political alliance with the very man whom the Republicans had run against him just four years earlier. And while we are contemplating the latitudinarianism with which presidents sometimes regard political parties, it may not be amiss to recall that a Republican President, not too far from here today, cast his first four presidential ballots for Franklin Roosevelt.

Jefferson put it classically in his first inaugural: "We have called by different names brethren of the same principle."

Today, to bring Jefferson up to date, we are all Democrats, we are all Republicans, as we join to honor a man who belongs not just to a party but to the essential history of this great Republic and to the intimate personal lives of most of us in this illustrious Chamber.

For Franklin Roosevelt led our Nation—led every one of us over the age of 50—through what have been, save for the Civil War, the two most grievous crises in our national life as a free state: the worst depression in American history and the greatest war in American history.

It is hard today to remember that America, now so rich and bountiful, was once, not too many years ago, a land of grim poverty and aching want, where millions who sought jobs could not find them, where factories stood empty and silent and crops rotted in the fields and men huddled in line to get a cup of soup and a piece of bread and children fought for food in garbage dumps.

Fifty years ago a blanket of despair was settling across the land. In the 1932 election, more than a million votes were cast for parties dedicated to the abolition of the capitalist system.

It is hard to remember today that America, now a great military super-power, was once, not too many years ago, a beset and embattled nation, its great warships sunk at Pearl Harbor, its new and inexperienced Army fighting for its life in North Africa and Italy, in France, and Guadalcanal, its gallant men dying on the Atlantic and the Pacific, in China, and in the skies over Japan. These terrible ordeals are now distant recollections. They recede in memory because we overcame them; and we overcame them in great part because of the exceptional qualities of leadership that Franklin Roosevelt brought to his high office—qualities that nerved his countrymen to fulfill their best and bravest selves.

An idealist in purpose, a realist in tactics, F.D.R. combined boldness and caution, openness and deviousness, compassion and ruthlessness, a genius for manipulation and a genius for inspiration. He not only enjoyed being President and communicated that enjoyment to the country, but he knew how to be President. He surrounded himself with singularly able and outspoken men and women and drove them successfully in the same harness. He fought depression and war with a White House staff far smaller than recent Presidents have required for less arduous challenges.

Roosevelt was a wonderfully effective President, because he had both the craft and the will to work steadily toward his objectives, and he was a great President because he loved this country, its meadows and plains, and forests, its spirited cities, it tranquil valleys, and its rushing streams; and because he imparted to the land he loved a noble vision of the future—the vision of a nation that could be humane and free and abundant, the vision of a world that could be ordered and peaceful and just.

He embodied this vision in a glittering personality—intrepid, exhilarating, and serene. In many ways a conventional man, he had a zest for unconventional ideas. Nurtured in the securities of a patrician past, he faced with equanimity the terrors of a shadowed future. The world, he understood, was in the throes of incessant and inexorable change. Like Lincoln before him, he regarded the dogmas of the quiet past as inadequate to the stormy present.

"We must disenthrall ourselves," as Lincoln said, "and then we shall save our country."

Franklin Roosevelt saw politics as an educational process, a process of intellectual liberation, and he saw experiment as the method of democracy. He doubted that democracy could endure when one-third of the Nation was ill-housed, ill-clad, ill-nourished. The urgent need, he liked to say, was to establish "a fair and just concert of interests"—to restore the balance of life and opportunity between business, labor, and agriculture, city and countryside, north and south and west, and he saw the national Government as the people's indispensable instrument in the abiding battle for balance, decency and justice.

We have a philosophical argument today between those who suppose that if we leave the economy to its own devices, our problems will solve themselves, and those who believe that Government has a vital role to play in promoting the general welfare.

No one can doubt where F.D.R. stood.

A laissez faire attitude in face of human suffering, he said, demanded "not only greater stoicism but greater faith in immutable economic law and less faith in the ability of man to control what he has created than I, for one, have."

Such views may not be popular at this moment. But the debate between private power and public purpose has gone on since the founding of the Republic. No one should think it to have been finally resolved in this particular year of grace.

F.D.R.'s response to economic crisis remolded the framework of American life, civilized our economic system, and restored popular faith in democratic institutions. Had the despair of the Depression deepened, the anti-Communist votes of 1932 would have become many millions in 1936 and 1940, but in fact by 1940, that vote had dwindled to a pathetic 150,-000.

Business leaders did not altogether appreciate Roosevelt's efforts on their behalf, and called him a traitor to his class. The achievement of the New Deal, it may be said, was to save capitalism from the capitalists.

Roosevelt's revitalization of democracy had impact far beyond our own borders. This was a time when across the world fanatic ideologies sacrificed human beings on the altar of dogma. Against the intoxication of creeds and the tyranny of absolutes, Roosevelt fought the fight of decent men and women struggling day by day to make a better life for their children. He steered between the extremes of orthodoxy and revolution, moving always, as he said, "slightly to the left of center."

"His impulse," said Winston Churchill, long before the glory of their wartime partnership, "is one which makes toward the fuller life of the masses of people in every land, and which, as it glows the brighter, may well eclipse both the lurid flames of German-Nordic self-assertion and the baleful, unnatural lights which are diffused from Soviet Russia."

Roosevelt understood that America could not be safe as a democratic island in the totalitarian world. He awoke us from our isolationist slumbers and led us superbly through the agony of war itself.

The generation that triumphed over the most devastating economic troubles and the most deadly military foes in our history showed the world what Americans are truly capable of.

We have our own great problems again, but it does no good to exaggerate their difficulty or our impotence in dealing with them. Crises ahead always look worse than crises surmounted. This does not prove that they are. Self-pity is not one of human kind's ennobling traits. The crises that confronted Franklin Roosevelt and Abraham Lincoln and George Washington were fairly considerable, too.

As we meet the problems of our own age—and meet them we must—we can surely take heart from the memory of F.D.R. from his boundless courage, his inextinguishable gaiety, his hard understanding of power, his instinct for innovation, his confidence in the ability of man to control what he has created, and, above all, from his indestructible faith in democratic institutions, his imperturbable trust in the strength of a free people, and his overflowing love of America.

Jennings Randolph's speech: Mr. Speaker, Mr. Vice President, I want to thank our colleagues of the Senate and House who by legislation, without partisanship, have brought this event into being. And ladies and gentlemen, and all those who may be listening and perhaps watching throughout America, today we commemorate the birth of Franklin Delano Roosevelt. He, as we know now in memory, and we knew then, was a national leader who sustained and enlarged the legion of a free society. As a youth he knew the world of wealth and privilege. As our President he gave hope to the homeless, he created jobs for the jobless and fostered the meaning of social and economic justice in American democracy.

Franklin Delano Roosevelt, more perhaps than any President, saved this Nation from being torn asunder by class conflict.

On March 4, 1933, President Roosevelt spoke to an anguished and anxious and a divided people. Two days later, to save the financial institutions of our Republic, he proclaimed a national bank holiday, closing all of the banks of our country. On the following Thursday, March 9, the first day of the new Congress, which he called into emergency session—Mr. Speaker, I say this to you and to all those who perhaps want to have something recorded which is a fact—the House passed, without a rollcall, that legislation. The Senate, by a vote of 73 to 7, passed that legislation. The President signed it. It was the Emergency Banking Act, and it was all done in that one day.

Thus began the New Deal, an experiment in using an unorthodox means to modify, but also to preserve the orthodox institutions of a free economy.

In that second week of March 1933 we were faced with the most extreme test of national purpose and will since the Civil War. Lincoln saved a Union divided against itself. Roosevelt saved a nation in disarray by calling forth a shared vision. In both crises the American people had the good sense to elect a leader who drew from the fundamental moral wellsprings of our nation.

Today we also commemorate the good fortune and the continuing wisdom of our American democracy.

The Roosevelt vision became the New Deal, and the New Deal worked. The New Deal created jobs, not leaf-raking jobs as was said by some then and mistakenly even repeated today, but jobs reclaiming and planting thousands of acres of forests, building more than 11,000 schools and thousands of libraries and other public facilities.

In 1933 millions of Americans were working for bare subsistence wages. Almost a third of our labor force was not working at all. Only 1 in 10 farm families was served by electricity. Annual per capita cash income for farm families had dropped to $48.

Now the New Deal brought hope where there was despair. It brought work where there was unwanted idleness. It brought unity of purpose where there was national chaos and much confusion.

The legislative reforms of the New Deal—I stress this—in banking and finance, in agriculture and conservation practices, in eliminating sweatshops and child labor and enabling working men and women to organize for collective bargaining, in creating some measure of security for the elderly, and in harnessing our rivers and generating electricity, that electricity going to farm and city homes alike, these reforms have changed the face of America and have been woven into the fabric of American life, and they will not be torn out. Between 1921 and 1933 more than 10,000 banks closed their doors in this country, destroying faith in our most basic financial institutions.

On October 1, 1936, with the President running for re-election and campaigning in West Virginia, I was with him at the time he received a telegram from Washington. It informed him that for the first time in 55 years we had completed a full year without a single national bank failure. This was the President, I say advisedly, who was reviled as an enemy of capitalism.

In his first inaugural address the President declared his constitutional duty to recommend the measures that a stricken nation in the midst of a stricken world may require. Roosevelt did just that.

The actions of that first administration were not always guided by consistent economic theory. They were experimental. Yes; they were pragmatic. They were guided, however, by consistent moral purpose.

In his second inaugural address the President made that purpose explicit. He stated, "The test of our progress is not whether we add more to the abundance of those who have much, it is whether we add more to those who have too little.

"In our personal ambitions"—he continued—"we are in- dividuals, but in our seeking for economic and political progress as a nation we all go up or else we all go down as one people."

Those words ring with truth, and they should, and I do believe they serve as a beacon for the generations of all Americans.

Thank you.

Claude Pepper's speech: Mr. Speaker, Mr. Vice President, my colleagues in the Congress, distinguished guests, and my fellow countrymen.

If beneficent providence—and we are happy to observe that providence has always seemed to be kindly disposed toward America—brought forth George Washington to gain our independence, Thomas Jefferson to teach us democracy, and Abraham Lincoln to save our Union, surely that same beneficent providence on March 4, 1933, lifted up Franklin Delano Roosevelt and his great wife Eleanor to rehabilitate and restore America and to lead the free world to a great victory over a terrible despotism and tyranny.

The nation upon which President Roosevelt looked that day was prostrate, almost, in body, and nearly broken in spirit. Not only were there millions unemployed, hundreds of thousands who had lost their homes and their farms to foreclosure; huts built in public parks were the only dwelling place for many more, with no food except what the soup kitchen would provide; and, perhaps even worse, groups of boys and girls out of school, hoboing from city to city like a pack of hungry wolves, seeking food, shelter, and a job.

But when that remarkable man began to speak to that audience standing in the snow around the inaugural platform and the millions listening over the radio in the land heard that marvelous voice, when they received the contagion of his dynamic spirit, when they sensed his own courage and confidence, in their hearts was born a new faith and a new hope, and upon that new faith and hope a new America was born.

I personally believe that when the man Franklin D. Roosevelt realized the awesome responsibility he assumed as he took the oath of office that day, his natural strength of character, refined in the crucible of long suffering, made a new Franklin D. Roosevelt—a man of even new courage and faith and confidence.

As long as free men shall write history, a brilliant chapter in the story of man will be about Franklin and Eleanor Roosevelt, about their years in the White House, their leadership of America, their leadership of the free world, and the kind of a nation and the kind of a world they left as legacies to their fellow citizens now and of succeeding generations.

It was my privilege from 1936 until he passed away to have enjoyed the privilege, like many of my colleagues, of working with President Roosevelt. I came from the South that needed help, and here was a helping hand. I proudly embraced it. And what he did for our South we shall never forget; what he did for America will live forever.

But those of us who had the privilege of personal contact with the President know that it was an immeasurable experience; always, to come into his presence was a thrilling exercise. You never knew exactly what sort of an experience you would have because he was full of ingenuity, full of innovation, full of doing things in his own peculiar way.

I remember one instance when I went to see him about a project that a lot of my people down in Florida were pressing me about. The President evidently knew what I was coming to talk about. He satisfied his mind that he had already done all he could to help me in that matter. So when I went in and sat down at the President's desk, he said, "Hello, Claude, how are you?"

I said, "Fine, Mr. President."

I got my breath and started to talk about my project. He said, "Claude, have you ever read very much about Robert Livingston?" He said, "Robert Livingston was one of my wife's ancestors. He was one of our greatest Americans."

Well, I was nodding my head and listening respectfully as the President went ahead, telling me about Robert Livingston. But he went on and on, and I was still nodding my head and had not said a word about my project. Finally, after a little while—and all of the Members of Congress know what that means—Marvin McIntyre, the President's appointment secretary, came in and took his place, standing there beside me. Well, of course, I knew that meant my time was up, and I had not said a word about my project. Well, I started to say, "Mr. President—" And by that time the cameramen were coming in, setting up their cameras, the press was pouring in and filling up the Oval Office, and in a little bit the President said, in his most ingratiating manner, "Claude, I am so glad that you came, I have enjoyed seeing you, come to see me again sometime." But I started to say, "But, Mr. President—" He said, "You know, I have got a press conference here now, Claude, and I cannot keep these people waiting. Thank you very much. I will see you soon."

Well, when I got back to my office I said, "Well, I did not make much progress on my project, but I am the best informed man on Robert Livingston there is on Capitol Hill."

There are three main legacies I venture to suggest which President Roosevelt left to our country and to the free world.

The first is: He showed by his own example and leadership that the government of the United States belongs to the people of this land and that whenever their troubles and their disasters and their needs impel its use, it is available. It is the mightiest institution on the face of the earth, and it can be a hand that will lift up the people if they call upon it.

There will be differences in the needs the people have for that government, there will be differences in the attitude of those in charge of that government toward the administration of such needs from time to time, but whenever the needs shall occur and be of sufficient gravity to make the demand proper and reasonable, you may be sure that the people of the United States will never let any President or any Congress forget that Franklin D. Roosevelt and the Congresses that worked with him came to the aid of a suffering people when they needed and they called upon it for help.

And a second great legacy President Roosevelt left to us, and that is that compassion, genuine concern for one's fellow man should be in the heart of every man or woman who assumes the awesome responsibilities of public office.

I rather believe that President Roosevelt would not have objected to every person, after taking the oath of public office, being required to reread Jesus' parable of the Good Samaritan, to be reminded that he was simply not to operate a cold machine, he was to help as far as would be proper and possible, people to live richer, healthier, and happier lives.

I remember a lady from Warm Springs saying when she was a girl in Warm Springs she always loved to see the President whenever she could, and he often came to her home, and she said that as a girl she always looked upon the President as sort of a kind uncle.

Everywhere he touched, Roosevelt left the warmth of his generous spirit.

The third legacy is the place where he left America in center stage of world affairs. No more would another President have to pull a reluctant country to an acquaintance with its responsibilities against terrible despotism in the world. America, as Roosevelt left it, will be in center stage among the nations of the earth, standing up for what is right, opposing what is wrong, and trying to build the institutions that will preserve the peace and the happiness of mankind.

So today we proudly commemorate the 100th anniversary of the birth of what they then called that fine baby boy to Sara Delano Roosevelt at Hyde Park. We proudly today attest our own respect, our admiration, and our affection for that great and good man, Franklin Delano Roosevelt, for his devotion to his God and his fellow man and his deep dedication to the service of both, and we leave him now again to sleep forever in honored glory with the lines spoken at Hyde Park by his old minister when he was laid to rest, the refrain of an old hymn:

> Father, in thy gracious keeping,
> Leave we now Thy servant sleeping.

DIGGING UP PARSON WEEMS[1]

ROBERT G. GUNDERSON[2]

Speaking to a highly select audience, Robert G. Gunderson delivered a significant and perceptive address on the importance of
heroes and myths at Western Kentucky University in Bowling
Green on May 1, 1981. The occasion was the annual awards dinner
of Phi Alpha Theta, a history honors society, and his audience
consisted of 50 to 75 history department faculty, graduate students, and undergraduate members of the organization.

Following the initiation of new members, Western Kentucky
University President Donald W. Zacharias, a former student of Dr.
Gunderson, introduced him at the dinner, which was held in the
banquet room of the Bowling Green Rib Eye Restaurant at 6:30
P.M.

After congratulating the new members of the society and acknowledging the awards and distinctions of earlier members, Dr.
Gunderson stated, "My theme tonight is that each generation invents its own heroes and its own distinctive mythology of success."
"The right myths are important," he contended, "because they
conceal, if alas they do not reconcile, clashing objectives in a society."

Dr. Gunderson was a particularly appropriate choice to speak
on this occasion because of his background and training. At Indiana University, he is Professor of Speech Communication and History, an indication of his scholarship in two separate disciplines.
He has written books and more than fifty articles on the subjects of
history, speech communication, and education and has been editor
of various speech and history journals.

Following Professor Gunderson's speech, the head of the university's history department presented awards for outstanding academic achievement.

Robert Gunderson's speech: Once when Chancellor Bismarck
faced an audience of German students in the last 19th century, he boldly gave the odds for their achieving fame and

---

[1] Delivered at the Phi Alpha Theta awards dinner of Western Kentucky University
in the banquet room of the Bowling Green Rib Eye Restaurant in Bowling Green, Kentucky, at 6:30 P.M. on May 1, 1981.
[2] For biographical note, see Appendix.

fortune: One-third, he predicted, would break down from the relentless university discipline. Another third, he warned, would be struck down by the ravages of dissipation. The remaining third would survive to run Germany.

Here tonight we see the third destined to run Kentucky, if not the country. I congratulate the new members of Phi Alpha Theta, and I am honored to be a part of this very happy occasion. The initiates are joining distinguished company. When I think of Phi Alpha Theta, I think of two of my teachers, Carl Wittke, once its national president, and Frederic Logan Paxson, once sponsor of its University of California chapter. I think of influential editors Wendell Stephenson, Boyd Shafer, and Oscar Winther; of university presidents Fred Harrington and Frank Van Diver; United States Senators William Fulbright and Mike Mansfield; and a host of Pulitzer, Guggenheim, and Fulbright winners like Frank Freidel, Roy Nichols, Tom Clark, Ben Wall, Lowell Harrison, and Holman Hamilton.

Although historians haven't been especially prominent in the presidential sweepstakes lately, two of the last fourteen—Teddy Roosevelt and Woodrow Wilson—were trained as historians and served as presidents of the American Historical Association before making it to the White House. A third, admittedly an amateur, John F. Kennedy, received a Pulitzer Prize for biography. The last historian to run as a major candidate, however, George McGovern, failed to make it into Phi Alpha Theta. Dakota Wesleyan, his alma mater, had no chapter.

My theme tonight is that each generation invents its own heroes and its own distinctive mythology of success. This explains why geriatric types are fond of digging up Parson Weems or William Holmes McGuffey, while younger Turks search for models consistent with Star Wars or the fantasies of Woody Allen. The right myths are important because they conceal, if alas they do not reconcile, clashing objectives in a society.

The founding generation of Puritans found unity in the eloquence of Governor John Winthrop, who, while still on the stormy North Atlantic in the spring of 1630, assembled the passengers aboard the Arabella to hear his altruistic statement of Puritan objectives. "The end," he said, is "to do more service to the Lord." For this, "wee must be knitt together . . . as one man. . . . Wee shall be as a Citty upon a hill." As God's vice-regent in Massachusetts Bay, Winthrop dedicated not only his whole estate but his life to the service of the colony. Three generations later, in 1702, Cotton Mather celebrated Winthrop's success as that of "The American Nehemiah."

By then, Winthrop's idealistic vision of success had become lost in Yankee materialism. Cotton Mather wrote some 450 titles, hoping to reactivate the dynamos of Puritan piety. In a persuasive analogy, he ingeniously explains the relationship between God and worldly success. The Christian, he said, is a man in a boat rowing toward heaven. If he pulls only the materialistic oar, he will make but "a poor dispatch to the Shoar of Eternal Blessedness." You should pull hard on the oar of worldly achievement, he admitted, but he warned against neglecting "the oar of your soul and its salvation." Row always "in the fear of God and strive to be holy and diligent in both your callings."

Mather's two-oared formula for success has been described as serving God by making money—a concept later promoted by Ben Franklin, who testifies in his *Autobiography* to Mather's influence. Franklin's hugely popular *The Way to Wealth* is one of America's first success manuals. But even Franklin, the American Prometheus who "snatched lightening from the sky," confessed that he "balanc'd some time between Principle and Inclination." Especially as a youth, what Ben preached about success was not necessarily what Ben practiced. Poor Richard's up-by-the-bootstraps philosophy is sometimes tinged with an iconoclastic cynicism. "A Ploughman on his legs," said Poor Richard in 1763, "is higher than a Gentleman on his knees." "God helps them that helps themselves," he said in the same edition; but some ten years later the Deity got more credit. "God heals," said Poor Richard, "and the Doctor takes the fees." In his 1754 edition he advised, "Love your neighbor, yet don't pull down your hedge."

George Washington provided the pattern for the leather-stocking models of success that flourished in the nineteenth century—models forged in frontier warfare and tested later in rough-and-tumble politics.

Aspiring young heroes took dramatic journeys over the Allegheny wilderness, stern rites of passage. Washington joined a surveying party to the Shenandoah at sixteen; at twenty-one he carried an ultimatum to the French beyond the Ohio, a mission, says Parson Weems, "as dangerous and disagreeable as Hercules himself could have desired." Weems vividly describes the terrors of the "country west of the Blue Mountains": "one immeasurable forest . . . the gloomy haunts of ravening beasts and of murderous savages. . . . the awful silence of those dreary woods . . . the hiss of rattlesnakes, the shrieks of panthers, the yells of Indians, and howling tempests." At eighteen William Henry Harrison marched on foot at the head of a company of recruits over the Alleghenies to Pittsburgh and then floated down the Ohio to Fort Washington (now Cincinnati), taking pains to stay in the middle of the river to minimize somewhat the hazard of Indian attack. Andrew Jackson at twenty-one rode horseback over the Great Smokies, armed with two pistols and a rifle and escorted by a pack of faithful dogs. At thirteen Davy Crockett made the reverse trip, escaping his indenture as well as a tyrannical father. Since Lincoln was born west of the mountains, he had to be satisfied with a flatboat trip down the Ohio and Mississippi at nineteen, miraculously surviving an attack by river pirates en route.

Architect for the success mythology of the early Republic was Mason Locke Weems, an itinerant Episcopal priest, book peddler, puppeteer, and country fiddler. The ninteenth child of an impecunious but obviously energetic Scottish immigrant, Weems exploited Mark Twain's principle: "To be good is noble, but to teach others to be good is nobler—and less trouble." Weems had "a penchant," as Dixon Wecter says, "for addressing the moral problems of adolescence." The feverish quality of his moralizing is evident in a few of his titles: *God's Revenge Against Murder* (1807), . . . *Against Gambling*

(1810), . . . *Against Adultery* (1815), . . . *Against Duelling* (1820), and *The Drunkard's Looking Glass* (1812), and *The Bad Wife's Looking Glass* (1820).

Weems's biographies of Washington, Franklin, Marion, and Penn served as guides to success for the adolescents of several generations. They were popular because they reflected the tastes and attitudes of an overwhelmingly rural clientele. Twenty-nine editions of his *Washington* were published before his death in 1825. Passages reprinted in Sunday school papers and in McGuffey *Readers* vastly expanded his influence. His experiences as a book peddler, traveling from parish to parish and from tavern to tavern, gave him a shrewd insight into exactly what the public wanted. There were many tearful pages, for the nineteenth century was an age of easy weeping. Someone has counted over thirty cases in the Washington biography, several describing Washington as the featured weeper. Anecdotes about the general's childhood and his athletic prowess appealed especially to parents seeking uplift more suitable for children than the tales found in some of Weems's racy tracts like *Hymen's Recruiting Serjeant* (1799). Stories of the cherry tree and the colt-breaking incident first appeared in the fifth edition (1806). In all his writing Weems specialized in passionate exhortation: "Young Reader! . . . think of Washington, and . . . delight in glorious toil."

Professional historians never took Weems seriously, dismissing the biographies with the scorn they reserve for fictionalized history. Even before Weems's death one critic labored the obvious by noting that his *Washington* was "full of ridiculous exaggeration." Later, John Fiske rejected it as a collection of "absurdities." And in 1889 Henry Cabot Lodge rejected it as a product of Weems's "imagination." Lodge described Weems as "destitute of historical sense, training, or morals," and claimed that he placed his subject in "a ridiculous light to an age that has outgrown the educational foibles" of an earlier generation.

Regardless of the opinions of historians, however, people make their own definitions of success and define the qualities that they want in heroes. By 1962 the public had supported some eighty-one editions of Weems's *Washington*, including five in German.

When Rupert Hughes brought out a realistic *Washington* in 1926 and attacked Weems's biography as a "slush of plagiarism and piety," the Parson's twentieth-century supporters were outraged. A newspaper reporter confronted President Calvin Coolidge for his view of this urgent conflict in historiography. Silent Cal pondered the debunking of the first President while staring a long time out a White House window. "Well," he said at last, "I see the Monument is still there."

Frontier models of success flourished from the presidencies of Jackson to that of "Old Rough and Ready," Zachary Taylor. Jackson, an orphan, became "symbol for an Age." "Talk of him as the second Washington!" exclaimed Philip Hone, the Whig Mayor of New York. "It won't do now; Washington was only the first Jackson."

Martin Van Buren's vice-president, Richard M. Johnson of Kentucky, had seventeen scars to testify to his heroism, and the nation's Democrats marched to the chant:

> Rumpsey Dumpsey,
> Colonel Johnson shot Tecumseh!

If Washington's generation took *liberty* as its watchword, Jackson's generation made linsey-woolsey the fashion and talked noisily of *equality*, a doctrine that encouraged nicknames. Jackson, "Old Hickory," became the first President to have one. Johnson became "Old Rumpsey Dumpsey"; Henry Wilson, a vice-president to be, was the "Natick Cobbler." The Senate had a "Mill Boy," an "Old Salt Boiler," a "Wagon Boy," and an "Old Bullion." A "Railsplitter" sat in Congress—but only for one term.

Success through self-improvement promoted a mania for knowledge. Penny newspapers and penny magazines widened horizons for the common man. Elihu Burritt, the "Learned Blacksmith," became the epitome of the common man as scholar. The American Lyceum, founded by Josiah Holbrook in 1826, spread from Massachusetts throughout the country, with a thousand local lyceums organized during the first five years.

Frontier heroes reveal a striking similarity. Presidents Jackson and Harrison both were born in the Old South and migrated to the frontier, Harrison rejecting his aristocratic heritage for the life of a soldier. As boys, both suffered at the hands of the British, Jackson far more intensely, surviving a sabre wound that left him permanently scarred. Harrison fled before Benedict Arnold's Redcoats, who sacked his James River home at Berkeley when he was eight years old. Both understandably remained anti-British, highly militaristic, and energetic champions of manifest destiny. (They were for it even before the phrase was coined.) Both were gullible enough to listen to the enticements of Aaron Burr. Although they ultimately repudiated him, Jackson cooperated with Burr's early schemes. Neither was the slightest bit disturbed to be dealing with the slayer of Alexander Hamilton. Both served as congressmen, senators, and territorial governors. Both fought Indians and aggressively negotiated land-grabbing treaties.

They of course had some substantial differences. As a youth in North Carolina, Jackson was a "roaring, rollicking, game-cocking" extrovert. Harrison, though not a drudge, was more prudent and decorous. In maturity, he became a "moral chameleon," changing from Federalist to Jeffersonian Democrat to Whig. Jackson, as Michael Rogin reports, retained a "spirit of infantile rage," and remained a Democrat. In 1840 Jackson called Harrison a "weak superannuated Federalist"—a "mock hero." Harrison's victories were fabian, conservative, calculating—Jackson's bold and dramatic. Even Jackson's ailments were spectacular. Old Tip suffered only commonplace complaints, sinus headaches and catarrh.

Nor was Harrison a ring-tailed roarer like Davy Crockett. He didn't ride upon a streak of lightning or slip without a scratch down a honey locust. No comet careened across the sky on the day of his birth. He never became a symbol for his age. Contemporaries described him as a common man in homespun, an Old Dominion aristocrat turned Buckeye farmer, a Cincinnatus ready to leave his plough for the White

House. During the campaign of 1840 he became a western Hercules ready to cleanse the Augean stables in Washington of its Jacksonian filth.

Crockett, with the help of a ghostwriter, emphasizes his modest heritage of "poor and respectable" parents. In his *Life and Adventures* Davy says that circumstances prevented him from spending much time in school. "No one," he admits modestly, ". . . could have foretold that he was ever to receive a commission to [wring] . . . off the tail of a comet."

Crockett was catapulted, as he said, "from the swamps" of the West Tennessee forest "into a *hair-bottom* chair" in Congress, where he served three terms without distinction. In fact he had properly apprenticed by serving two terms in the Tennessee Legislature, where he voted against Jackson in the critical contest for the U.S. Senate. A rather stiff colleague from South Carolina claimed that he never heard Davy "utter a word that savoured of wit or sense." If one goes by the published record, the romantic bear hunter was a grizzly bore in Congress. In 1836 his constituents voted him out of office, favoring instead Adam Huntsman, a man with a wooden leg and Jacksonian principles. "Since you have chosen a man with a timber toe to succeed me," said Davy at a farewell in the Union Hotel bar in Memphis, "you may all go to hell and I will go to Texas."

Leatherstocking models of success can be found wanting when measured by the standards of today. The charisma that Davy enjoyed in the 1830s tarnishes when exposed to twentieth-century scrutiny. He belonged to a nomadic way of life. He was not yet ready for agriculture. As a farmer, he was "indolent and shiftless." In his relationships with women, he hardly provides a role model for emancipation. Davy can never be a hero to Betty Friedan or Gloria Steinem. Nor does he provide inspiration for prospective lawyers. As a qualification for serving as justice of the peace, he boasted of never having read a page of law in his life. In spite of his lack of education, he did anticipate contemporary linguistic scholarship: Correct spelling, he said, was "contrary to nature"—and grammar was "nothing at all."

By present-day standards, frontier heroes had no proper

sense of ecology, including human ecology. Respect for life
was at best indifferent or casual. Crockett boasted of killing
105 bears in a day. Bill Cody brought down 69 buffalo in a
single shootout. Even the saintly Washington dismays us.
Young George, said Weems, would blaze away with his
"fouling piece" at the swans on the Potomac, killing "seven or
eight at a shot."

Standing quite apart from the leatherstocking heroes and
promoters of a materialistic success ethic is Henry David
Thoreau, who brilliantly dramatizes contradictions in American thought, as Stanley Edgar Hymen has demonstrated.
Using amusing epigrams, Thoreau in *Walden* contrasts tran-
scendental and pragmatic goals. As the railroad shatters the
bucolic quiet of Walden Pond, he notes that the smoke is
"going to heaven" while the cars clatter pragmatically on to
Boston. He thinks it "might be worth while" to keep chickens
for the "sound of cock-crowing"—"to say nothing of the eggs
and drumsticks." Thoreau's outlook is remarkably contemporary, as members of the counter-culture will testify. He even
provides a pragmatic answer to dress codes. "Bare feet," he
reminds us, "are older than shoes." "Beware," he says, "of all
enterprises that require new clothes."

The theology of success reached its zenith in the Gilded
Age. Andrew Carnegie provided the text in an essay appro-
priately entitled, "Wealth." Preachers like Russell Conwell
spread the joyful word, delivering "Acres of Diamonds" over
6,000 times, often enough to provide Temple University with
a comfortable endowment. "To make money honestly," Conwell said, "is to preach the Gospel."

Even the satirist of the age, Mark Twain, succumbed to
gold fever. Like his fictional mountebank, Colonel Beriah
Sellers, who daydreamed about making a fortune in eyewash,
Twain hoped to get rich by developing an ill-fated typeset-
ting machine. Twain bet on the wrong gadget. As Mr. Dooley
proclaimed, "the cash raygister" is the "crownin' work in our
civilization."

Because of his more than 100 novels, Horatio Alger's
name has become synonymous with the rags-to-riches syn-

drome. But as John Cawelti and Michael Zuckerman have demonstrated, Alger's heroes found success not by practicing the Puritan virtues of hard work and frugality, but by good luck. The stories are "studded" with kidnappings, robberies, and contrived excitement. Max Weber's long-faced Puritan Ethic is lost in derring-do. Self-made girls and boys are alas nowhere to be found in the world of Ragged Dick.

A reaction to Gilded-Age excesses came in 1906, when Harvard psychologist William James denounced "the moral flabbiness born of the exclusive worship of the *bitch-goddess,* SUCCESS." James insisted that the "squalid cash interpretation put on the word success" is "our national disease."

Since James, the success gurus have emphasized positive thinking. In 1910 French psycho-therapist Émil Coué popularized a naive formula for self-help that returned with the troops from World War I. When Coué came to America in the early twenties, enormous crowds heard him incant his shibboleth: "Every day, in every way, I am becoming better and better." Although Coué is now forgotten, little less sophisticated systems of positive thinking still flourish.

The startling contribution of the 1970s is the new fashion of success through intimidation. Robert J. Ringer published *Winning Through Intimidation* in 1974. Shirley S. Fader tells *How to Get Ahead By "Psyching Out" Your Boss and Co-Workers,* and Sydney C. Schweitzer describes *Winning With Deception And Bluff.* Workshops and classes are readily available to provide practice in the art.

For those too timid to make it to class, every Friday night there is "Dallas" with its quintessential hero-villain. J. R. is a multi-national success. Bantam has published his wisdom, *The Quotations of J. R. Ewing.* Bumper stickers say "J. R. for President." Twenty-four million people in Britain, almost 45 percent of the population, watched BBC's re-run of the episode in which J. R. was shot. One British fan made a trans-Atlantic phone call to Parkland Hospital to inquire about his condition.

Today's aspiring heroes suffer through their own agonizing rites of civilized passage. They wander about like Bobby

Ewing in the howling, plush-carpeted wildernesses of New York and Dallas, skirting gingerly among Halston-clad panthers like Sue Ellen and J. R.

Dr. Joyce Brothers has been called upon to explain the J. R. phenomenon, and she has decreed that "Evil is more fascinating than good." "His appeal," she says, is in his having "that certain mixture of good and bad."

Larry Hagman confirms Dr. Brothers's analysis. "The time is ripe for a real bad guy and I'm it," he says. "People are sick of good guys." Hagman says he has received only one hate letter—and that was sent from a mental institution.

Although J. R. is hardly the first celebrity to wear both a halo and horns, aggrieved traditionalists still long for sturdy virtues celebrated by Parson Weems. Sunday supplements, even those in the *New York Times*, keep asking, "Where Have All the Heroes Gone?" They recall that Lindbergh became immortal overnight, while astronauts, including some who have walked on the moon, are quickly forgotten—lost or minimized in a technology of interchangeable parts.

Lost, also, are Viet Nam heroes, who find their plight beyond comprehension. Real green berets remain unknown and unrecognized, while John Wayne, a cinematic green beret, is a legend.

Today the most visible celebrities may be entertainers, demi-gods enhanced by echo-chambers and enshrined in strobe lighting. Elvis Presley, the Beatles, and later the appalling spectre of Punk Rockers. Some contemporary personalities have exploited satire and one-liners. In true Algerlike fashion, Bob Hope, Johnny Carson, and Woody Allen made it—from gags to riches.

It's a long way from John Winthrop's "Citty on a hill" to J. R. and Punk Rock. But those who are uncomfortable with contemporary heroes, and with contemporary definitions of success, should remember that these, also, will, as Carl Becker has said, "be relegated to the category of discarded myths."

TECHNOLOGY AND THE FUTURE

A TIME FOR DECISION[1]
JOHN H. GLENN JR.[2]

On March 27, 1981, Senator John H. Glenn Jr., delivered the keynote address to the 24th annual Goddard Memorial Dinner of the
National Space Club. In his remarks, Senator Glenn stressed that
the United States stood at a critical crossroad with respect to the
exploration of space and indeed all research and development. He
suggested that while government had to deal with the problems of
inflation, it also must look ahead and make certain that we do the
research that will provide for tomorrow's innovation and productivity growth.

Senator Glenn was remarkably well-qualified to discuss this
subject before members of the National Space Club. In 1962, he
became the first American astronaut to orbit the earth in Mercury-Atlas Friendship 7, circling the planet and he subsequently
assisted in planning Project Apollo. As a result of his space ex-
ploits, Glenn emerged as a national hero: "the first American to
orbit the planet . . . the clean-cut Marine who showed the Russians
America was still in the space race. A man celebrated like few in
the nation's experience. . . . 'America's first flesh-and-blood Buck
Rogers' was how the *New York Times* described Glenn." (Roth-
berg, Associated Press, Baton Rouge *Advocate*, Fe. 21, '82,
p 1)

After leaving the space program, Glenn entered politics and in
1974 was elected United States Senator from Ohio and, in 1980, he
was re-elected by a large majority. By October, 1981, in the opinion of political experts—and supported by polls—Glenn was
emerging as one of the leading contenders for the Democratic
presidential nomination in 1984.

Glenn's delivery as a speaker has been described variously as,
he "can outgrin Dwight D. Eisenhower," he "speaks in a relaxed
voice," which has a "dry settled quality." He is also said to have a
"reputation as a man who does his homework" and has "a taste for

[1] Delivered at the 24th annual Goddard Memorial Dinner of the National Space
Club in a banquet room of the Hilton Hotel, Washington, D.C., at 9 P.M., March 27, 1981.
[2] For biographical note, see Appendix.

understatement." According to one observer, "his biggest asset is his personality, which projects his true strength of character." (Kennedy, "John Glenn's Presidential Countdown," *New York Times Magazine*, O. 11, '81, p 32)

The National Space Club is a non-technical organization of individuals and companies affiliated with the missile space field in government, industry, the military, and the press whose purpose is to encourage American space leadership and stimulate the advancement of peaceful and military application of space flight and related technologies. The dinner honored Dr. Robert H. Goddard who laid the foundation for many of today's space developments, for in 1914, he obtained the first United States patent on multistage rockets and another on the use of liquid propellants for rockets. In his lifetime, Goddard was awarded a total of 214 patents, and he has been described as "the true father of modern dry-fuel and liquid rocketry."

The dinner, held in a banquet room of the Hilton Hotel in Washington, D.C., was attended by approximately 1,350 persons, including members of the National Space Club, members of Congress, Congressional staffers, and representatives from NASA. Senator Glenn's address was preceded by the introduction of distinguished guests, an invocation, the presentation of colors by a Joint Armed Forces Color Guard, and welcoming remarks by the president of the National Space Club. It began around 9 P.M. and was followed by the presentation of eight special awards and scholarships. The occasion had an aura of the military, with an Air Force general giving the invocation, the Armed Forces color guard, and military music by the United States Marine Corps Band.

John Glenn's speech: Thank you, Jim (Hart) for that most gracious and generous introduction. You know, I find it almost unbelievable that we are fast approaching the 20th anniversary of my flight in Friendship 7. Twenty years! Although I was reminded tonight that my own adventure in space is now almost two decades old, I am delighted to be here and am deeply honored that the National Space Club asked me to participate in this year's Goddard Memorial Dinner. Tonight's dinner is particularly special, since we are standing on the threshold of the Space Shuttle launching. It is altogether fitting that the calendar has brought these two events together. For just as Robert Goddard's rocket experiments in 1926 ushered in the Space Age, so the launching of the Space

Shuttle will open a whole new era—an era in which man will probe ever deeper into this Last Frontier.

With the Space Shuttle, the possibilities are as exciting as they are unlimited. It is the largest, most powerful and most complicated space vehicle ever launched. Because it is reusable and can return from space to land like an airplane, it is both versatile and economical. It will dramatically increase our knowledge of Earth and its resources—and perhaps even provide us with clues as to how we can someday become independent of the Earth's environment. In 1983, the Shuttle will launch the Space Telescope, a 22 thousand-pound piece of equipment that will enlarge our view of space seven-fold and bring us closer to answering age-old questions concerning the origins and nature of life, matter and energy. And as important as these cosmic questions are, the principal justification of our space program lies in the benefits it provides not just to us in the future alone, but to us in the here and now— benefits which will enhance the lives of each and everyone of us. And, although estimates vary, some experts have suggested that the space program has had a cost-benefit ratio as high as 8 to one. But, perhaps equally important, the Space Shuttle will signal America's return to space after an absence of almost six years—an absence that has not gone unnoticed in the world community.

Let us reflect for a moment on the theme of this evening's program: "A Time for Decision." In the Spring of 1981, that theme is particularly appropriate. It is appropriate because America today truly stands at a critical crossroad—not only with respect to space, but also with regard to the broader issue of all U.S. research and development. And like the traveller in Robert Frost's immortal poem, the road we choose will have enormous impact on our future—and that of our children today.

Today, man's most fundamental tool in the quest for knowledge—basic research—is under sharp attack. Evidence of this hostility is all around us. It manifests itself in the shrinking number of research grants available to our universities. It is apparent in the devastating slashes that have been proposed in the NASA and National Science Foundation budgets. And it shows up even in the halls of Congress where important basic research is often cynically disparaged and presented with facetious "awards" which imply that it is little more than a clever rip-off.

Similarly, many Americans greet our return to space with something less than enthusiasm. For these people, space exploration is too costly, too visionary and too far removed from such "real world" problems as hunger, disease and poverty.

Does research sometimes seem unrealistic? To those enmeshed in the complexities of the "real world," it is bound to seem that way at first—just as it always has in every historical epoch. But let us remember that we ourselves live in a "real world" created by previous generations of emigrants who set sail from another "real world" in pursuit of a dream.

Is exploration of the unknown merely an "escape" that we can no longer afford? Was our first human ancestor who rose on two legs to discover new horizons "escaping" the problems of his age? We could go back in our minds to see a group of cavemen. Perhaps we could see one adventurous caveman in the group who is sitting with his peers, wondering what's over that nearby hill. And his fellow cavemen are telling him he's crazy to think about going beyond the hill. "We have enough food here, and only 15 percent of our people died in the cave last year. Why go over there?" they're asking him. Well, he goes over the hill anyway, and he finds some different types of food; there's even more sun than he had in his own valley. He returns home with his treasures, finding years later that his people are living longer, becoming more healthy because of the treasures he brought them.

Did Columbus, Vespucci and Cabot "escape" the problems of their age or contribute to their resolution by going beyond that next hill or ocean? Again and again history demonstrates that when solutions at hand don't solve the problem, it is time to reopen the quest. Only by doing so can we reap those marvelous by-products of the inquisitive, innovative and inventive mind and discover the unexpected possibilities that emerge when we encounter unknown worlds either at the end of a telescope or a microscope.

Does research and development seem a fanciful extravagance unlikely to produce tangible results? Let us remember that the one thing we know about research is that it is not amenable to the rigors of cost accounting. How can we know in advance what we're looking for? Or, what we'll find? Rarely can we see at the outset what ultimate benefits research will bring us. If you doubt that, listen to what the astronomer, William Pickering, said about air flight after the invention of the airplane:

... the popular mind often pictures gigantic flying machines speeding across the Atlantic carrying innumerable passengers. ... It seems safe to say that such ideas (are) wholly visionary, and even if a machine could get across with one or two passengers, the expense would be prohibitive.

Or, let us recall that the Edison Power Company once offered Henry Ford a managerial job, but only, as Ford put it, "on the condition that I give up my gas engine and devote myself to something really useful." And before we condemn specific scientific undertakings as foolish, let us recall that in 1945, Admiral William Leahy chided the development of the atom bomb by telling President Truman:

"That is the biggest fool thing we have ever done. ... The bomb will never go off, and I speak as an expert in explosives."

Or, we could go back and look at the technologists' record at forecasting the future. Their long-range record is even worse than that of today's economists. Technology forecasters in the 1930s, for example, missed the development of the computer, atomic energy, antibiotics, radar, and the jet engine.

I'm also reminded of a statement Daniel Webster made in the U.S. Senate when the Senate was trying to decide whether to spend more money to get west of the Mississippi River. His statement was to the effect that he could see no reason why to go out into this area of prairie dogs and wild savages, of howling winds and blowing sands. He finished his remarks by saying:

"Mr. President, I would not devote one cent from the U.S. Treasury to bring the West coast one inch closer to Boston."

It will be twelve years ago this summer that Neil Armstrong and Buzz Aldrin walked the cratered barrens of the moon. Many people assumed that the sole practical value of our space program lay in the political victory we achieved in beating the Soviets to the lunar surface. Many regarded our space effort as a cosmic drag race with the Soviets. And, if the moon was the finish line in the minds of those Americans, then we won the race and could quit our space efforts.

But, there was a significance to our landing on the moon that goes far beyond the satisfaction which comes from a dramatic and spectacular victory in international competition.

The success of the Apollo program gave mankind initial access to the literally infinite resources of the universe. Few Americans fully realize the extent to which the uses of space have already affected our daily lives since we achieved that initial success. Consider the following:

We now make quick, clear intercontinental telephone calls at half of what it cost 10 years ago, thanks to the ever more versatile and reliable communications satellites pioneered through our space program.

Satellite technology also permits us to transmit sharp, full-color television coverage of events transpiring anywhere on the globe having a mammoth impact on how man relates to man around the world. I think it would be fair to say that we've lived in a time when television stopped the first war—as we found in Vietnam.

Countless thousands of human lives and many millions of dollars have been saved through satellite warning of hurricanes, typhoons and other severe storms. The increased knowledge of Sun–Earth relationships acquired through such efforts as the Space Shuttle will permit far more accurate weather forecasts in the future and perhaps even the ability to modify weather and climate. We have found, for example, that during times of high solar activity, the Van Allen Belts moved, changing the heating of the upper atmosphere as well as the flow of the jet-streams. The result was a change in our weather here on Earth.

Our digital watches, hand-held calculators and desk-top computers are direct derivatives from the integrated circuit technology developed for the Apollo spacecraft.

We can now navigate ships and aircraft to within yards. This equipment is even available for pleasure craft on the Chesapeake Bay, providing navigational fixes with the help of satellites.

Aircraft, automobiles, ships and even buildings are now more structurally sound and thus safer, due to the use of a computerized structural analysis technique developed for the construction of spacecraft.

And, worth every penny spent on the entire space program is the increased security our nation has because reconnaissance and early warning satellites make a surprise attack on the United States more costly, less feasible and, therefore, much less likely.

And yet, despite these life-enhancing spin-offs, despite the fact that space research and development, even in its infancy, has provided the cutting edge of our technological superiority for almost 20 years, we are not pressing our advantage in space. We are all but abandoning portions of our civilian space program. The Administration's proposed NASA budgets for 1981 and 1982 will provide even less money, given inflation, than that agency had in 1969, the year Apollo 11 landed on the moon. The depressing result is that, except for the shuttle, the only new space missions that will be undertaken between now and 1986 are two that had been planned but previously deferred.

This is especially disturbing in light of the stepped-up space activities of other nations. Since the last manned American Flight in 1975, there have been 21 manned Soviet flights. During that period, America remained earthbound while Soviet cosmonauts accumulated two years of space-flight time.

The Soviet Union plans to orbit a permanent, 12-man space station by 1985. And some observers believe that the U.S.S.R. will soon announce its intention to send a man to Mars by the end of the decade. In addition, France and West Germany are hard at work on a low-cost booster that could corner the launch business. In a joint venture, China and Japan hope to orbit two astronauts for a full week by the end of 1986.

The loss of our once commanding lead in space should both embarrass and frighten us. We should be embarrassed because we are consciously choosing to default rather than to compete. We are consciously choosing that we will let other nations be the "first to know, to discover the new, to have available to them, first, the new information on potential energy source, of earth resources analysis, of space weightless manufacturing, and of so many other things."

And we should be frightened because that default could some day prove literally fatal. Many experts are convinced that much Russian work aboard Salyut has been directed toward military applications of space research—applications such as electronic surveillance and satellite interception. Although I'm not one who sees a threatening Soviet behind every lamp post, but, given what we see going on in the world, God help us should we ever reach a decidedly inferior position in space while the Soviets develop not only "eyes and ears" in space but weaponry systems as well.

Currently, the Soviets are believed to devote 2 to 3 percent of their GNP (Gross National Product) on space—six times more than we spend. If we allow these trends to continue, we may soon find ourselves worrying about far more than balanced budgets or the relative wisdom of supply-side economics.

But a crucial point I wish to emphasize tonight is that the challenge confronting America in the areas of research and development is by no means confined to our space program. On the contrary. Whether we speak of national defense, industrial strength or energy independence, research and development is an indispensable tool for realizing our objectives.

Historically, America's willingness to facilitate and invest in research has been the touchstone of her pre-eminence. This point is well-understood by our international neighbors. In 1969, for example, Jean Jacques Servan-Schreiber, the French author and politician, wrote a book entitled, *The American Challenge*. One of his central themes was that the United States surpassed the rest of the world economically and industrially not simply because of our waving fields of grain or purple mountains' majesties but because from our inception as a nation we have always promoted and financed inquiry into the unknown. We had devoted a larger part of our GNP to research than any other nation in history.

Piece by piece, increment by increment, new advances in knowledge multiplied—until, finally, a quantum leap forward was made possible. Research, and the technology we developed to exploit the fruits of that research, made America the wealthiest, most powerful and most productive nation on Earth in a tiny time frame in history.

In the 12 years since the publication of *The American Challenge,* however, there is mounting evidence that we are killing the proverbial goose that laid the golden egg. Over the past 15 years, the proportion of America's GNP invested in research has steadily declined, dropping over 20 percent between 1965 and 1979. During that same period, West Germany's investment in R & D (Research and Development) climbed by 41 percent of her GNP, Japan's rose 27 percent and the Soviet Union's increased by 21 percent. These figures take on added economic significance when it is recognized that 50 percent of all U.S. research is defense-related, while less than 1 percent of Japan's and only 8 percent of Germany's is spent in the same fashion.

It is, therefore, hardly an accident that since the close of World War II, other nations have become alternative sources of industrial innovation. We're seeing employment leave our nation far too often. Nor is it coincidental that U.S. productivity and economic growth have lately been falling. Studies by such renowned economists as Edward Denison have shown that "advances in knowledge" constitute the single most important source of productivity gain, as well as of overall economic expansion. So while the U.S. economy may still be the world's largest, it is no longer the most efficient or the fastest growing.

Fortunately, American industry has recognized the danger and has been moving to meet it. According to a recent study by the National Science Foundation, industrial research and development has been rising in real terms since 1972. In January, Battelle's Columbus Laboratories forecast a continuation of this trend in 1981 and predicted that industrial R & D funding would climb 13 percent over last year's level.

Welcome as this news is, we must not be lulled into a false sense of security. For one thing, much of our industrial R & D is devoted simply to meeting the requirements of government regulation, rather than to the kind of risk-taking research that promises true technological breakthroughs. Historically, American industries have concentrated their efforts on applied R & D, leaving basic research mostly to the government and academia.

Each side works in relative isolation and collaborative research is often studiously avoided. In contrast, our competitors in Europe and Japan link industrial research to government and academic science. The result is that they are now surpassing us in a growing number of fields, perhaps the most conspicuous of which is the production of new scientific instruments. In my view, America can simply no longer afford a continuation of our traditionally "arms-length" research relationships. If we are to meet the challenges ahead, it is vital that we begin to encourage cooperative research ventures between the public and private sectors.

But even that will not be enough. We must also recognize that expanding industrial R & D does not mean that the federal government can now begin to reduce its own commitment to research. Much of the basic research needed to achieve energy independence, for example, is of so large a scale and requires so long a development period that it is simply unrealistic to expect the private sector to shoulder the burden alone.

America's dependence on foreign energy sources cost us about $100 billion last year—and it is estimated by some economists to account for between 40 and 60 percent of the increased inflation we have suffered over the past four years. Because our energy dilemma threatens both our national security and our national economy, involvement by the federal government is, to my way of thinking, clearly appropriate.

So, I am appalled that under the Administration's latest budget proposals, energy R & D has been mercilessly slashed. If these proposals are adopted, by 1982 conservation programs will be cut by 79 percent and solar energy development by 66 percent. Similarly, research on electrical energy storage—which could make solar, wind, geothermal and other alternative energy sources practical and usable—is being cut by 28 percent in 1981 and by almost 33 percent in 1982.

If I had one energy wish tonight, it might surprise you what it would be. My wish would be for better electrical energy storage that would enable us to take the power generated by wind, wave, tidal and solar power and store it for later use. If we could store this electricity, and bring it back when needed, as some research indicates we could do in the near future, we would have one of the biggest breakthroughs we've had for some time.

Electrical energy storage would also enhance development of the electrical automobile which could take care of 92 percent of the non-commericial driving we do within 20 miles of our homes. If we let the Japanese and the Germans beat us to the world's first practical electrical automobile, we will have nobody to blame but ourselves. And if that happens, we won't be bailing out Chrysler, we'll be asking for money to make Detroit a great national park on a scenic river.

Now, I fully recognize the need for budgetary restraint in these inflationary times and I support these efforts. But let us not be penny-wise and pound-foolish to what is going to happen to this country in 1985. Let us not seek fiscal frugality by mortgaging our future. And let us recognize that if the energy crisis constitutes the moral equivalent of war, as Jimmy Carter called it, failing to develop alternative energy sources could well be the economic equivalent of suicide. There are many areas today in which it is desirable and necessary to reduce federal involvement. But surely research and development is one area where even greater government support is clearly justified.

In today's world, failing to meet the R & D challenge is

the surest way to forfeit our claim to world leadership. It's just that simple.

Let me close this evening with one final thought. In 1962, just before Wally Schirra's Mercury flight in Sigma 7, President Kennedy declared that:

> The exploration of space will go ahead, whether we join it or not. . . . It is one of the great adventures of all time, and no nation that expects to be the leader of other nations can expect to stay behind in the race for space.

I submit that those words are equally applicable today—not just with respect to the space race, but also with respect to the global competition in research and development. For that competition may be the most compelling challenge of our age. History has shown that missing or retreating from such challenges almost inevitably leads to a loss of national eminence. Perhaps that is what the Immortal Bard, William Shakespeare, sensed nearly 400 years ago when he wrote:

> There is a tide in the affairs of men which, taken at the flood, leads on to fortune; omitted, all the voyages of their life is bound in shallows and in miseries. On such a full sea we are now afloat, and we must take the current when it serves or lose our ventures.

Thank you very much.

TECHNOLOGY AND MORAL RESPONSIBILITY[1]

George D. Snell[2]

In a commencement address at the University of Maine, on April 18, 1981, Dr. George D. Snell, senior staff scientist emeritus at the Jackson Laboratory in Bar Harbour, Maine, said:

> Nature has given us a world both unique and beautiful, its diversity being part of its beauty. . . . In the United States, a free and democratic society is also part of our

[1] Delivered at the commencement exercises of the University of Maine at Presque Isle in the Widen Gymnasium at 1:30 P.M. on April 18, 1981.
[2] For biographical note, see Appendix.

inheritance. . . . It would be a tragedy beyond belief if we lost either our freedom or the loveliness of the world that nature has given us. The preservation of these inheritances is the greatest single task which we face.

Snell, who was awarded the 1980 Nobel Prize in Medicine for pioneering work in genetics, addressed the 201 graduating seniors and approximately 1,200 parents, faculty members, staff, and friends at the University of Maine at Presque Isle. The seventy-seven-year-old scientist called for a renewal of moral and ethical responsibility in making decisions related to the environment and technological innovations. "My generation, now largely retired, and the succeeding middle-aged generally," he said, "have done a very imperfect job in carrying out this task. While many conscientious and intelligent decisions have been made, we also have made decisions incompatible with the preservation of a free and livable world."

Dr. Snell delivered his address at approximately 1:30 P.M. in the Widen Gymnasium on the Presque Isle campus. His speech was preceded by the faculty procession, the invocation, greetings from the school's acting president, brief remarks by the senior class president, and the conferment of a University-wide honorary degree of Doctor of Science on Snell. After the Nobel laureate's address, the ceremonies closed with the benediction and recessional.

George Snell's speech: In the last 100 years, technology has undergone an enormous expansion, in the process, altering our lives and our world. Dozens of miraculous devices, undreamed of in 1881, are commonplace today. Many of these technological developments have occurred in my lifetime.

The Wright brothers made their first flight at Kitty Hawk on December 17, 1903. This was two days before I was born. For at least another ten years, airplanes were still a rarity of primitive construction. Automobiles were invented in the last century, but were uncommon when I was a small boy. My first recollections of an auto are of an electric vehicle, more like a carriage than what we now think of as an auto, that a middle-aged lady used to drive by our house. The milkman and the iceman still brought their wares in horse-drawn wagons. The street lights outside our house were gas; a lamp lighter went by every evening to turn them on. Our house was still lit by gas, though newer houses were equipped with electric lights, still Edison's original carbon filament bulb. Wireless telegraphy was in existence, but it had little effect on our lives, and broadcasts of the human voice and of television were part of the future. The first computer was built in 1944.

Back of each of the technological marvels produced by applied research has lain a long and complex history of basic research. The pathways by which basic research leads to usable methods or products are often winding and full of surprises. I can testify to this from my own experience; that is part of the fun and excitement of science. The essential point here is that the basic and applied aspects of research are both necessary ingredients in the progress of technology.

Looking to the future, I think we must assume that the expansion of science and technology which we have witnessed in the past century will continue. Nature still hides many secrets from us, and there is much to learn. The pace of discovery may indeed accelerate rather than slacken. I see no barriers in natural law to further developments, though shortages of natural resources may limit some applications. The institutionalization of science, both in the universities and in industry, to which much of the past century of progress is due, is firmly in place and provides the necessary setting for continuing discovery. There may be ups and downs due to fluctuations in financing, but the long range prospect is for further advances in technology, medicine, and human understanding.

While technology has brought us great benefits, it also is a source of great risks. It is to these risks that I now turn.

The immediate end product of applied research is options—ways of doing new things and new ways of doing old things. At some point the decision must be made as to whether and how each option is to be exercised. The multiplicity of options also is expanded on down the line. We have, in our daily lives, more ways of doing things, more products on the market to choose from, a greater diversity and complexity of jobs. The decision whether or not to exercise a given option is often far from trivial. Do we market a new drug which has proven benefits but also known deleterious side effects? Do we equip a new coal burning facility in Ohio with scrubbers, thereby reducing the risk of acid rain in Maine and Canada? In the ultimate military crisis, do we use the atomic bomb? And in our personal affairs, what line of work do we seek to enter? No one, I think, can doubt the importance of the correct exercise of these options.

We are faced, in this matter of options, with a third domain, the domain of value judgments. It is a domain with very different properties from the two already discussed, the domains of basic and applied research. It is not and never can be a science, although science interacts with it in important ways. It is, however, akin to ethics or morals. The exercise of an option we are evaluating can have significant effects on the welfare of others and, insofar as it does, our judgment takes on moral qualities. The question of whether and how to use a given technology can bring us face to face with questions of right and wrong.

Let me interject here a story which I heard when I spent some time in Texas many years ago. A Texan, so the story goes, was driving in southwest Texas between San Angelo and San Antonio when he noticed a hitchhiker and stopped to pick him up. The hitchhiker turned out to be a young New Zealander who was seeing the United States on a shoestring budget. The part of Texas through which they were driving was flat as a pancake and so covered with cactus and thornbushes that even a goat would hardly manage a living. It was also scorching hot. As they were driving along, the hitchhiker noticed a bird running across the road.

"What's the bird? he asked.

"That's a bird of paradise," replied the Texan.

"A bird of paradise? Gosh! He's a hell of a long way from home!"

Despite the comment of the hitchhiker, we *do* live in a paradise. Nature has given us a world both unique and beautiful, its diversity being part of its beauty. The more I learn about life and evolution and, from space probes, about other worlds in our solar system, the more convinced I am that planet Earth is a very rare and special place, adapted in extraordinary ways to the development and support of complex forms of life. We are indeed blessed with a priceless inheritance.

In the United States, a free and democratic society is also part of our inheritance. This social component of our environment, like the natural component, can be tarnished or destroyed by unwise or unethical decisions. If we, as free citizens, fail to cope with the complex problems created by modern technology, we will become the puppets of those who offer authoritarian and ultimately totalitarian solutions.

It would be a tragedy beyond belief if we lost either our freedom or the loveliness of the world that nature has given us. The preservation of these inheritances is the greatest single task which we face.

My generation, now largely retired, and the succeeding middle-aged generation, have done a very imperfect job in carrying out this task. While many conscientious and intelligent decisions have been made, we also have made decisions incompatible with the preservation of a free and livable world. The technological explosion created new situations for which we were philosophically and ethically unprepared. Of course there were warning voices and we did, at times, listen to them, as in the creation of the National Parks, but like all generations before us we did not face up to major and novel problems in time to institute orderly and adequate solutions before substantial damage had been done.

The great need, I submit, was and is a renewed sense of moral responsibility. The increase in our options requires a realization that, although basic ethical principles have not changed, the complexity of their applications has changed. It may be, too, that the consequences of moral failure have expanded. The areas of past deficiency and future need are many, but a few deserve especial emphasis.

The ethical obligations created by technology rest on all of us, not just on our leaders who have to make the most momentous decisions. The fabric of mutual confidence on which a free society depends is woven from the honest and considerate choices made by each and every one of us. The fabric is weakened whenever dishonesty and selfishness are condoned.

All of us, but especially those in positions of major responsibility, need to expand our circle of consideration. We need to think not only of our friends, our business associates, our state, our nation, but of people everywhere. In the world as it exists today, ethics must be universal, not parochial.

We need to expand our circle of consideration in time as well as in space, thinking of the welfare of people decades, centuries, or, as in the case of the disposal of long-lived radioactive wastes, even millenia beyond our time. Only a long-range point of view can insure that the powers conferred on us by technology are well used.

We need to realize that many of the decisions we face are enormously complex, and prepare ourselves to deal with these complexities. This requires the assembling of all possible relevant facts. This is an area where the basic sciences impinge on the domain of value judgments. They can help us, by adding to our knowledge, to foresee the outcome of our acts, and hence to choose wisely.

If your generation has inherited problems, it has also inherited and, indeed, has helped to generate, encouraging trends.

You begin your careers in a world made beautiful by Nature and enriched by the wonders of technology, yet a world which we, its inhabitants, have defiled and not so often through ignorance as through greed. It is a very different world from the one I remember as a boy. Those were simpler times and we tend to look back on them with nostalgia. But they also were times when many essential undertakings, now done by machine, were done in sweat shops or by underpaid manual labor and when diseases now almost forgotten were still prevalent and dreaded.

But have we traded our past problems for permanent disillusionment and disaffection? I reject that conclusion. Along with the disillusionment has come a ferment of intellectual and civil involvement, a ferment directed to the discovery and implementation of solutions.

In the past few decades, an extraordinary number of organizations have been formed, seeking to help the consumer, protect the environment, reform the government, or in some other way deal with the problems which we face. The multiplication of these voluntary organizations and their success in enlisting public support recalls the comment of Alexis de Tocqueville in his classic, *Democracy in America*, that "whereas at the head of some new undertaking you see the government in France, or a man of rank in England, in the United States you will be sure to find an association." Even though the accomplishment of these associations is still far short of the need, the spirit of active citizen involvement in the search for solutions which they represent will not be thwarted in the long run.

Though the times you face are not easy, they are nevertheless challenging times, times full of hope. Problems that have been recognized can be solved. I think I can say for members of my generation, you carry our warm good wishes, our cheers, and our faith.

THE FUTURE OF COMPUTER DATA SECURITY[1]

JOSEPH F. COATES[2]

In speaking at the plenary luncheon of the Eighth Annual Computer Security Conference on November 11, 1981, Joseph F. Coates expressed anxiety concerning unprecedented corporate and national disasters brought about by the abuse or misuse of computers. Specifically, he stated:

> My belief is that the computer industry is so complacent, its buyers and users so beguiled by the equipment, and regulators so enchanted by the calm sea as computers slowly expand across this nation, that the industry needs its equivalent of Hiroshima to alert the nation in a

---

[1] Delivered at the plenary luncheon of the Eighth Annual Computer Security Conference, at 1 P.M., November 11, 1981, in the New York Statler Hotel.
[2] For biographical note, see Appendix.

timely fashion to the enormous risks latent in the current
way in which we organize our computer affairs.

A fundamental law, which he called "Coates' Law," is that "no
one who designs, plans, builds, operates, maintains, supplies, or
sells a large computer system understands what it can do." The
danger, according to Coates, is that these people are unaware of
the potential limits of the system in terms of side effects, abuse,
and latent capabilities.

Coates delivered the address at 1 P.M. to an audience of approximately 400 people in a banquet room of the New York Statler
Hotel on the third day of a four-day conference. Members attend-
ing the conference were mostly employees of organizations using
large computer assisted systems, some law enforcement officials,
and representatives of vendors such as large computer manufacturers. The meeting included buyers, users, sellers, overseers of security computer systems, and other consultants and researchers.

Coates employed a problem-solution method of division in organizing his speech. His use of three specific examples to illustrate
the problem added interest.

Joseph Coates's speech: There has been tremendous progress
in the eight years since the founding of the Computer Security Institute in developing the arts and crafts of safeguarding
data. A company now victimized by a routine security violation is likely to be as much at fault as it is a victim. The craft
level in this field has developed in terms of technique, management, tools and procedures for ensuring routine computer
security. There are all kinds of objective and subjective measures of this enormously improved state of the arts. Just a few
years ago it was not difficult to read all the books and articles
on computer security. Today that is nearly impossible unless
one chooses to make that a near full-time occupation. Questions of computer security are now widely and relatively
freely spoken of, which is a good sign insofar as it indicates
that there are ways of coping with the problem. We generally
do not speak of the intractable or the insoluble. Donn B.
Parker, of SRI International, has noted the maturation of this
field in terms of the substantial number of established specialists, full-time administrators, and security products available
at reasonable prices, a federal cryptographic standard, and

management support. In addition, there are well-developed security review methods, many cases of documented loss. Literature is proliferating, along with laws and regulations. Even insurance is now available.

Against the background of a firm base of computer security craft, I draw attention to a far less satisfactory structural situation. The built-in ways in which we conduct our business, and our orientation toward personal, corporate, and national affairs have latent within them the possibilities of unprecedented corporate and national disasters. Some three years ago I forecast that within five years there would be a half billion dollar scam based on using computers. So far, as well as we can tell, that has not yet come to pass. My anxieties are rising but I figure I have at least another four years, two for events to occur and two for it to be discovered. My anxieties, however, aside from the personal embarrassment of being wrong as a forecaster, carry a more serious negative message. My belief is that the computer industry is so complacent, its buyers and users so beguiled by the equipment, and regulators so enchanted by the calm sea as computers slowly spread across this nation, that the industry needs its equivalent of Hiroshima to alert the nation in a timely fashion to the enormous risks latent in the current way in which we organize our computer affairs. Let me first point out that as with my anxiety about the half billion dollar theft, there is ambiguity implicit in almost every new positive development with regard to computers and security.

We have all seen the widely presented IBM advertisement in newspapers and magazines which shows a group of middle-class men in a police lineup. The caption is "The Computer Didn't Do It"; the message is that people commit computer crimes by misusing computers. While the good side of that ad is that IBM as a major manufacturer is prepared to come out of the closet and talk about computer crimes, the regrettable part is that the ad is so reminiscent of Detroit's approach to auto safety in the mid-sixties. Remember those now bizarre ads which claimed the problem with auto safety is not the automobile but "the nut behind the wheel." We have outgrown that belief in automotives. The sooner we outgrow that belief in computers, the better off we will all be, including IBM. The minimum that one can say is that computer systems involve people/machine interactions and that there is the opportunity to deal with the person or the machine. The reality, however, is that we have relatively little control over people, but we have substantial control over the machine. Insofar as crimes do occur, one can look at them as technological malfeasance, not human operator failures. In contrast to the basic reality of technological society—poor systems design—almost all our efforts are directed at administrative, organizational, and procedural techniques for preserving computer security.

Another element of good news is that the Congress has sponsored several major studies on computers in relation to security and privacy. The Privacy Protection Study Commission, the Electronic Funds Transfer Commission, the recent series of reports of the Office of Technology Assessment, are steadily increasing our sophistication with regard to the problems. Nevertheless each of those studies has shied away from the long-term future and structural problems. They have all shied away from radically different public policy strategies for dealing with security and privacy issues.

Encryption is another source of good news. Encryption, using modern techniques, promises to provide at low cost the opportunity for corporations and even individuals to enjoy an unprecedented degree of security in the messages that they send. Curiously enough, encryption does not seem to be permeating the economy as rapidly as one might have expected. Perhaps it is a combination of fear and ignorance raised by the National Security Agency's insistent intrusion into this private sector opportunity. So long as the true intentions and needs of the national security apparatus remain unclear, it is rather reasonable for businessmen to be skittish about adopting this new technology. On the other hand, NSA's intense concern about encryption should go a long way toward legitimating its importance in the eye of even the most skeptical businessman.

A fundamental law, one might call it the "Coates' Law," about large systems is that no one who designs, plans, builds, operates, maintains, supplies, or sells a large computer system understands what it can do. It is the case that, as with most articles of commerce, these people involved in the buyer-seller chain do understand what the product is designed to do, and design it to perform those tasks. But those very designers are unaware of the potential limits of the system in terms of side effects, abuse, and latent capabilities. The public is increasingly becoming aware of this fundamental law of systems and it can only work to the advantage of the American and world society when we realize that there are intrinsic not accidental limitations on the knowledge of those designing, using, and servicing computers. Let me illustrate the situation with three cases. In New York City a group of private high school students, the Dalton boys, were apprehended after they had broken into a commercial computer system using their computer consoles at the school. They proceeded to bollix up some Canadian business records. One curious thing about the case is that they were never brought to trial, apparently never punished, and no particular sanctions were laid on them. While it would be difficult to state with full confidence why that is so, I propose that the primary reason is that it is in no one's interest connected with that computer incident to take these young people to court. A trial would require that what happened and its technological base be made a matter of public record. No one would want to lay bare the vulnerability of that system on the public record. The second case was a recent rash of red alerts. When one realizes the implications barely latent in a red alert—that we are X minutes from a nuclear exchange with the Soviet Union—the failure of the computer systems initiating those red alerts are enough to cause a billion hours of nightmares among thoughtful people. There is probably no government computer system that has more sophistication brought to it than that associated with the management, control and use of nuclear weaponry. My favorite example of the lack of understanding of large systems is already several years old. In Great

Britain, a group of young people were apprehended by the Postal Service (which maintains the telephone system). They were making telephone calls free of charge around the world from public pay telephones. The game they were playing, the challenge to each other, was deliciously anti-technological. It was to make the telephone calls with the maximum number of linkages. It seems that they had cracked the routing code for the British telephone network and the game was to see how many links one could make in calling one's self up at the next telephone booth. Again, the fundamental basis of law of large systems is made clear when one realizes that the amnesty offered to them had a very low price. "Tell us how you did it."

Other good news is that the veneer of complacent satisfaction within the industry is being chipped away. The 1978 Sentry Life Insurance Company survey on dimensions of privacy showed that 64 percent of the population surveyed were concerned with threats to privacy. Fifty-four percent felt that computers were a threat to privacy. More striking and a sounder basis for public and governmental alert is that 53 percent of those in the computer industry agreed.

Other good news has to do with developing technologies that help in computer security. Technologies for identifying handprints and fingerprints, devices with ability to identify voice prints, and the technology for signature verification all promise to add a new degree of certitude to the question of who has access to, and who is operating, a particular computer. However latent in those very technologies is their application beyond the mere question of computer security. The techniques, if just permitted to be freely and haphazardly used without civil rights controls, give the corporation or the government agency an unprecedented degree of intrusion into the rights of workers to work at their own pace and in terms of customary practices.

Let us turn to the big open issues relating the structural habits of American society and the structural components of the computer and computer user industries.

Privacy as a computer-related issue will be forever more

an issue of the post industrial society. While the focus of attention and the sensitivity to issues is shifting, if anything, the matter is becoming more, not less important. Each of the key areas of privacy—personal preferences, customs and practices, personal economics, personal sexual behavior and preferences, and personal political beliefs—are each at special risk from computer systems. The fundamental realization that the long-term risks to privacy are not from the corporation and the private sector, but from government, is still a matter enjoying virtually no public airing. Without doubt, the annoyances, the insults, the affronts, the day-to-day abrasive abuses of privacy come from the private sector. But they are relatively trivial and in my judgment relatively manageable compared to the long-term risks from government itself. The great irony, of course, is that these private sector violations of privacy, real and potential, are not being approached through the tools most likely to be effective in the private sector, namely, economic measures. Commissions recommend, lawyers advocate, and government attempts to apply, but ends up misapplying regulation, control, and administrative procedures while ignoring the most important tool—monetizing privacy. By no means will hanging a price on privacy deal with all problems but it will certainly clear the field of many of the present annoyances. Let me illustrate. I subscribe to *Time* magazine. I do not particularly care who they sell my name to or why they sell it. I am just one among tens of millions. But let us say I were a subscriber to Gynecologic Monthly (a.k.a. Hustler), I might be somewhat reluctant to have that bandied about but might be willing to accept a 25, 50, 75-cent or $1 discount if the publisher could assure me of the scope and kind of use of my name. Readers could be offered the option of $1 discount if the name were sold or circulated or no discount if it were not. Finally, there are other magazines of such an extreme affront to my sensitivities that I would be so reluctant to have them in my house or be associated with them that I would expect the publisher to pay me for accepting a subscription, much less for selling my address.

We are doing virtually nothing to monetize the privacy of the nation.

Other aspects of privacy that have received relatively little attention are the technological opportunities for giving the individual fuller control over personal information. It is now technically feasible for each of us to have a full life's medical history on a card that would fit in pocket or purse. In a future system your totally portable medical record could be produced in the doctor's office, the hospital, the clinic, or whatever; the data called up ad hoc for diagnosis and evaluations; and after decisions and prescriptions are given, the modified medical record returned to the patient and the central system records destroyed. Again, the option and the opportunity to do that could be monetized and would be a major step forward in dealing with the obvious abuses of the present medical information system.

Other aspects of privacy, however, are virtually unspoken of. The aggregation of information can be used as an anti-group tool to create an anti-group basis. Suppose, for example, that statistical surveys of questionable validity show socially undesirable characteristics are common in Hispanics or Armenian Americans or Italian Americans or American Jews. In some sense, a group's privacy might be violated by making such information available. We have no mechanisms for coping with that kind of computer assisted abuse.

The question of fake input into computer systems is virtually unspoken of. I am not thinking of the fake inputs for theft or manipulation, but fake inputs to distort someone's reputation or to muddy up a situation. Recall the case of the would-be vice presidential candidate about whom it was learned that he had had psychotherapy. What are the potentials in future systems of polluting someone's job opportunity or someone's political career by intruding fake information, which eventually could be purged or corrected but not in time to undo the damage.

Physical integrity of computer systems has received no significant public attention commensurate to the risks. Computer systems are not designed against natural and man-made disasters. For decades the telephone company operated with a maximum disaster being a hurricane. There is no reason to believe that computer designers operate with any greater sense of physical integrity but let me point out that it is well known that computer systems are terribly vulnerable to both man-made and natural intrusions.

Computers are the great field day for crime. But as I suggested, most potential routine crimes can be handled at the craft level. One structural problem is that large municipal, state, and federal agencies have not tooled up to deal with computer related crime in a way commensurate with the problem. Catch-up will undoubtedly occur but sooner rather than later would be desirable. Business and industries now appear by all reports to find it in their short-term interests to suppress information about crime. We need legislation or other mechanisms for letting those crimes be known so the system can evolve faster to protect us all. A typical situation might be: a bank suffers a $500,000 loss but rather than let it be known that it is vulnerable, the bank eats the loss. Thus the record of the crime and the criminal is lost to other computer users and law enforcement agencies.

The fundamental notion that the computer is a political tool is difficult for businessmen, government agencies, and the computer industry to swallow. Yet it is a political tool as is everything associated with the techno-economic system and its ideology. In Italy extremists on the left and right, the Red Brigade and others, have already destroyed some 30 computer centers, recognizing that computer centers are new nerve centers of the multinational and large national corporations. Similar acts have occurred in other countries. The potential for future disruption is enormous. My scenario for the future is that we will have far more, rather than far less, important system terrorism over the next decade or two.

Some antisocial uses of computer systems will occur merely because we have not exercised the foresight to anticipate what may legally happen. Suppose, for example, that a highly credible forecast of a major earthquake in California were to occur. It would be in the short-term interests of many national corporations to withdraw assets from California. It would quickly seem to be to the advantage of other citizens to withdraw their resources, leaving the people strapped for resources at the very time that protective measures were called for. There are scores of other potential uses of computer information which would not work in the public interest and for which there is little public awareness, no public discussion, and no government plan.

As computer systems, particularly in finance, spread across the world, there will be banking arrangements involving Middle Easterners, Europeans, Africans, and Latin Americans. Cultural differences across societies are a commonplace in anthropology. But cultural differences seem to the private sector a constant source of fresh amazement. There is every reason to believe that people in different cultures will approach the computers with a different orientation, a different regard for truth, a different sense of completeness, a different sense of security, a different sense of loyalties, a different sense of appropriate manipulation. And yet, we blindly go ahead linking up and making connections with little attention to the implications for the security of the U.S. society and economy. National security is itself a separate and distinct item for which relatively little planning has been done on these large systems. Harking back to the illustration of the Dalton boys and the British telephone bandits, it is not unreasonable to think that a foreign power hostile to the United States, for a few million dollars would have an agent set up a bank in Iowa or some other nice part of the country. Being a new bank, being avant garde, it would adopt all the latest technologies and become thoroughly enmeshed in the EFT system. At the critical moment after years of operation, with the word from abroad, it would foul up the EFT system, a system in which tens of billions of dollars would be circulating every day in the form of electronic accounts. That such a thing could occur is at this stage conjectural. But the public discussion does not exist to assure reasonable people that there is not a reasonable likelihood of it occurring. Several simultaneous ventures of this sort entailing a sunk investment of less than $25 million would be a piddling investment for a foreign power wishing to disrupt the U.S. economy.

The implication of none of these risks and problems is to abandon the computer. The implication is certainly to understand better and to determine what the proper unit is in which it should be organized. The endless linking together into bigger and bigger systems may be the single most pathological thing we can do if we allow short-term marginal economic gain to create a structural disaster.

There are a half dozen factors that inhibit progress along the lines suggested above. First, no one has a plenary interest in the impacts of computers on society. Unlike other advanced nations, we have no Nora-Mink study, that marvelous study rendered to the President of France. We have no association or organization, not even a national commission which looks at the overall problem. Our typical piecemeal approach is so sadly characteristic of current politics, the politics of post World War II America. Even the piecemeal approach of the Privacy Protection Study Commission and the EFT Commission fails to take a full bite of their pieces. Second, there is little future orientation in government and almost no future orientation in the industry. The marketing of computers is just like the marketing of Christmas toys. Buy it now, enjoy it immediately, and the next wave of development will take care of itself. Never in history has a rapidly moving revolution been implemented with such myopia, as the computer revolution in American society. Three, there is no positive model for privacy. There is only continuing niggling and picking away at issues and topics as they burst forth or evolve and come to attention. Fourth, the technical infrastructure of big users is just penurious beyond belief. Bankers are penny pinchers. Some $7½ billion is spent every year on check processing. Those big users are complacent, defensive and effectively indifferent to long-term implications and to true technological choices. Bankers won't put a nickel into studying the future of their own systems and its choices.

Curiously enough, in a knowledge-based society, in a society in which over half the work force is in the information business, we literally have no economics of knowledge. There is no way of evaluating information from a monetary point of view. Its cost and, hence, the value of security, are without a theory. One could literally read within a week every English language article on the economics of information.

The ten specific suggestions below may be useful in two ways. As suggestions, they may themselves be worth adopting. They also may open up the discussion and point out that there are strikingly new options and strategies in managing our affairs.

Innovation 1: Set an IQ ceiling on computer operators. Some of the finest minds in the nation do and must design and build large computer systems. However, it is not at all clear that it is desirable to have highly intelligent people responsible for the operation and day-to-day maintenance and control of computers. As an anecdote illustrating this point, years ago I had a friend who designed a psychological test for a milk company. The test was directed at choosing routemen. The milk company had found that the routemen had to be bright enough to deliver the milk, keep the records, collect the money, get the horse to and from the stable. However, if he were too smart, the job was not challenging enough. He had lots of slack time, and he could quite easily cook up ways to cheat the company. So the problem for the applied psychologist was to find the proper IQ and aptitude window through which to select the candidates.

Innovation 2: Stop blaming the computer. The industry has allowed users of computers to blame their own incompetence and ineptitude on the computer. I am sure that each of us, once a month if not more often, receives a note or telephone excuse or some other kind of nonsense that blames a management failing on the computer. It cannot be good for the industry. So long as users of computers can fob off their ineptitude onto the machine, the technology will enjoy a poor reputation.

Innovation 3: Let the computer manufacturers hold the insurance. When Louis Sullivan designed the first skyscraper in Chicago, the municipal authorities were concerned about its safety. As a condition for granting a license, they made Sullivan set up his own office on the top floor of the new building. The present dissociation between computer manufacturers and computer users has created and aggravated our risks. If large computer manufacturers were required to hold insurance against the failures of the system, it would radically alter the present way in which computer risks are handled. It would rapidly lead to the next innovation.

Innovation 4: Cost out choices of risks and vulnerabilities. It seems to me that the industry must acknowledge that there is an intrinsic error rate in every system. The acknowledgement of the error rates would put everyone on notice that there is no such thing as a foolproof system and would lead to the development of price schedules of risks and price elasticities of risk. Acknowledging error rates and incorporating them into the system design as a positive recognized planning and purchasing factor will be increasingly important as electronic funds transfer, electronic mail, crime records and other large systems flourish.

Innovation 5: Design portable records. As already described, much of the privacy matters affecting individuals in several areas, notably health, could be dealt with by portable records. The industry should give some attention to this. Federal systems subsidizing health care should give further attention to promoting this.

Innovation 6: Require companies to keep records of all debts. A recurrent problem in computer security is the wipeout of records. Several companies have failed through viciousness or accident when accounts receivable have been wiped out. If companies were routinely required to keep records of all debts to be called up under certain circumstances, the situation could effectively be dealt with.

Innovation 7: Customize all information. The long-term trend in the industrial society has been toward uniform quality products. Every issue of a national magazine, every copy of a book, ideally should be identical and letter perfect. Digitalized technology, however, now makes it possible to take advantage of a radically new strategy, namely the introduction of customized variations to make literally each copy of each issue unique. To illustrate specifically it is my understanding that today all German typewriters are manufactured with minor variations on the keys and typefaces so that should one come across a kidnap note or an illegal message, one can immediately identify the specific machine by manufacturer, date of sale, and so forth, just from the typeface. Customized information could make major inroads into the counterfeiting of records, recorded music, all kinds of other computer stored data.

Innovation 8: Call in all the money and reissue machine readable bills. Strange as it seems, 26 percent of all money now in circulation is in hundred dollar bills or larger. A monitoring of the daily press shows that a sizeable portion of that is certainly the medium of quasi-legitimate, illegitimate, organized criminal and terroristic activities. Large boodles of money flowing from one hand to another outside the record system are most conveniently done in hundred dollar bills. If all money were called in and issued as machine readable, we would be able to instantly identify large blocks of money that were caught up in various kinds of illegal activities. Furthermore, the very fact of calling the money in would tremendously discount the money collected by terrorist organizations, large-scale criminal thefts, and organized crime.

Innovation 9: Tax information transfers. Taxing information transfers would move all users very sharply toward an awareness of the cost, price, and the value of information. It would lead to the purging of data bases of gratuitous information. It would provide a basis of accountability on transfer. It would cause those so liberal, if not overly liberal, in dispensing information about their fellow citizens to be more careful. Banks, credit companies, large retailers would be forced, by the transfer tax, to keep records of their gross volume of information flow. Similarly, government might in some regards once we had established the value of information pay for it as it does any other commodity in the industrial society.

Innovation 10: Monetize information and privacy. As already suggested, great inroads could be made into commercial abuses by monetizing privacy, setting up a fee schedule and giving those who wish security some real choices. Similarly one could set up tax systems to tax the use of information rather than attempting to maintain tight security over it. Remember what John Kenneth Galbraith has taught. There are no secrets, only varying times to release information. We could use the power of money to moderate those release times.

In closing, the challenge I throw down to the computer industry, its customers, and its guardians, is to come up with ten better innovations.

APPENDIX

BRINK, DAVID R. (1919–   ). Born, Minneapolis, Minnesota; B.A. *cum laude*, University of Minnesota, 1940, B.S.L., 1941, J. D., with honors, 1947; honorary doctors of law degrees from Capital University, 1981, Suffolk University, 1981, William Mitchell College of Law, 1982; member, Dorsey and Whitney law firm, 1947–   ; member, House of Delegates of the American Bar Association, 1968–79, finance committee, 1974–77, executive committee, 1976–77, board of governors, 1974–77, president 1981–82; author, articles and monographs on problems of the legal profession and organized bar, specialization, word processing, and probate subjects.

BURGER, WARREN EARL (1907–   ). Born, St. Paul, Minnesota; student, University of Minnesota, 1925–27; LL.B., *magna cum laude*, St. Paul College of Law (now William Mitchell College of Law); Doctor of Laws, 1931; honorary degrees, LL.D., William Mitchell College of Law, 1966, and New York Law School, 1976; admitted to Minnesota bar, 1931; faculty, William Mitchell College of Law, 1931–53; partner, Faricy, Burger, Moore & Costello (and predecessor firms), 1935–53; assistant attorney general in charge of Civil Division, US Department of Justice, 1953–56; judge of U.S. Court of Appeals, District of Columbia, 1956–69; Chief Justice, U.S. Supreme Court, 1969–   ; lecturer, American and European law schools; faculty, Appellate Judges Seminar, New York University Law School, 1958–   ; member and legal adviser, US delegation to International Labor Organization, Geneva, 1954; contributor, law journals and other publications. (See also *Current Biography*, November 1969.)

CANNON, MARK WILCOX (1924–   ). Born, Salt Lake City, Utah; student, Deep Springs College, 1944–46; B.A. University of Utah, 1949; M.A., 1954, M.P.A., 1955; Ph.D., Harvard University, 1961; research analyst, Utah Foundation, 1953; secretary, Utah Scholastic Merit Study Commission, 1954; instructor, 1955, chairman of department of political science, 1961–64, Brigham Young University; administrative assistant to U.S. Congressman Henry A. Dixon, 1956–61; legislative assistant to U.S. Senator Wallace F. Bennett, 1961–64; member, staff of the Institute of Public Administration, New York City, 1964–72; director, Urban Development

Program, Venezuela, 1964–65; director, international programs, New York City, 1965–68, 1968–72; administrative assistant, Chief Justice of the United States Supreme Court, 1972–   ; awards, West Point Science Association, 1963; co-author, *The Makers of Public Policy: American Power Groups and Their Ideologies*, 1965, *The Challenge of Urban Government in Valencia*, 1966; author with others, *Partnership for Progress: Atlanta-Fulton County Consolidation*, 1969.

GLENN, JOHN HERSCHEL JR. (1921–   ). Born, Cambridge, Ohio; student, Muskingum College, 1939, D.Sc. 1961; naval aviation cadet, University of Iowa, 1942; graduate flight school, Naval Air Training Center, Corpus Christi, Texas, 1943; Navy Test Pilot Training School, Patuxent River, Maryland, 1954; commissioned second lieutenant, United States Marine Corps, 1943, advanced through grades to lieutenant colonel; assigned to the 4th Marine Aircraft Wing, Marshall Islands campaign, 1944, 9th Marine Aircraft Wings, 1945–46, 1st Marine Aircraft Wing, North China Patrol and Guam, 1947–48; flight instructor, advanced flight training, Corpus Christi, 1949–51; assistant G-2/ G-3 Amphibious Warfare School, Quantico, Virginia; with 25th Fighter Squadron, United States Air Force, Korea, 1953; Navy Bureau of Aeronautics, Washington, 1956–69; astronaut, Project Mercury, NASA, 1959–64; pilot Mercury-Atlas 6 orbital space flight from Cape Canaveral, Florida, 1962; vice president for corporate development and director, Royal Crown Cola Company, 1962–74; United States Senator from Ohio, 1975–   ; awards; decorated D.F.C., Air medal, Astronaut medal of United States Marine Corps, Navy unit commendation, Korean Presidential unit citation, Distinguished Merit Award of Muskingum College, Medal of Honor of New York City; co-author, *We Seven*, 1962; author, *P.S., I Listened to Your Heartbeat*. (See also *Current Biography*, March, 1976.)

GUNDERSON, ROBERT G. (1915–   ). Born, Madison, Wisconsin; B.S., University of Wisconsin, 1937; M.A., Oberlin College, 1941; Ph.D., University of Wisconsin, 1949; instructor to professor of speech, Oberlin College, 1938–58; military leave, private to captain, United States Army, 1941–46; professor of speech, Indiana University, 1958–75, director, American Studies, 1969–78, professor of speech communication and of history, 1975–   ; visiting professor, University of Michigan, 1958, University of Hawaii, 1964; executive vice-president, Speech Communication Association, 1961–64; parliamentarian, Southern Historical Association,

1976–   ; Henry E. Huntington Library Fellowship, 1971–72; Visiting Scholar, University Center of Virginia, 1973; National Endowment for the Humanities—Henry E. Huntington Library Senior Fellowship, 1979; interim editor, *Journal of American History*, 1977–78; editor, *Quarterly Journal of Speech*, 1966–69; author, *The Log-Cabin Campaign*, 1957, *Old Gentlemen's Convention: The Washington Peace Conference of 1861*, 1961, *"Stoutly Argufy": Lincoln's Legal Speaking*, 1963, more than fifty articles in history, speech, and education journals; contributing, *Smithsonian Conference on Political Campaigning*, 1967.

ILCHMAN, ALICE STONE (1935–   ). Born, Cincinnati, Ohio; B.A., Mt. Holyoke College, 1957; M.P.A., Maxwell School of Citizenship, Syracuse University, 1958; Ph.D., London School of Economics, 1965; assistant to president and faculty member, Berkshire Community College, 1961–64; assistant research political scientist, Institute of Governmental Studies, University of California at Berkeley, 1968; program director, Center for South Asia Studies, 1966–68, 1969–70; director, Professional Studies Program, India, 1968–69; assistant professor and director, Pakistan Education Program, 1971–73; professor of education and economics and dean, Wellesley College, 1973–1981; president, Sarah Lawrence College, 1981–   ; international assistant to John F. Kennedy, 1957; director, Peace Corps Training for India, 1965–66; assistant Secretary of State, 1978; association director, International Communication Agency, 1978; author, *The New Man of Knowledge and the New States*, 1968; co-author, with W.F. Ilchman, *Education and Employment in India, The Policy Nexus*, 1976.

JACOB JOHN E. (1934–   ). Born, Trout, Louisiana; B.A., Howard University, 1957, M.S.W., 1963; began work with National Urban League in 1965 as Director of Education and Youth Incentives at the Washington Urban League, where he later filled a series of administrative positions, Acting Executive Director, 1968–70; Director of Community Organization Training, Eastern Regional Office, National Urban League, 1970; Executive Director, San Diego Urban League, 1970–75; President, Washington Urban League, 1975–79; Executive Director, National Urban League, 1979–81, President, 1982–   ; member of board, Local Initiatives Support Corporation, "A Better Chance, Inc.," National Advertising Review Board; is member of several District of Columbia councils and societies.

KIRKLAND, JOSEPH LANE (1922–   ). Born, Camden, South
Carolina; student, Newberry College, 1940; graduate, United
States Merchant Marine Academy, 1942; B.S., Georgetown University School of Foreign Service, 1948; LL.D. (honorary), Duke
University, Princeton University; Deck officer, United States Merchant Marine, 1942–46; nautical scientist, Hydrographic Office,
Navy Department, 1947–48; American Federation of Labor, research staff; 1948–53; assistant director AFL–CIO, department of
social security, 1953–58, director, research and international education, Union Operating Engineers, 1958–60, executive assistant
to president, 1961–69, secretary treasurer, 1969–80, president,
1980–   ; member, Commission of Foundations and Private Phi-
lanthropies, Commission on Financial Structure, Blue Ribbon Defense Panel, President's Labor-Management Advisory Committee,
President's Commission on CIA activities Within the United
States, Commission on Critical Choices for America; board of
directors, American Institute of Free Labor Development, National Urban League, American Arbitration Association, Rockefeller Foundation, Brookings Institution, Carnegie Endowment for
International Peace, and Council of Foreign Relations; awards,
Distinguished Public Service medal, Department of Defense; fel-
low, American Public Health Association; member, International
Organization of Masters, Mates, and Pilots, Council of Foreign
Relations. (See also *Current Biography*, May 1980.)

LEONARD WILLIAM AUGUSTUS, II (1916–   ). Born, New
York, New York; A.B. Dartmouth College, 1937; reporter, Bridgeport (Conn.) *Post-Telegram*, 1937–40; radio researcher, Newell-
Emmett Advertising, 1940–41; CBS, Inc., New York, 1945–   ;
programs include "This Is New York" (radio), 1945–57, "Eye on
New York" (television), 1950–61, "6 O'Clock Report" (television),
1952–56, "Voice of America" (radio), 1960–64, "Let's Find Out"
(radio), 1955–59, "Bill Lawrence Show" (radio), 1957–59, CBS
news correspondent, 1959–64, vice-president, programming, CBS
News, 1965–72, senior vice-president, 1972–75, vice-president,
CBS News Inc., Washington, D.C., 1975–78, president, CBS News,
Inc., New York, 1978–1982; retired March 1, 1982; United States
Naval Reserve, ensign to lieutenant commander, 1941–45; awards,
Albert Lasker award for medical journalism, 1956, Ed Stout award
for best Latin American reporting, 1960; co-author, *This Is New
York Guide*, 1955.

McGOVERN, GEORGE STANLEY (1922–   ). Born, Avon, South
Dakota; B.A., Dakota Wesleyan University, 1945; Northwestern

University M.A., 1949, Ph.D., 1953; professor of history and political science, Dakota Wesleyan University, 1949–53; executive director, South Dakota Democratic Party, 1953–55; member, 85th-86th United States Congress 1957–61; director, Food for Peace, 1961–62; Democratic candidate for President of the United States, 1972; United States Senator from South Dakota, 1963–80; chairman, Americans for Common Sense 1980–   ; pilot, United States Army Air Force in World War II; decorated D.F.C.; author, *The Colorado Coal Strike, 1913–14*, 1953, *War Against Want*, 1964, *Agricultural Thought in the Twentieth Century*, 1967, *A Time of War, A Time of Peace*, 1968, *An American Journey*, 1974, *Grassroots*, 1978; co-author, *The Great Coalfield War*, 1972. (See also *Current Biography*, March 1967.)

NEWSOM, DAVID DUNLOP (1918–   ). Born, Richmond, California; A.B., University of California, 1938; M.S., Columbia University, 1940; Pulitzer traveling scholar, 1940–41; publisher, *Walnut Creek Courier-Journal* (California), 1946–47; served in American embassies in Karachi, Pakistan, 1948–50, Oslo, Norway, 1950–51, Baghdad, Iraq, 1952–55; officer in charge of Arabian Peninsula affairs, Department of State, 1955–59; 1st secretary, American embassy, London, 1960–62; deputy director, Office of North African Affairs, Department of State, Washington, 1962–63; director, 1963–65; ambassador, Libya, 1965–69; assistant secretary of state for African affairs, 1969–74; ambassador, Indonesia, 1974–77; ambassador, Philippines, 1977–78; under-secretary of state for political affairs, 1978; currently, director, administration and programs, Institute for the Study of Diplomacy, Georgetown University; special advisor to U.S. delegation to United Nations General Assembly, 1972; public service awards, United States Information Service, 1955, Department of State, 1958, National Public Service League, 1972, the Rockefeller Public Service award, 1973, the Department of State Distinguished Honor award, 1981.

PEPPER, CLAUDE DENSON (1900–   ). Born, Dudleyville, Alabama; A.B., University of Alabama, 1921; J.D., Harvard University, 1924; LL.D., McMaster University, 1941, Toronto University and University of Alabama, 1942, Rollins College, 1944; D.Sc., University of Miami, 1974; instructor of law, University of Arkansas, 1924–25; admitted to the bar, 1924; member, Florida House of Representatives, 1929, Florida Board of Public Welfare, 1931–32; United States Senate from Florida, 1936–51; United States House of Representatives, 88th Congress-1963–   ; served with armed forces, 1918; awards, Mary and Albert Public Service award, 1967, Eleanor Israel Humanities award, 1968; member, Phi Beta Kappa, Omicron Delta Kappa, Phi Alpha Delta. (See also *Current Biography*, February, 1941.)

RANDOLPH, JENNINGS (1902–   ). Born, Salem, West Virginia; A.B., *magna cum laude*, Salem College, 1924, D. Aero Science, 1943; honorary degrees from 17 colleges; member, editorial staff, Clarksville (W. Va.) *Daily Telegraph*, 1924; associate editor, *West Virginia Review*, 1925; head, department of public speaking and journalism, Davis and Elkins College, 1926–32; professor, public speaking, Southeastern University, Washington, 1935–53, dean, college of business administration, 1952–58; instructor, Leadership Training Institute, Washington, 1948–58; member, United States House of Representatives, 73–79th congresses; U.S. Senator from West Virginia, 1958–   ; awards, B'nai B'rith award, 1961, gold medal of merit, Veterans of Foreign Wars, 1969, President's award, National Rehabilitation Association, 1971, other awards from organizations concerned with aviation, the environment, and the handicapped; co-author, *Speaking That Wins* and *Mr. Chairman, Ladies and Gentleman*; author, *Going to Make a Speech*. (See also *Current Biography*, January, 1962.)

REAGAN, RONALD WILSON (1911–   ). Born, Tampico, Illinois; B.A., Eureka College (Illinois), 1932; sports announcer, radio station WHO, Des Moines, Iowa, 1932–37; motion picture and television actor, 1937–1966; program supervisor, General Electric Theater; president, Screen Actors Guild, 1947–52, 1959; captain, US Air Force, 1942–45; governor, California, 1967–74; unsuccessful candidate for Republican presidential nomination, 1976; US President, 1980–   (See also *Current Biography*, February 1967.)

ROSENTHAL, ABRAHAM MICHAEL (1922–   ). Born, Sault Ste. Marie, Ontario, Canada; came to the United States in 1926, naturalized in 1951; B.S., City College of New York, 1944, LL.D., 1974; member, staff of the *New York Times*, 1944–   , United Nations correspondent, 1946–54, assigned to India, 1954–58, Poland, 1958–59, Switzerland, 1960–61, Japan, 1961–63, metropolitan editor, 1963–66, assistant, associate, and managing editor, 1967–77, executive editor, 1977–   ; awards, citations by the Overseas Press Club, 1956, 1959, 1960, and 1965, the Pulitzer Prize for international reporting, 1960, George Polk memorial award, 1960 and 1965, Page One Award of the Newspaper Guild of New York, 1960, and Elijah P. Lovejoy award, 1981; president, Foreign Correspondents Association in India, 1957; author, *38 Witnesses;* co-author, *One More Victim.*

SCHLESINGER, ARTHUR JR. (1917–   ). Born, Columbus, Ohio; A.B., *summa cum laude,* Harvard University, 1938; member, Society of Fellows, 1939–42; Doctor of Letters, Muhlenberg College, 1950; associate professor, Harvard University, 1946–54; professor, 1954–61; member, Adlai Stevenson campaign staff, 1952, 1956; special assistant to President of the United States, 1961–64; Albert Schweitzer Chair in the Humanities, City University of New York, 1967–   ; member, Board of Trustees, American Film Institute; trustee, Twentieth Century Fund; awards, Pulitzer Prize for history, 1945, Guggenheim fellowship, 1946, American Academy of Arts and Letters grant, 1946, Pulitzer Prize for biography, 1965, National Book Award, 1965; author, *The Age of Jackson,* 1945; *The Coming of the New Deal,* 1958; *Kennedy or Nixon,* 1960; *A Thousand Days: John F. Kennedy in the White House,* 1965; *The Bitter Heritage,* 1967; *The Crisis of Confidence,* 1969; *The Imperial Presidency,* 1973; *Robert F. Kennedy and His Times,* 1978; and other works. (See also *Current Biography,* January, 1976.)

SENESE, DONALD JOSEPH (1942–   ). Born, Chicago, Illinois. B.S., Loyola University, Chicago, 1964; M.A., University of South Carolina, 1964, Ph.D., 1970; studied at Sophia University, Japan, 1970, and National Chengchi University, Taiwan, 1971; Department of Agriculture Graduate School, 1973–74; professor, history, Radford College, 1969–74; legislative assistant to U.S. Representative Bill Archer, 1973–76; senior research associate, House Republican Study Committee, 1976–78, concurrently legislative assistant to U.S. Senator William L. Scott, 1973; assistant secretary for educational research and improvement, U.S. Department of Education, 1981–   ; author, *Indexing the Inflationary Impact on Taxes—the Necessary Economic Reform,* 1978.

SILBER, JOHN ROBERT (1926–   ). Born, San Antonio, Texas; B.A., *summa cum laude,* Trinity University, 1947; postgraduate work, Yale Divinity School, 1947–48; University of Texas Law School, 1948; M.A., Yale University, 1952, Ph.D., 1958; instructor, philosophy, Yale University, 1952–55; assistant professor, philosophy, University of Texas at Austin, 1955–59, professor, 1962–70, chairman of department, 1962–67, professor of arts and letters, 1967–70, chairman, Comparative Studies Program, 1967, dean, College of Arts and Sciences, 1967–70; president of the university and professor of philosophy and law, Boston University, 1971–   ; visiting professor, University of Bonn, 1960; fellow, Kings College, University of London, 1963–64; awards, Harbison award for teaching, Danforth Foundation, 1966, Fulbright research fellowship, Germany, 1959–60, Guggenheim fellowship, 1963–64; member, Phi Beta Kappa, Royal Institute of Philosophy; author, *The Ethical Significance of Kant's Religion*, 1960; editor, *Religion Within the Limits of Reason Alone*, 1960, *Works in Continental Philosophy*, 1967.

SMITH, WILLIAM FRENCH (1917–   ). Born, Wilton, New Hampshire; A.B., *summa cum laude*, University of California, 1939; LL.B., Harvard University, 1942; admitted to California bar, 1942; attorney and senior partner, Gibson, Dunn, and Crutcher, Los Angeles, 1946–80; director, several California corporations; member, Los Angeles Commission on Foreign Relations, 1954–74; chairman, California delegation to the Republican National Convention, 1968; United States Attorney General, 1981–   ; member, executive committee of the California Roundtable, 1975–   ; United States Naval Reserve to rank of first lieutenant, 1942–46; member, California Chamber of Commerce (director, 1963–   , president, 1974–75), Phi Beta Kappa, Phi Gamma Mu, Pi Sigma Alpha.

SNELL, GEORGE DAVIS (1903–   ). Born, Haverhill, Massachusetts; B.A., Dartmouth College, 1926; Sc.D., Harvard University, 1930; instructor, zoology, Dartmouth College, 1929–30, Brown University, 1930–31; assistant professor, Washington University, St. Louis, 1933–34; The Jackson Laboratory, Research Association, 1935–37, senior staff science administrator, 1949–50, senior staff scientist, 1957–   , emeritus, 1969–   ; National Research Council fellow, University of Texas, 1931–33; Guggenheim fellow, 1953–54; National Institute of Health grantee for study of allergy and immunology, 1958–62; awards, Bertner Foundation award, 1962, National Cancer Institute award, 1964–68, Gregor Mendel medal of the Czechoslovak Academy of Sciences, 1967, honorary M.D., Charles University, Prague, 1967, honorary Sc.D., Dartmouth College, 1974, Gairdner Foundation award, 1976, Wolf Prize in Medicine, 1978, Nobel Prize in Medicine, 1980; member, National Academy of Science, Transplantation Society, Genetic Society of America, American Academy of Arts and Sciences, British Transplantation Society, Phi Beta Kappa, Sigma Xi; editor, *The Biology of the Laboratory Mouse*, 1941; editor-in-chief, *Immunogenetics*.